P9-CEG-618

drama
SKITS & SKETCHES 3

THE *ideas* LIBRARY

FOR YOUTH GROUPS

THE IDEAS LIBRARY

drama
SKITS & SKETCHES 3

THE ideas LIBRARY

FOR YOUTH GROUPS

Youth Specialties

ZONDERVAN™

A DIVISION OF HARPERCOLLINS*PUBLISHERS*

Drama, Skits, and Sketches 3 for youth groups

Copyright © 2001 by Youth Specialties, except for the following scripts, which are published by permission:

© by Curt Cloninger: Flunking English, Flunking Life; In the Dark; and Waiting for the Commercial.

© by Bryan Belknap: A Day in Court; I'm Almost Ready; American Master; Going Up?; You Don't Have to Pay; I'm Listening; and The Big Question.

Youth Specialties Book, 300 S. Pierce St., El Cajon, CA 92020, are published by Zondervan Publishing House, 5300 Patterson Ave. S.E., Grand Rapids, MI 49530.

Library of Congress Cataloging-in-Publication Data

Drama, skits, and sketches 3 : for youth groups.
    p. cm. — (Ideas library)
  Includes index.
  ISBN 0-310-23823-4 (alk. paper)
  1. Drama in Christian education. 2. Church group work with youth. I. Title: Drama,
skits, and sketches three. II. Youth Specialties (Organization). III. Series.

BV1534.4 .D73 2001
246'.72—dc21

2001017557

Web site addresses listed in this book are current at the time of publication. Please contact Youth Specialties by email (YS@YouthSpecialties.com) or by postal mail (Youth Specialties, Product Department, 300 South Pierce Street, El Cajon, CA 92020) to report URLs that are not operational and to suggest alternate URLs if available.

Edited by Amy Jacober and Lorna McFarland Hartman
Cover design by Curt Sell
Interior design by Tom Gulotta

Printed in the United States of America

01 02 03 04 05 06 07 / / 10 9 8 7 6 5 4 3 2 1

CONTENTS

ALPHABETICAL LIST OF SCRIPTS

Looking for a skit or drama for your meeting on faith? Materialism? Forgiveness? Dating and marriage? Salvation? Simply glance down the list of topics and find the perfect script for your purpose and for your group.

SCRIPTURE
SKETCHES

SCRIPTURE SKETCHES

Some students can tell Beelzebub from Barnabas. Others need help finding the New Testament. But the Bible is brought to life for *all* teens when they can act out scriptural episodes, stories, and passages. These scripts can be used as no-rehearsal reader's theater, memorized performances, or anything in between. (Other scripts that illustrate or portray particular Scriptures are indexed by Bible reference on page 7.)

RECIPE FOR A QUIET TIME
2 TIMOTHY 2:15, MARK 1:35, PSALM 10:17

Absorbing God's word through osmosis by using the Bible as a pillow does not count as devotional time. Specific things need to happen. This sketch offers a quick recipe—courtesy of two girls deciding on breakfast and a pushy waiter—for spending time with God. The basics—a quiet and consistent place, consistent time, God's Word, prayer, and the desire to have a quiet time—are all covered along with the Bible references. This can be played as straight or as funny as you want it to be.

The sketch contains a few specific lines and Bible verses to be quoted. Luckily a cheat sheet is built in as a prop—the menu. You can find the script on page 16 and a reproducible menu on page 18. Add a few chairs and a table, and you're ready to go. Bon appétit! *Gary Canfield*

ABSOLUTE POWER

What was on Pontius Pilate's mind when the Pharisees asked him to have Jesus crucified? We may never know for certain, but the sketch on page 19 certainly gives one idea of what may have occupied his thoughts. He gives a speech, rules people, deals with a couple of annoying Pharisees, and faces a choice he'd rather pass on to, well, anyone he can. This sketch walks the audi-

ence through the events that lead up to Jesus' crucifixion from Pontius Pilate's self-absorbed perspective.

The sketch definitely takes a lot of rehearsal and preparation, and it's longer than most of the other sketches. It's set in a modern day office complete with desks, phones, computers, and a fax machine. This sketch works well near Easter, but you can use it any time to segue into the passion story and how personal perspectives can warp reality. *Andrew Davey*

IN THE DARK
MATTHEW 5:14-16

Being a light in the dark is supposed to come naturally to Christians. Unfortunately for one of the characters in the sketch (page 30), that's just not the case. As one character makes an obvious cry for help, the other character judges and rejoices that she's not in that place.

This sketch requires a dark space, two spotlights, and a flashlight for effect. It's a serious piece that can lead into Bible study, a youth service, or a discussion.
• Why are some "lights" brighter than others?
• How can you hide your light? How can you let it shine?
• What does your brightness say about your relationship with Christ?

Curt Cloninger

A Day in Court

The ruling in this court is almost as ridiculous as the rulings on Ally McBeal! The crazy part is that it's right in line with the way God says we should treat sinners. Sins have consequences. However, once they're forgiven, they're forgotten. Now if we could only get that through our dim brains!

The sketch on page 32 uses a courtroom example of trying to keep someone out of church for past mistakes. Luckily, the judge knows the payment has already been made, and he rules for the defendant. *Bryan Belknap*

As the Cookie Crumbles: The Search for Fig-nificance

Sometimes the toughest lessons are taught in the weirdest ways. This sketch is not that deep, but the discussion that follows can be. We eavesdrop on Isaac and Newton, two Fig Newtons, discussing the struggle of comparing ourselves with others and feeling worthless. The dilemma on page 34 is not resolved, which makes it an ideal discussion starter.

The sketch requires some preplanning. Make cookie costumes from cardboard. Add soap-opera-type music to create the melodrama mood. This is not a serious sketch, but it should be polished to make its point. The two main characters have quite a few lines.

Incorporate a few of the following scriptures to direct thinking and discussion: Romans 8:17; Ephesians 1:5, 2:10; Colossians 2:10; 2 Timothy 1:7. Questions may include—
• Where do we get our significance?
• Who decides what's valuable?
• How do you accept the way you were created?
• What does God have to say about where we should get our worth?
Larry Marshall

Who Am I?

I.D. please. For everything from registering for school to writing a check, you've got to have identification. That's a little tough when your name is John Doe, and no one can give you a clue about who you are, including your own father! Ultimately, the sketch on page 36 shows that the only true identity we can rely on is the one given by God alone.

Just as in real life, on the stage the people who surround John Doe can't help him. They offer lots of words, but only when John turns to God's Word does he discover who he is. The characters on stage

remain frozen until it is their turn to talk. Blocking for this one is simple so spend some preparation time memorizing lines before rehearsal. *Kevin Spurlock*

The Building Permit
Genesis 5-9

Red tape is as old as, well, Noah. The sketch on page 39 gives your students a whimsical look at a man trying to obey the law and get a permit to build a boat. Sometimes obedience to God doesn't fit with policies already set in place. *Douglas Twitchell*

I'm Almost Ready
1 Thessalonians 5:2

Some people just can't seem to get anywhere on time. If they're on time, you can bet something didn't get done! The sketch on page 42 shows us what it may be like when our time comes to go to heaven. It won't be quite what you expected, and you'll never be totally ready for it. As much as she wants to, Amy will never be totally prepared to leave.

Both characters wear everyday clothes. Amy is frantic and a bit scattered. First Thessalonians 5:2 says Christ will come like a thief in the night. We never know when it's going to happen. Just like Amy, we need to live so that we're ready to leave anytime! *Bryan Belknap*

Community Kitchen
Matthew 25:31-46

In the sketch on page 44, an interviewer talks to three kitchen volunteers and three food recipients. Each person has a story—some are touching, and others remind us how crooked people can be. Following one disappointing interview after another, the questioner finally talks with someone who truly understands what serving is all about. The mixed emotions and uncertainty about serving end when he realizes that whether someone takes advantage or not, whether someone has a bad attitude or not, Jesus would still take the time to meet these people's needs.

You can make this sketch as simple or as elaborate as you want. A pantomime of serving and eating can be just as effective as using props and costuming. Each character has a distinct personality, so remember this when you cast your actors. Reading one of the suggested Bible passages between the first and second parts adds depth to the presentation. This sketch provides an opportunity to talk about what your group believes about helping others and what they can do as a result.

You can also use this sketch to examine the servers' attitudes. Some serve out of the goodness of their hearts. Others serve for selfish reasons. Use this sketch to explore what's more important—the attitude or the action. *Stephen C. Deutsch*

PARABLE ON JUSTICE

LUKE 18:1-8

The sketch on page 48 serves up a silly spoof based on Luke 18:1-8. As a widow goes to a judge for help, the judge just wants her to go away. Undaunted, she returns over and over—not just to ask for his help but to present her request as a serenade. The judge finally gives in and helps her. *Dewey Roth*

DAVID AND JONATHAN

1 SAMUEL 18-20

Not quite a chick flick, the sketch on page 49 tells the touching story of a friendship between two guys who face many obstacles and go against family and society just to be friends. In the end they're willing to die for their friendship. David and Jonathan have captivated audiences for years. Their story illustrates everything from loyalty to overcoming difficult odds.

First Samuel 18-20 and Proverbs 17:17 give insight into the Christian perspective of friendship.

Some of the props can be imagined if you'd like a simpler production. *David E. Ruiz*

THE WONDER YEARS

Catch a rare moment with Jesus, not as miracle worker, Savior of the world, or remarkable teacher, but as a cousin to John. Being around family can be hard since they know you best. Imagine Jesus telling John that he's the Messiah while they're on a fishing trip. The sketch on page 56 offers striking familiarity between the two characters, which makes their friendship and blood relation seem genuine. It may or may not have happened this way, but it's a good guess! *David Ruiz*

TRUST

PSALM 33:22 AND PSALM 119:42

We all take a lot of things in life for granted—that the car will work, the radio will play music, and the library will have a book we like. We trust that these parts of life will always happen. But is that what trust is—knowing that something just *is*? The sketch on page 61 explores the real meaning of trust and raises questions about these things. The sketch reminds us that the only trust we need to have is in God, his Word, and his promises. Instead of getting caught up in the world, we need to look past these everyday things and realize that God is the only constant.

Your students learn this important lesson by listening to a quick conversation between three very different friends. They all have ideas about what they can count on. In the end two of them still aren't so sure about the whole God thing but the third has made up her mind!
• Name some of the things you place your trust in. What do they say about you?
• Is trust earned? How does God earn our trust?
• What would you tell a person about the benefits in trusting our Lord?
• When confidence in a person is broken, what steps must be taken to restore it?
Michael Hotchkiss

NTTV PRESENTS: NEW TESTAMENT NEWS—GOOD NEWS, ALL THE TIME

If CNN had been around 2000 years ago, it might have looked something like this. See the crucifixion, death, and resurrection delivered through sound bites and short reports. The sketch on page 62 includes a full script for anchors, live reporting shots, and built-in spaces for your own original video commercials.

This sketch gets everyone involved! You'll need 25 characters (many can play two parts—live and recorded). Set design, video, music, and more complete the presentation. Read through this longer and more complicated sketch and plan carefully for rehearsals and special effects coordination. The performance will amaze people as it all comes together, and they witness the reason for Christianity live through broadcast news! *Sheri Gruden*

RUNNING FROM GOD

JONAH 1-4

Grab your fishing pole, we're gonna revisit Jonah. The sketch on page 69 takes you on a quick sail through Jonah 1-4. Ultimately, the lesson is the same: you can't run away from God. If he wants you, he will find you—even if it's at the bottom of the ocean.

A lighthearted trip through Jonah's experience running from God's command and call leads him right where he was supposed to go in the first place. Funny how it seems to work that way! This sketch takes place in several locations. If you're feeling ambitious, by all

means rent a boat, catch a really big fish, and build a town. If not, well, small sets or make-believe will do.
Danny Formhals

HELL'S BARBERSHOP

Even Satan sometimes needs a therapist, and in hell the therapist is the barber. This creative rendition on page 72 shows the end times from Satan's perspective. Following the final judgment no one even recognizes Satan as a celebrity inhabitant of hell. While the barber cuts his hair, Satan whines and relives some of Christ's most glorious moments as he tries to figure out what he could have done differently. His barber nods, half listens, and sends him on his unmerry little way.

This sketch requires a little planning and someone with memorizing skills. A few simple but necessary props turn your stage into a barbershop. Satan has quite a few long lines as he retells the life of Christ on earth. Be prepared to laugh as you present one hell of a sketch!
Troy Price

BIBLE WALK THROUGH THE BEATITUDES

MATTHEW 5

A time machine takes you back to a small village in Israel where you eavesdrop and participate in some activities that reflect the truths of the beatitudes. The sketch on page 75, based on the Beatitudes in Matthew 5, offers interactive, experiential learning to the extreme. It resembles walking through the Stations of the Cross, but live actors at each station help explain the lesson and offer an example or activity to accompany the beatitude.

Organization is the key for this sketch. Eight scenes take place in eight different locations. In some scenes a biblical character delivers a monologue. In some scenes activities such as hand washing, snacks, or a game demonstrate the point. Have at least one strong leader at each location. Recruit people to serve as guides to help the group along its path and to answer any questions about the beatitudes and what they just experienced. You can also use this sketch to let your students host the rest of the church or families as an outreach tool! *Michael Murdock*

GENESIS 1-3

If only these walls could talk! Well, in the Garden of Eden there were no walls but there were plenty of trees and bushes. In the tell-all exposé on page 77, a tree and bush break the code of silence. The audience hears the story of Genesis 1-3 via a little gossip as this tree and

bush catch up on what's been going around the garden. National Enquirer has nothing on this exclusive conversation.

You can use these questions after the sketch to kick off a discussion.
• Do we all have the qualities of Adam and Eve in us? Explain.
• How does Genesis demonstrate God's dominance over his creation?
• What can we do to prevent ourselves from falling to the temptations of our own particular fruit of the biblical tree?
• Knowing that we all sin like the first people, how can that affect the way we speak to our God?
Michael Hotchkiss

WALKING ON WATER

MATTHEW 14:22-36

Open mouth, insert foot. That could be Peter's mantra. Once again we see his mouth getting him into a tough place. But, in the sketch on page 79, that place is actually *closer* to Jesus. Matthew 14:22-36 tells a tale of high seas adventures and ghosts on water. At least that's what the disciples thought at the time. And then it happened—Peter was called out of the boat. Even though he stumbled and had to be rescued, he got out of the boat while the others were left sloshing and shaking!

This sketch has great possibilities for Bible study. After the sketch, ask each person to consider what role they would take if they'd been in that fishing boat. Would they recognize Jesus but observe from the boat, be scared, want to go to him, or mock the one walking on water? Use the following questions to get the discussion going.
• What have you been asked to step out on faith for?
• How do you react when people make fun of you or don't understand why you do things?
• How can you learn to get out of the boat more?
• Why do you think Peter ended up sinking?
• What makes you sink when you started out strong in a decision?
John C. Madvig

LOVE THAT WILL NOT LET ME GO
ZEPHANIAH 3:17

People don't usually like the idea of being tied to something. In this case, Alma is tied to Jesus—even when she tries to push him away. This demonstration of unconditional love and forgiveness makes the sketch on page 81 a visual reminder of the forgiveness Jesus has for us, every time we sin.

This sketch focuses on blocking and visual images.

The characters don't speak any words—they just mime to a Steve Camp song in the background. You'll need a few simple costumes and several signs made ahead of time. You can use Microsoft PowerPoint to project the verses or have someone read them. Use rehearsals to get timing down with the music for a flawless presentation. *Larry Marshall*

IN THE NEWS THIS WEEK

We interrupt these regularly scheduled introductions to bring you the latest breaking news. Just discovered—the lost tapes reporting Jesus' birth. The sketch on page 82 is the transcription of the original broadcast event just after Jesus was born. Use this sketch to capture sound bites of the blessed event from many different angels, I mean angles.

This sketch offers a framework for a Christmas program but not the entire program itself. Between interviews use singing, activities, recitations, or any other Christmas tradition your church has. The logistics can be complicated so be certain you prepare before the first rehearsal. Keep the technical directions in mind—they add to the overall news broadcast theme. This sketch sheds new light on an old, familiar story! *Douglas Twitchell*

Recipe for a
Quiet Time

- -

CAST

- Corina
- Latisha
- Waiter

PROPS

- Restaurant table with two chairs
- Waiter outfit
- Two menus
- Order pad and a pencil
- Sign that reads THE RIGHTEOUS RESTAURANT

- -

(Girls enter the restaurant and sit at a table.)

CORINA: I'm starving; let's eat. Those few potato chips last night didn't last very long.

LATISHA: *(sarcastically)* Few potato chips! You mean the whole bag didn't last you very long.

CORINA: I didn't eat the whole bag!

LATISHA: You most certainly did. I sure didn't get any.

CORINA: You did too! I wouldn't eat the whole bag; I'm watching my figure.

LATISHA: Oh, you are?

CORINA: Yes, I am. So I most certainly would not stuff myself with fat, cholesterol-laden snacks.

LATISHA: Yes, you would.

CORINA: No, I wouldn't.

LATISHA: Would too!

CORINA: Would not!

WAITER: *(hesitantly)* Excuse me, ladies. I hate to break up your discussion, but would you like to see some menus? *(has two menus, an order pad with a pencil, and two glasses of water in his hands)*

CORINA: Uh, yes, please. *(waiter hands each girl a menu)* I'm *so* hungry. *(looks at waiter)*

WAITER: Yeah, I've heard. Well, what can I get you to eat?

CORINA: I'd like a breakfast omelette, but I can't read this menu.

LATISHA: Yeah, this is confusing. What's all this "God's Word" and "Quiet Place"?

WAITER: *(interrupting)* That's a recipe for a quiet time.

LATISHA: A quiet time?

WAITER: Yeah, a quiet time. You girls are Christians, aren't you?

CORINA: Well, *(hesitantly)* of course, I go to church every Sunday. A lot of cute boys go to my Bible study class.

WAITER: A quiet time has nothing to do with going to church. It's time you spend every morning with God.

LATISHA: What do you mean?

WAITER: See? Look. *(points to the menu)* The recipe for quiet time is just like making an egg omelette. You start with God's Word. Like the egg, it is the most important ingredient. Second Timothy 2:15 says, "Do your best to present yourself to God as one approved, a workman who does not need to be ashamed and who correctly handles the word of truth."

LATISHA: What does "correctly handling the word of truth" mean?

WAITER: It means that you know what the Bible says and what the Bible means. You can't really know what it says unless you read it.

CORINA: What does Mark 1:35 have to do with it? "Very early in the morning, while it was still dark, Jesus got up, left the house, and went off to a solitary place, where he prayed."

WAITER: That verse represents the other ingredients that make an omelette taste good: the milk, the cheese, and the seasonings.

LATISHA: *(sarcastically)* So, what you're saying is if I'm not an early bird, I can't have a quiet time.

WAITER: Not necessarily. Jesus started his day with God to help get him through all the difficulties that would be coming his way. It's kind of like brushing your teeth. You wouldn't dare go out of the house in the morning to meet your friends with bad breath and gunk on your teeth. Jesus realized he had to have God's help before

he could face anyone. That's why he started his day with God. The important thing is to have a quiet place where you won't be bothered, a consistent time every day, and a consistent place.

CORINA: So what do the heat and pan and spatula signify?

WAITER: Psalm 10:17 says, "You hear, O Lord, the desire of the afflicted; you encourage them, and you listen to their cry." If you want to mature to a healthy adult you have to take care of your body. You know, get plenty of rest, watch what you eat, get exercise.

LATISHA: *(interrupting)* Not eat a whole bag of potato chips before bed. *(glares at Corina)*

CORINA: I didn't eat the whole bag. *(pause)* I, I, left three in there.

WAITER: Anyway, if you want to mature as a Christian, you must have a strong desire to grow closer to God. That happens when you hear what he has to say to you by reading his Word and talking to him in prayer about your hurts, disappointment, and joys.

CORINA: Sounds like a lot of work to me.

WAITER: It is. But it's worth it. Anything worth having takes work.

CORINA: *(hesitantly)* I don't know.

LATISHA: That sounds pretty good to me. I think I'll try the egg omelette with the works.

CORINA: Yeah, okay, me too. I'll give it a try.

WAITER: Wise choice. Remember, we don't need to make a schedule and try to fit God in it. We need to make our schedule around God.

END

RECIPE FOR A QUIET TIME

An Egg Omelette

EGG (God's Word)

Do your best to present yourself to God as one approved, a workman who does not need to be ashamed and who correctly handles the word of truth.

—2 Timothy 2:15

MILK (Quiet Place)
CHEESE (Consistent Time)
SEASONING (Consistent Place)

Very early in the morning, while it was still dark, Jesus got up, left the house and went off to a solitary place, where he prayed.

—Mark 1:35

HEAT (Strong desire to have a quiet time)
PAN AND SPATULA (Prayer)

You hear, O Lord, the desire of the afflicted: you encourage them, and you listen to their cry.

—Psalm 10:17

*We don't need to make a schedule and try to fit God in it.
We need to make our schedule around God.*

ABSOLUTE POWER

CAST

- Pontius Pilate
- Debra, Personal Assistant
- Leah, Junior Secretary
- Pharisee
- Junior Pharisee
- Jesus

PROPS

- Large desk
- Impressive chair
- Laptop computer
- Inkstand
- Folders
- Modern telephone
- Picture window overlooking the city
- Couple of generic office armchairs
- Two small desks
- Desktop computer
- Fax machine
- Telephones
- Jars of pencils
- In and out trays
- Little stuffed animals
- Stack of mail
- Royal robe stained with blood
- Bowl of water on stand

The scene opens in Pilate's office. To the left of center stage sits a large desk with a laptop computer, an inkstand, some folders, and a modern telephone. An impressive chair is behind the desk, facing center stage. At the back of the stage, a large picture window overlooks the city. Just to the right of the window, sit a couple of generic office armchairs pushed against the wall.

Below the stage on the far right, sit two desks with a desktop computer, a fax machine, telephones, jars of pencils, folders, in and out trays, stuffed animals, and other secretarial items.

In this important office everything, especially Pilate's desk, is very clean, tidy, and tasteful. Added ornamentation, like a potted plant or a portrait of Caesar, may be added to complete the effect.

You will need prerecorded cries of a crowd shouting, "No! Release Barabbas! Release Barabbas!" "Crucify him! Crucify him!" and "No! Crucify him!" and "Let his blood be on us, and on our children." and a tape player.

Act 1, Scene 1

(The lights come up on PILATE at his desk, practicing a speech. He's alone on stage long enough to display his poise and bureaucratic aptitude. He recites the speech with that tone of bright sincerity universally adopted by politicians making insincere speeches.)

PILATE: Friends, Romans, countrymen. We live in dark and difficult times. It seems that every day brings to our attention some new crime, some new outrage, and some new act of injustice. The people ask us, "How long must we endure the crimes of evil men?" It is time we answered them. Rome believes in peace. Rome believes in stability. Rome believes in justice. These are the simple answers. And it falls upon us, the leaders of this land, to see that the people hear them.

(DEBRA, his personal assistant, a smartly dressed woman of about 50 with an overcoat thrown over one arm, enters from stage right, sorting through the day's mail. She jumps slightly when she sees PILATE.)

DEBRA: Oh, you startled me, sir. I wasn't expecting to see you here.

PILATE: I had an important speech to write, and I find it easier to concentrate here than at home. I don't usually beat you to the office, do I?

DEBRA: No, sir.

PILATE: I should try it more often. The traffic's easier, for a start. Plus I got to see the sunrise through this window.

DEBRA: Didn't those men at the gate give you any trouble?

PILATE: What men?

DEBRA: Didn't you see them?

PILATE: They must have arrived after I did. Who are they?

DEBRA: I didn't speak with them, but I gather they were from the temple of the Jewish god down in the city.

PILATE: It's probably another one of their festivals.

DEBRA: There were an awful lot of them, sir, and the sun's only just up. I think it might be something serious.

PILATE: If it's serious, and they want to see me, they can make an appointment. Buzz the gate, and tell security to move them on.

DEBRA: Yes, sir.

(DEBRA takes her seat at her desk and picks up the phone to make the call. Her junior secretary, LEAH, arrives stage right.)

LEAH: Good morning, Debra. Good morning, Mr. Pilate.

PILATE: Good morning, Leah. Did you have any problems getting in?

LEAH: The security men helped me get in, thank you, Mr. Pilate. I couldn't have gotten in otherwise. There must be a hundred of them out there.

PILATE: Really? A hundred?

LEAH: Yes, Mr. Pilate. They seemed angry. I think they had some sort of prisoner with them.

PILATE: A prisoner? Why would a crowd of priests have a prisoner?

LEAH: I don't know Mr. Pilate *(takes her seat at her desk and begins to look through her work. DEBRA finishes her call and looks over at PILATE.)*

DEBRA: Mr. Pilate, the guards at the gate say that the priests refuse to move on. They demand to see you. I think it's something about a man they want tried.

PILATE: And what's stopping them from making an appointment like everyone else?

DEBRA: I don't know, sir. What should I tell the gate?

PILATE: I suppose I'd better see them. Do I have any windows today?

DEBRA: *(checks computer or large day planner)* I've allowed three hours for your lunch meeting with the tetrarch. If you cut that down to two and a half, I can slot them in at 2:30.

PILATE: Half an hour less with the tetrarch won't hurt me. Write them in, and tell the gate to inform them.

DEBRA: Yes, sir. *(gets to it)*

(PILATE practices his speech.)

DEBRA: Excuse me, sir, I've got the gate on the phone. They say the priests demand to see you now.

PILATE: They demand to see me?

DEBRA: They say the matter is urgent.

PILATE: Who are they to demand to see me?

DEBRA: I don't know, sir.

20

PILATE: Hmmmm. They should know better than this. I'm intrigued. Send their leader up, and he can have ten minutes.

DEBRA: *(passes message into phone and listens to reply. Gulps.)* Mr. Pilate?

PILATE: Yes, Debra.

DEBRA: Apparently they want you to come down and see them.

PILATE: Do they now?

DEBRA: Yes, sir.

PILATE: And why is this?

DEBRA: Apparently we're nearing one of their holy days, and…

PILATE: And?

DEBRA: They say if they enter the building, they'll become ceremonially unclean.

PILATE: *(long, tense pause)* My palace will make them unclean?

DEBRA: That's what they say, Mr. Pilate.

PILATE: I would think it's the other way around. I don't remember any public baths in Jerusalem before the Roman army arrived.

DEBRA: No, sir.

PILATE: If it were any others, I'd have them all flogged. But these Jews are so precious about their clergy. Inform security that I'm coming down to speak with the priests.

DEBRA: Yes, sir.

PILATE: *(as he exits)* And this had better be good.

Act 1, Scene 2

(PILATE crosses the auditorium to the back where the PHARISEE and the JUNIOR PHARISEE wait for him. The PHARISEES wear long, dark robes. The CHIEF PHARISEE stands aloofly, while the JUNIOR PHARISEE fidgets.)

PILATE: Good morning, gentlemen.

PHARISEE: Good morning, my lord Pilate.

PILATE: *(pause)* Are we going to stand in the cold all day, or is there a point to this meeting?

JUNIOR PHARISEE: My lord, we have apprehended a dangerous criminal.

PILATE: A criminal? Are you priests or soldiers?

PHARISEE: He is a criminal, my lord, and criminals must be delivered into the proper hands.

PILATE: I'm pleased to see that the Jewish church has become so civic-minded. Who is this criminal?

PHARISEE: His name is Jesus, my lord. *(gestures for JESUS to be brought forward. As he comes, he stumbles, and the two PHARISEES leap back in alarm. PILATE steadies JESUS, more out of decorum than real care.)*

PILATE: I see you've handcuffed and beaten him, gentlemen. I don't think he's going to hurt you.

JUNIOR PHARISEE: Oh, it's not that. We can't get any blood on us, or we'll become unclean.

PILATE: You should be more careful to stand back the next time you order a beating. What charges do you bring against this man?

PHARISEE: If he were not a criminal, we would not have handed him over to you.

PILATE: *(slowly, sensing that something is not quite right)* Well, take him yourselves, and judge him by your own law.

JUNIOR PHARISEE: But we have no right to execute someone.

PILATE: Execute?

(JUNIOR PHARISEE realizes he said too much and looks to PHARISEE.)

PHARISEE: His crimes warrant execution, my lord.

PILATE: I see. *(pauses thoughtfully)* Bring the prisoner to my office. I doubt it'll make him any more 'unclean.' *(turns and leaves, to return to office)*

Act 1, Scene 3

(PILATE strides into his office, goes to his desk, and gives orders to his secretaries as he goes.)

PILATE: Do we have any information about a man names Jesus?

LEAH: Is that the name of the prisoner outside?

PILATE: Yes. He's got the Jewish priests more riled than I've ever seen them. He must have spread some slander about their God.

LEAH: Yes sir, I read about him on the Internet. He's popular with the people, Mr. Pilate.

PILATE: Is this true, Debra?

DEBRA: Yes, sir. If you'll look in your current events file, I've printed out some material on him. He caused a lot of fuss when he arrived in Jerusalem a few days ago, and I thought the information might be useful. *(hands him a manila folder)*

PILATE: This is why I pay you so much. *(goes to his own desk, missing DEBRA's skeptical look. Leafs through folder as JESUS walks in. Secretaries look, shocked at the blood. JESUS stands before the desk, and PILATE gives him a cool professional stare.)*

PILATE: I've read about your activities, Jesus, son of Joseph. You've done many things in the past few years. You've made quite a name for yourself. And claimed a good many interesting things.

(JESUS is silent.)

PILATE: For example, are you really the King of the Jews?

JESUS: Is that your own idea or did others talk to you about me?

PILATE: Have you murdered someone? Stolen something? Exploited widows and orphans? Cursed your god? Have you committed any crimes against the Empire?

JESUS: My record speaks for itself.

PILATE: Nothing is recorded here. So, are you the King of the Jews?

JESUS: My kingdom is not of this world. If it were, my servants would fight to prevent my arrest by the Jews. But my kingdom is from another place.

PILATE: You are a king, then!

JESUS: You are right in saying that I am a king. In fact, for this reason I was born, and for this I came into the world, to testify to the truth. Everyone on the side of truth listens to me.

PILATE: Really? When you've been in politics as long as I have, you learn that there is one unanswerable question. "What is truth?" *(He gets up and walks down to his secretaries)* This man is simply deranged. I ave him sent back to the gates, and I will release him. *(PILATE strides to the back of the auditorium to meet the priests.)*

Act 1, Scene 4

(PILATE stands before the PHARISEE and JUNIOR PHARISEE.)

PILATE: I find no basis for the charge against this man. I shall release him, and anything that he brings upon himself after that is his concern.

JUNIOR PHARISEE: But we found that this man is subverting our nation. He opposes payment of taxes to Caesar!

PILATE: Really? Is that true?

(JUNIOR PHARISEE suddenly realizes that he has lied. Looks stricken.)

PILATE: I asked you, is that true?

PHARISEE: *(smiles coldly)* Well, we all get a little irritable at tax time. Even I sometimes resent the amount I have to pay. I find no basis for a change against him.

JUNIOR PHARISEE: But he stirs up people all over Judea with his teaching. He started in Galilee and came all the way here.

PILATE: *(with a vulture's smile)* I'm sorry, did you say Galilee?

JUNIOR PHARISEE: *(panicking at PILATE's look)* No.

PILATE: No?

JUNIOR PHARISEE: I mean yes.

PILATE: You're sure?

JUNIOR PHARISEE: I think so.

PILATE: Ah, well then, gentlemen, the decision is not in my hands at all.

PHARISEE: But you are the Roman governor.

PILATE: Yes, but this man is Galilean, and thus comes under the jurisdiction of Herod. You see, we Romans have a chain of command. I cannot announce any sort of sentence on this man without the approval of Herod. I shall send him to Herod. Fortunately he's visiting Jerusalem at the moment, so it shouldn't take long. I'm sure we are both eager to see justice done as soon as possible. Am I right?

PHARISEE: Yes, my lord Pilate.

PILATE: Hand him over to my guards, and I will have him transported to Herod without delay. Good day, gentlemen. *(strides back to his office)*

Act 2, Scene 1

(PILATE sits at his desk, reading from his laptop screen and chuckling occasionally. His secretaries work at their desks. After a particularly loud chuckle, DEBRA looks over at PILATE.)

DEBRA: Has someone sent you an e-mail joke, Mr. Pilate?

PILATE: No, Debra. It's from Herod. He interviewed this Jesus person and found no basis for the charge against him. He's sending him back to me for final dismissal.

23

DEBRA: And that's funny?

PILATE: No, but he described the antics of the Jews trying to trump up charges against Jesus—like little children trying to blame the weakest one for breaking the cookie jar.

DEBRA: I though you didn't approve of Herod.

PILATE: He's a fat disgusting old leech, but he's still canny enough to see through these Jews. Some poor idiot thinks he's God, the hypocrites get offended, and suddenly they want him put to death in the most painful way we Romans have devised. They're just like spoiled children.

(DEBRA's telephone rings. She answers and speaks silently into receiver.)

LEAH: So what's going to happen to Jesus?

PILATE: Herod had him flogged and ridiculed; that should appease the priests. Then I'll make a proclamation and set him free.

DEBRA: *(covers receiver with hand)* Sir, the guards say Jesus has been returned. What should they do with him?

PILATE: Keep him there. I'd better go down and speak with the priests again. *(strides down to gate, where he meets the two PHARISEES and JESUS, who now wears a royal robe stained with his blood)*

Act 2, Scene 2

PILATE: Gentlemen, as requested, I examined the charges against this man and sent him to Herod for further consideration of the matter. We both find no substance to the charges against this man, and so I intend to release him.

JUNIOR PHARISEE: No!

PHARISEE: That will not be acceptable, my lord.

PILATE: You brought him to me as one who is inciting the people to rebellion. I have examined him and found no basis for these charges. Neither has Herod, or he would not have sent him back to me. He has done nothing to deserve death. I will punish him for his impudence, and then I will release him.

PHARISEE: No, my Lord. He must be crucified.

PILATE: I have told you. By the law of Rome he has done nothing wrong. As an upholder of Roman law I cannot in good conscience condemn him to death. You're priests. You know all about good conscience.

PHARISEE: No, my lord. He must die for his crimes.

PILATE: Then you take him and crucify him. I will not.

JUNIOR PHARISEE: We cannot.

PILATE: Why? Because you'll become unclean?

PHARISEE: Jesus claims to be the Son of God. Under our law he must die. Under Roman law we cannot put him to death. So you must do it.

PILATE: I am under no such compulsion. I will not condemn a man because he has irritated a gang of priests.

JUNIOR PHARISEE: The offense is not against us. It is against God.

PILATE: Unfortunately, I don't care about your God.

PHARISEE: But the people do. It is they who demand his death.

PILATE: Is that a fact? It's odd that I don't see any of them here with you.

PHARISEE: They await your presence in the square. It is tradition at the Feast of Passover.

PILATE: Oh yes, you're right. I think I'll go and speak to them now, and see what's on their minds. Your prisoner will come with me. *(returns to his office with JESUS)*

Act 2, Scene 3

(PILATE enters his office.)

PILATE: I am dealing with madmen here.

DEBRA: Sir?

PILATE: They are consumed with jealousy because a man has gained a following among the peasants. Then they risk incurring the wrath of the empire by demanding his execution without any evidence. Does this sound like the work of sane men?

DEBRA: It sounds like the work of dangerous men, sir.

PILATE: Unfortunately, yes. Are the Jews assembled out in the square?

DEBRA: Yes, sir. They're waiting for your Passover address.

PILATE: It'll be brief. *(gestures at JESUS)* Keep an eye on him. *(starts to go out onto balcony, but DEBRA calls to him)*

DEBRA: Oh, Mr. Pilate!

PILATE: Yes, Debra?

DEBRA: I just remembered. I had a call from your wife. She left a message for you about him.

PILATE: She did? What is it?

DEBRA: *(reading from a pad)* Do not have anything to do with that innocent man. I have suffered a great deal today in a dream because of him.

PILATE: *(pause)* If she calls again, tell her it's too late. I'm already involved.

(PILATE walks onto the balcony. A single spotlight falls on him to delineate the balcony from the rest of the stage.)

PILATE: *(speaks with authority)* Good day to you, people of Jerusalem. Today is the eve of the Feast of the Passover, and on this day it is traditional for me to release a prisoner from our jails and grant him a full and unconditional pardon. This year, we have in our custody a man named Jesus, also called the King of the Jews. Is this the man that you would have me release today?

(Play prerecorded cries of the crowd shouting, "No! Release Barabbas! Release Barabbas!" from the back of the room.)

PILATE: Barabbas is a thug and a murderer, while Jesus is innocent of all wrongdoing. If I release Barabbas, what shall I do with Jesus?

(Play prerecorded cries of "Crucify him! Crucify him!" from the back of the room.)

PILATE: What you say makes no sense. You ask for the freedom of the guilty and the death of the innocent. Is this really what you want?

(Prerecorded cries of "Crucify him! Crucify him!" play from the back of the room. PILATE returns from the balcony and steps back into his office.)

DEBRA: Mr. Pilate, I have a man on line one that wants to talk to you. He says it's about Jesus, and it's urgent.

PILATE: Put him through to my phone. *(gestures at JESUS)* And have the guards take him away and flog him.

DEBRA: Sir?

PILATE: Don't question me, Debra. Maybe they can beat some sense into him.

(DEBRA leads JESUS offstage then returns to her desk. PILATE picks up his phone and takes the call.)

PILATE: This is Pontius Pilate of Jerusalem… Yes…Go on…I beg your pardon, you did what?…I see…Yes, I'd worked that much out for myself…Yes, I know he's not guilty…Well, what do you want me to do about it?…That's your concern, not mine…I'm not surprised, that you feel bad…Look, I don't care how upset you feel. You were foolish enough to deal with these people, and now you must pay the price. It's not my fault that you're the only person around here who has a conscience. You'll just have to deal with it as best as you can. I don't have time for this, Mr. Iscariot. Good day! (hangs up and thinks briefly)

PILATE: Debra, would you sell someone who loved you for thirty pieces of silver?

DEBRA: Of course not, Mr. Pilate.

PILATE: Leah?

LEAH: No, sir. Why?

PILATE: Just curious. I'm beginning to really dislike these Jews. What sort of God would choose them to be his people?

DEBRA: One with a forgiving heart, I suppose.

PILATE: He'd need it.

(DEBRA's phone rings. She answers it, listens to a message, then speaks to PILATE.)

DEBRA: Mr. Pilate, the guards have beaten the prisoner, but they're worried that he can't take much more.

PILATE: Tell them to send him back up here.

(DEBRA does as she is told. After a pause of about ten seconds, the secretaries get on with their work and PILATE hacks at his speech. JESUS returns to stage with more blood on him.)

PILATE: Are you feeling a little more cooperative now?

(JESUS is silent.)

PILATE: Fine. Come with me. (takes JESUS out onto the balcony) People of Jerusalem. You see before you Jesus of Nazareth, also called the Christ, King of the Jews. As you can see, he has been duly punished for such crimes as he has committed. Shall I release him?

(Prerecorded cries of "No! Crucify him!" play from a speaker at the back of the room.)

PILATE: He committed no crime punishable by crucifixion. By all our laws, I must release him. He is innocent.

(Prerecorded cries of "No! Crucify him!" play from a speaker at the back of the room. PILATE and Jesus come in from the balcony.)

PILATE: What have you done to make these people hate you so? What foul crime did you commit to make them thirst for your blood like a pack of starving wolves? What hole did you crawl out of that offends them so much that they want to see you nailed to a cross and left out in the sun to die?

(JESUS remains silent.)

PILATE: Speak up! I can't hear you.

(JESUS remains silent.)

PILATE: Do you refuse to speak to me? Don't you realize that I have the power to either free you or to crucify you?

JESUS: You would have no power over me if it were not given to you from above. The one who handed me over to you is guilty of a greater sin.

PILATE: I don't care about sin. I care about justice. I want to see justice done.

JESUS: You're not alone.

26

PILATE: And yet you will not help me. I've heard you can speak eloquently on the law of the Jews. Why will you not use that eloquence in your defense?

JESUS: It's not needed. It's not wanted.

PILATE: I need it! I want it! I can't do this alone.

JESUS: I say again, you're not alone.

PILATE: I may as well be. I'm alone in my sanity, of that I'm sure. *(leaves the office and goes to the priests)*

Act 2, Scene 4

(PILATE confronts the PHARISEES again.)

PHARISEE: Well, my lord Pilate, did you ask the people of Jerusalem about Jesus?

PILATE: I did.

PHARISEE: I'm eager to hear their response.

PILATE: I'm surprised to hear that. I thought you'd already orchestrated their response.

PHARISEE: The people simply respect authority, Pilate.

PILATE: The people are mindless sheep. One day they adore Jesus as if he were some heavenly being, and the next they're baying for his blood.

PHARISEE: In any case, their wishes have been made known. Jesus must be crucified.

PILATE: You seem to be forgetting something. Jerusalem has been part of the Roman Empire for over 50 years now, and the Roman Empire is not a democracy. Caesar decides who lives or dies, and I am Caesar's representative here. The people do not make the decisions.

PHARISEE: But if the people are denied this, they may become uncontrollable.

PILATE: Is that a threat?

PHARISEE: Of course not, my lord. I simply state a fact.

PILATE: Well, it's amazing how easy it is to reestablish control with a few well-armed soldiers. Just look at what happened to Barabbas.

PHARISEE: That is true. Such an event would be regrettable. No doubt Caesar would view it as such.

PILATE: I'm not sure that I follow you.

PHARISEE: I only suggest that when Caesar hears that some of this loyal subjects were killed while protesting the release of a man who claimed that he, not Caesar, was their rightful king, it might appear neglectful.

PILATE: I don't believe Caesar is that naïve.

PHARISEE: Of course not. But it seems to me that a true friend of Caesar's would not take the risk.

PILATE: Are you questioning my loyalty to Caesar?

PHARISEE: I would be foolish if I did so.

PILATE: Indeed you would be. But I'm not concerned with my allegiance to Caesar. I'm more interested in yours.

PHARISEE: Mine?

PILATE: Yes. I hold the King of the Jews in my office. And yet it seems to me that you would prefer that Caesar be your king.

PHARISEE: Caesar *is* our king, my lord Pilate.

PILATE: Caesar, the ruler of the empire that enslaves your nation, the ruler of the empire that took away your right to administer your own justice, the ruler who is officially recognized as a god by our civilization—he is your king?

PHARISEE: *(cold pause, then)* Yes.

JUNIOR PHARISEE: *(in a loud whisper)* But sir, we have no God but Jehovah!

PHARISEE: *(tersely)* Quiet!

PILATE: I'm sorry. I think I missed that. Who is your king?

PHARISEE: *(through clenched teeth)* Caesar, my lord Pilate.

PILATE: And Jesus, who preaches salvation for eternity, who healed the blind and the lame and the leprous, who performed miracles before thousands of witnesses, who shows nothing but love and patience for his enemies. He is a criminal to be executed?

JUNIOR PHARISEE: He must be crucified!

PHARISEE: He is a criminal, Pilate, and must be crucified.

PILATE: Well, gentlemen, it's good to know where we all stand. I think I can take it from here. You may return to your temple.

PHARISEE: But what of Jesus?

PILATE: I will deal with Jesus. As for you, you have my permission to leave.

PHARISEE: Leave?

PILATE: Now. *(PHARISEES bow. PILATE turns and returns to office.)*

Act 2, Scene 5

(Back in PILATE's office.)

PILATE: Debra, take this man out to the guards, and tell them to take him out to Golgotha and crucify him.

DEBRA: But, sir, he's innocent!

PILATE: Thank you, Debra. I'm well aware of that. Please do as I say.

DEBRA: You can't execute an innocent man!

PILATE: I can, and I will. Take him to the guards, Debra. *(DEBRA pauses in indecision.)* Debra! Do as I say!

(DEBRA takes JESUS and slowly leads him off stage. PILATE watches them go, then steps out onto the balcony.)

PILATE: Good day to you again, people of Jerusalem. I come before you once more to give you an opportunity to save the life of an innocent man. That man is Jesus of Nazareth, the King of the Jews. His life is in your hands. What shall I do with this man?

(Prerecorded cries of "Crucify him!" play from the back of the room.)

PILATE: Why? What crime has he committed?

(Prerecorded cries of "Crucify him!" play from the back of the room.)

PILATE: Very well then. *(washes his hands in a bowl of water on the balcony)* Do you see, people of Jerusalem? I wash my hands of this affair. I am innocent of this man's blood. It is your responsibility.

(Prerecorded cries of "Let his blood be on us, and on our children." play from a speaker at the back of the room.)

PILATE: You fools. *(returns indoors)* May their God have mercy on their putrid little souls.

LEAH: Mr. Pilate, you can't allow Jesus to be crucified.

PILATE: Leah, I'm getting a little tired of people telling me what I can and can't do.

LEAH: You don't have to listen to them. You're Pilate. You can do what you like.

PILATE: Theoretically, yes, that's true. But reality rarely coincides with theory.

LEAH: But why, Mr. Pilate?

PILATE: Because sometimes politics takes precedence over justice. Sometimes one person must be sacrificed for the good of many. Sometimes the rules need to be bent so they don't snap.

LEAH: That's not true, Mr. Pilate. It's better to have broken rules than to have rules that are bent out of shape.

PILATE: Don't be so naive as to think in absolutes, Leah. All great rulers and empires are forged in compromise.

LEAH: That's just an excuse! Great rulers have the strength to follow justice and not compromise.

PILATE: By that logic, Jesus is a more powerful ruler than I. And yet who is being led to Golgotha at this moment?

LEAH: At least Jesus didn't allow himself to be corrupted!

PILATE: Be careful of who you accuse of corruption, Leah.

LEAH: I'm sorry, Mr. Pilate, but that's what this is!

PILATE: I tell you it is politics, not corruption. Granted, an innocent man will die. But what if he doesn't? The Jews would riot by nightfall. Because of my decision, the city has peace, and I have those priests firmly by the throat. They made their allegiance to Caesar before witnesses. They will behave themselves from now on, or they will find themselves in the next round of crucifixions. Do you see why I made this decision now?

LEAH: Yes I do, Mr. Pilate. You made it because you're a coward who cares more about being comfortable than about justice!

PILATE: Get out of my office.

(LEAH runs out in tears. PILATE leans back in his chair and massages his temples. He leans forward again and catches sight of DEBRA standing in the shadows.)

PILATE: Did you hear all of that, Debra?

DEBRA: I did, sir. *(crosses to her desk and collects her coat and her handbag as PILATE delivers his next line)*

PILATE: Could you please get me a cup of coffee? Then phone the newspaper and put in and advertisement for a new secretary.

DEBRA: I'm sorry, sir, but you'll have to get your own coffee. And you'll need two advertisements, not one.

PILATE: Debra?

DEBRA: If politics really is more important than justice, sir, then I don't want to work in politics any more. Good-bye.

(PILATE watches her leave. He sits silently at his desk for a while, then looks down at his papers and finds his speech. He picks it up, sits up straight, smoothes his suit, and practices his speech. Only now his voice is not polished and optimistic, but dead. Lights slowly fade as he delivers the speech.)

PILATE: Friends, Romans, Countrymen. We live in dark and difficult times. It seems that every day brings to our attention some new crime, some new outrage, some new act of injustice. The people ask us, "How long must we endure the crimes of evil men?" it is time we answered them. I give you these answers. Rome believes in peace. Rome believes in stability. Rome believes in justice. These are the simple answers. And it falls upon us, the leaders of this land, to see that the people hear them.

(Lights go off completely.)

END

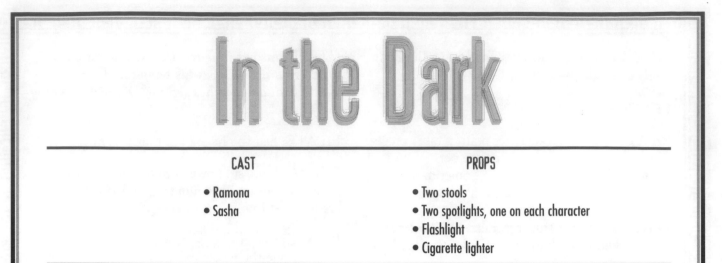

In the Dark

CAST	PROPS
• Ramona	• Two stools
• Sasha	• Two spotlights, one on each character
	• Flashlight
	• Cigarette lighter

RAMONA is an unloving, self-righteous bigot who thinks she's a Christian because she's better than everybody else. RAMONA sits on a stool stage left in a pool of light that is somewhat dim but makes her visible. RAMONA has one flashlight, which she turns on herself throughout the whole sketch. During the sketch, the pool of light on RAMONA gets slowly, but steadily, dimmer until she's in total darkness at the end except for the dim glow of her flashlight.

SASHA is a happy-go-lucky type, a pagan who's nervous about the dark. SASHA sits on a stool stage right, holding a cigarette lighter. The pool of light that surrounds her is very dim, and we can barely make her out in the darkness. Her pool of light remains constant through the whole sketch. We hear SASHA's voice in the semi-darkness. The melody for the song at the end of the sketch can be accessed at http://apk.net/~bmames/ht0147_.htm.

SASHA: Excuse me; do you have a light?

RAMONA: *(condescendingly)* No, I do not have a light. I don't smoke and, quite frankly, I'm offended by cigarette smoke. So, I'd appreciate it if you wouldn't.

SASHA: Oh, no problem. I won't smoke. But I meant a flashlight. You wouldn't happen to have another flashlight, would you?

RAMONA: No, I don't happen to have another flashlight. This is my special flashlight, and I don't give this away to just anybody.

SASHA: Sure, I understand. It's just all this dark. It's kinda got me spooked. Maybe if I just lit my cigarette lighter, that would help me out a little bit. Would you mind if I did that?

RAMONA: *(coldly)* As long as you don't light a cigarette.

SASHA: Sure. I won't. *(lights her lighter)* I know cigarette smoke can be a bother. I've been trying to quit for, gosh, I don't know how long. They sure do calm me down, though. Cigarettes. This dark is really making me nervous. I won't smoke, though.

RAMONA: *(colder)* Fine.

SASHA: *(after a nervous pause)* It just seems a little darker than usual, doesn't it? I sure hope my thumb holds out. I really don't like the dark. Never have.

RAMONA: *(a brush-off)* Well, good luck to you.

SASHA: I don't know what it is about the dark. It just always makes me nervous. Sometimes when I get nervous about it, I have a couple of beers. That'll usually settle me down for a while.

RAMONA: *(interrupting, fed up with the conversation)* Well, I don't drink, so I don't happen to have any beer here. And I don't smoke, so I don't happen to have any cigarettes. All I have here is light, which happens to be *my* light. Now, if you're nervous over there in your darkness, I suggest you go get your own light.

SASHA: *(pause, then simply, almost wistfully)* Boy, that would be great. My own light. I'd love that. I'm just a little nervous about getting off this stool to go look for one. It's so dark out there. I might trip or something. *(gets an idea)* Say, you wouldn't want to shine your light on these steps over here so I could sorta get started, would you?

RAMONA: *(almost sickeningly sweet and self-righteous lecture)* No, I wouldn't want to do that. You're over there in the dark, and that's your own doing. I, on the other hand, have chosen to be in the light. Now, if you want to go find you some beer or some cigarettes or whatever else you people need, you just stumble off and do that. But I've got my own light here, and I don't intend to waste it on you.

SASHA: *(not bitter, just simple understanding)* Oh, sure, I understand. You've got your own light. *(pause)* What kind of light is that, that light you've got?

RAMONA: *(condescendingly)* Well, I wouldn't expect you to recognize it, but this is my God Light.

SASHA: *(in awe)* Oh, that's a God Light?

RAMONA: *(proudly)* Yes, it is.

SASHA: *(almost reverently)* A God Light. I haven't seen one of those in years. Not since I was a little girl. My grandmother lived in God Light. *(thinking)* Hers seemed a lot brighter though. *(realizing she might have offended RAMONA with that statement)* But, I was just a little kid. Everything seems different, bigger, brighter when you're a kid, I guess.

RAMONA: *(offended, coldly)* Yes, I suppose it does.

SASHA: *(remembering, almost wistfully)* My grandma used to sing me a song about God Light. She lived way out in the country. I'd visit her in the summer, and I'd get scared at night because it was so dark in the country. She used to sing me the same song every night when I was at her house. I remember it to this day.

RAMONA: *(condescendingly, at the end of her patience)* Yes, well that's very nice, but your grandmother is not here right now, and quite frankly, I've got better things to do than listen to you sit over there in the dark and reminisce about your childhood.

SASHA: Sure, I understand.

RAMONA: *(now completely in the dark, disgusted)* Oh, great!

SASHA: What's the matter?

RAMONA: What do you think's the matter, you idiot? My light has failed me.

SASHA: Oh. *(pause, then she sings a cappella, with the stage completely dark, except for her cigarette lighter)*

> Jesus bids us shine with a clear pure light
> like a little candle burning in the night.
> In this world of darkness we must shine.
> You in your small corner, and I in mine.

END

A DAY IN COURT

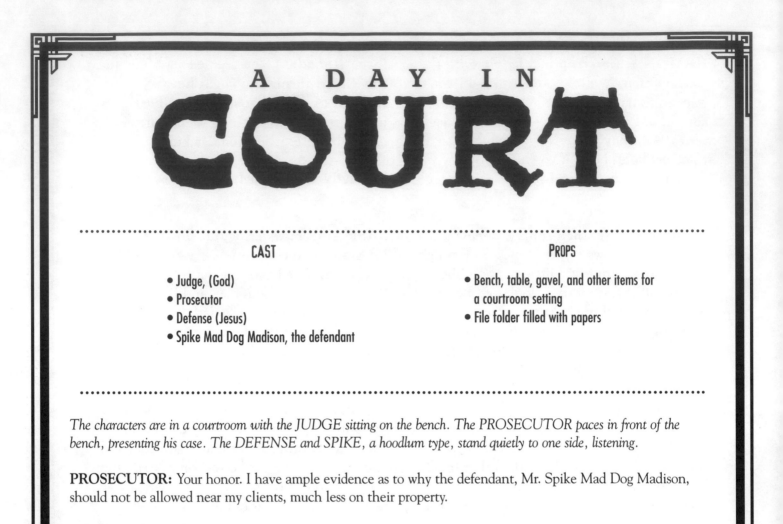

CAST

- Judge, (God)
- Prosecutor
- Defense (Jesus)
- Spike Mad Dog Madison, the defendant

PROPS

- Bench, table, gavel, and other items for a courtroom setting
- File folder filled with papers

The characters are in a courtroom with the JUDGE sitting on the bench. The PROSECUTOR paces in front of the bench, presenting his case. The DEFENSE and SPIKE, a hoodlum type, stand quietly to one side, listening.

PROSECUTOR: Your honor. I have ample evidence as to why the defendant, Mr. Spike Mad Dog Madison, should not be allowed near my clients, much less on their property.

JUDGE: What evidence?

(The PROSECUTOR holds up a large file filled with papers.)

PROSECUTOR: I have evidence that he was a drug user and that he lied and cheated his way in and out of everything. He also has a short temper, which he displays to his friends and family quite regularly, as well as his foul mouth. And that's just the tip of the iceberg, your honor.

DEFENSE: Objection, your honor. The things on that list have been paid for and forgotten.

PROSECUTOR: You may have forgotten, but my clients haven't.

JUDGE: Sustained. The crimes in question have been paid for in full and have no bearing on the current case.

PROSECUTOR: I disagree, your honor. My clients ask that you grant the injunction against the defendant so he cannot take part in any of their gatherings.

JUDGE: I don't see on what grounds they can make this request.

PROSECUTOR: The people I represent hold a high moral standard. The entire community looks up to them. They do service for people who are poor and needy, and they open their doors to young and old, rich and poor alike.

JUDGE: What's your point?

PROSECUTOR: If we start allowing riffraff and scum...

DEFENSE: Objection. The prosecution is slandering the defendant.

JUDGE: Sustained.

PROSECUTOR: Pardon me, your honor. If the defendant is allowed into my clients' organization, it will cause detrimental repercussions. Their standing in the community would suffer. People might start gossiping about them, and the city at large might not view them in the same way.

DEFENSE: You're worried about how people will view you, not your organization.

PROSECUTOR: Hey! I'm not the one on trial here.

JUDGE: That's enough. Spike, do you have anything to say?

SPIKE: Everything he's saying about me is true. I done all them things and more that I wasn't caught for.

PROSECUTOR: You see! He admits his guilt!

JUDGE: Order! *(pause)* Go on, Spike.

SPIKE: I'm different now. I'm trying to stop doing all them things. I just want to go to church so I can know more about living right and meet other people who want to do right. I'm sorry for what I done, and going to church'll help me learn right from wrong.

JUDGE: Prosecution?

PROSECUTOR: It's too late. Maybe if he'd come while he was in junior high or before everyone knew what a sinner he is.

DEFENSE: You were a sinner when you came to me.

PROSECUTOR: That was different! I never did drugs.

DEFENSE: Your honor, I died for both of these men. Both of them have equal right to enter the church and worship me. In fact, I'm very disappointed in the prosecution for even bringing this case to trial.

JUDGE: In light of the evidence, I rule that Spike is free to attend church. This court finds for the defendant.

SPIKE: Great! *(to PROSECUTOR)* See ya Sunday!

PROSECUTOR: *(mutters)* This is ridiculous! Next thing you know they'll be letting in prostitutes and tax collectors.

END

AS THE COOKIE CRUMBLES:
The Search for Fig-nificance

CAST

- Announcer
- Isaac, a Fig Newton
- Newt, a Fig Newton
- CC, a chocolate chip cookie
- DS, a Double-Stuff Oreo
- NB, a Nutter Butter cookie

PROPS

- Bench
- Cardboard costumes

• •

Isaac and Newt sit on a bench, asleep. They are two Fig Newtons in a cookie jar. The other cookies lounge nearby. Sappy soap-opera-type music begins.

ANNOUNCER (*or show on a screen*): It's been said that, "You are what you eat." For many, that's just a cute, over-used phrase to make a point about diet or lifestyle. But for a cookie, well, it could mean life or death. Join us now as we take a bite out of life and look in on our star characters, Newt and Isaac, two Fig Newtons trying to make the best of their place in the cookie jar.

ISAAC: *(yelling frantically)* No, no, put me back! Take the chocolate chip! Put me back!

NEWT: Isaac, Isaac, wake up! You're having another bad dream. It's over now.

ISAAC: Oh, thanks, Newt. I never should have watched that movie last night. I had no idea it would give me nightmares like that.

NEWT: Yeah, that *Jaws* movie gets me every time!

ISAAC: I've gotta stop watching that stuff. I almost *never* got over that new movie: *Star Wars: The Phantom Nutter-Butter.* **(*pause*)** Maybe I'll take up reading. You like to read, don't you?

NEWT: Yeah, it's not bad. I just picked up a few books yesterday. One is *How to Have your Cake and Eat It, Too!* I thought it was a history book, about our ancestors or something. Turns out it's all about success, positive attitudes, and junk like that.

ISAAC: Oooh, sounds boring to me. I like classic stories, like *Snow White and the Seven Keebler Elves, The Three Little Figs,* and *20,000 Figs under the Sea.*

NEWT: I did finish one last week that made me think a lot. It was called *The Search for Fig-nificance.*

ISAAC: Really? Who's the author?

NEWT: It's the same guy who wrote *How to be King of the Cookie Jar—Fifteen Strategies to Get off the Shelf and into the Shopping Cart.*

ISAAC: So what's it about anyway?

NEWT: It's one of those self-help books. You know, to make you feel good about yourself. To make you feel like you really matter or something.

ISAAC: Gee, I could use that. Sometimes I feel kinda crummy.

NEWT: Actually, it's kinda hard. The whole first part of the book is about trying to be good at things so other people will like you. That's how you feel important.

ISAAC: Sounds like the time I tried to be an Oreo. I thought everyone would like me if I could just be a fat-laden, tasty Oreo. Instead, I learned that I am what I am—a low-fat, boring Fig Newton. I'll never be an Oreo, a molasses cookie, or even one of those cool fortune cookies. I'm me. It's easier just to accept who you are and go on!

NEWT: Then, the author says I should always find some person or thing to blame my problems on. You know, my horrible upbringing, the stigma of being called "fruit and cake" all my life, and always being passed up for the fattening cookies. Those things aren't my fault!

CC: *(sits up)* Yeah, your problems don't go away just because you blame them on someone else. Sounds like a figment of some guy's imagination. *(lies back down)*

NEWT: The last part of this book says that we carry all of our bad breaks with us the rest of our lives, even if they were someone else's fault! Can you believe that?

DS: *(sits up)* Really? You mean, like the time I accidentally broke that Nutter-Butter in half? Come on! That wasn't my fault! I was dropped out of the package into this giant cookie jar. I can't help it if the Nutter-Butter was in my way! *(lies back down)*

ISAAC: Sounds like, according to the book, you'll carry that mistake with you the rest of your life.

NB: *(sits up)* With stuff like that hanging over your head, how can a decent, cream-filled, respectable cookie ever find meaning and fig-nificance? It's days like this that I wish I had never come out of the oven. *(lies back down)*

NEWT: I don't know. I mean, we've tried everything from frosting to different flavors. And still, it just seems useless. We're just a mass of baked goods at the bottom of the cookie jar.

ISAAC: I mean, I know I'm special and all. We're not just cookies—we're fruit and cake! But it just seems like there should be something more.

NEWT: Yeah, how do you find real fig-nificance?

(Music begins. A giant cardboard hand comes from offstage and picks up double-stuff.)

DS: I've been chosen! I've been chosen! Na-na-na-na-na-na!

(Dejected look from ISAAC and NEWT. Bring lights down.)

ANNOUNCER: Join us next week when our two heroes, Newt and Isaac, in their search for meaning and significance, er, uh, fig-nifi-cance, find themselves fighting over the same gal for this year's prom date, Ginger Snap. Until next week, that's the way the cookie crumbles.

(Music swells and fades)

END

Who Am I?

CAST	PROPS
• John Doe, a teenager searching for his identity	• Legal pad
• Dad, John Doe's Dad	• Bible
• Horace, John Doe's friend	
• Julie, John Doe's school counselor	

JOHN DOE stands on the right-hand side of the stage. The people who try to help John find himself stand across the stage from left to right. These characters (DAD, HORACE, and JULIE) do not move until JOHN speaks to them.

JOHN DOE: My name is John Doe, and I'm on a quest to find out who I am. Unfortunately, most of the time this quest seems like a wild-goose chase. Last week when I went down to the department of motor vehicles to get my driver's license, the first question they asked me was, "Who are you?" When I realized that after 16 years of life, I didn't know the answer to that question, I went outside and wept. In the past week my search to find out who I am is at full throttle—something has to be on full throttle in my life since I can't get my driver's license until I can answer one simple question—"Who am I?" Over the past seven days, I've asked many people to help me with my quest.

(JOHN DOE walks over to his DAD. DAD unfreezes and looks at JOHN DOE as JOHN DOE begins to speak.)

JOHN DOE: Dad, I need to ask you a serious question.

DAD: Sure, you know I've always got time for my favorite son Jim, Jacob, Jeremiah…*(DAD fumbles through the names of all his sons before he finally remembers John's name.)*

JOHN DOE: *(interrupting his dad, almost in tears)* Dad, my name is John Doe. Why can't you ever remember which one of your sons I am?

DAD: Oh, I guess that's because you and your brothers are all the same to me.

JOHN DOE: Dad, my problem is that I don't know who I am, and I can't get my driver's license until I find out. So could you tell me who I am?

DAD: *(already forgetting John Doe's name)* Jordan, I can tell you exactly who you are. You are a descendant of your great-great-great grandfather Jedidiah Jackson—one of the world's greatest inventors. Your great-great-great grandfather Jedidiah, like all Jacksons, had a problem with excessive nose hair. So he invented the nostril hair nullifier—a specially shaped instrument to pluck out those pesky hairs by the root. During the Civil War, General Robert E. Lee noticed that after spending a few weeks on the battlefield in winter, his troops had a hard time breathing. Their nose hair froze together and blocked their nasal passages. So in 1861 your great-great-great grandfather Jedidiah had the monumental task of using his nostril hair nullifier to trim the Confederate Army's nose hairs so the soldiers could breathe. That's who you are Jordan—the proud descendent of Jedidiah Jackson.

JOHN DOE: That's definitely something to stick my nose up in the air about. By the way Dad, my name is John Doe.

(DAD freezes. HORACE unfreezes when JOHN DOE speaks to him.)

JOHN DOE: Horace, you've always been there for me, even though I don't know who "me" is. And that's what I need help with. Could you tell me who I am?

HORACE: You're one of us; you're one of the guys. You act like us, you talk like us, you dress like us, so you are definitely one of the gang. You like four-wheel-drive trucks, fishing, camping in the woods in the fall, and country music. Your favorite foods are pepperoni pizza and apple pie.

JOHN DOE: Are you sure that's who I am?

HORACE: Of course. You're one of the guys, and I'm into that kind of stuff so you must be too because you're just like us.

JOHN DOE: Thanks.

(HORACE freezes again as JOHN DOE walks to the front of the stage.)

JOHN DOE: Now I'm more confused than when I began my quest. My dad says that I'm the proud descendant of a woolly-nosed Civil War hero, and Horace thinks I'm just like him. But I want to know who I am, not who my friends or family say I am. Someone has to know the answer to my question.

(JULIE unfreezes as JOHN DOE begins to speak. JULIE is a school counselor and is holding a legal pad of paper.)

JOHN DOE: *(timidly)* Could I talk to you for a minute?

JULIE: Sure, who are you?

JOHN DOE: *(exasperated)* Why does everyone have to ask me that?

JULIE: Oh, I'm sorry. That's always the first question school counselors ask. How can I help you?

JOHN DOE: I want to get my driver's license, but I don't know who I am. I know I've never talked to you before, but I guess you're here to help. So could you tell me who I am?

JULIE: I'll try. You see, many millions of years ago an explosion occurred that sent all the matter in the universe flying outward from a central point. Some chemicals got together on this planet and formed a single-cell organism. That single-celled creature eventually turned into a monkey, and then it mutated into one of your ancient ancestors. After a long adaptation time, you were finally born into this world. Since then, many things happened in your environment that shaped who you are. *(with deep concern)* I hope that helps.

JOHN DOE: So, you're saying that I'm a product of evolution and shaped by my environment.

JULIE: That about sums it up.

JOHN DOE: *(dejected)* Thanks for nothing.

(JULIE freezes when JOHN DOE turns to walk away. JOHN DOE returns to the position he was in when the skit started and picks up a Bible. JOHN DOE walks in front of the frozen actors. After pacing for a while he begins to pray.)

JOHN DOE: God, it's been a while since we talked. Do you remember me? I guess that's a stupid question—no one else knows who I am, why should you be any different? *(opens Bible to Jeremiah 1:5 and reads)*

"Before I formed you in the womb I knew you, before you were born I set you apart." *(pause)* You know who I am. You created me to be somebody special, to have an identity. I just wish you would tell me who that somebody is that you created me to be. *(opens Bible to Deuteronomy 26:18 and reads)*

"And the Lord has declared this day that you are his people, his treasured possession as he promised. *(turns to John 1:12 and reads)*

"Yet to all who received him, to those who believed in his name, he gave the right to become children of God." *(pause)* A treasured possession and a Child of God. A son of the King, that makes me a prince in his kingdom. *(turns to 1 Peter 2:9-10)*

"But you are a chosen people, a royal priesthood, a holy nation, a people belonging to God, that you may declare the praises of him who called you out of darkness into his wonderful light. Once you were not a people, but now you are the people of God." *(pause)* A son of the king of the universe, a priest, a man who has been set apart to be holy in your sight. Thanks for adopting me into your family, God.

(As JOHN DOE runs by DAD, DAD unfreezes.)

DAD: Where are you going, Jeremiah?

JOHN DOE: I'm going to get my driver's license, because I finally know who I am—I'm a child of the King.

DAD: Before you get your picture taken for your license, you might want to use this nostril hair nullifier. It would make your great-great-great grandfather Jedidiah proud.

(JOHN DOE waves off his DAD's suggestion and runs off stage.)

END

THE BUILDING PERMIT

CAST

- Noah, dressed in overalls
- Jabal, dressed in business suit

PROPS

- Clipboard with papers
- Stack of forms
- Calculator
- Business card

NOAH: *(knocks)*

JABAL: Come in. We're open!

NOAH: Hi. I want to get a building permit. Is this the town office?

JABAL: *(holding clipboard)* This is the C.M.O.B.O.N.I.A.R.T.

NOAH: Excuse me?

JABAL: I said, this is the C.M.O.B.O.N.I.A.R.T.

NOAH: Sorry, I didn't catch that. I never was very good at spelling.

JABAL: It's not a word. It's an acronym.

NOAH: Well, I was never much of an acrobat either.

JABAL: Acronym! Not acrobat! C.M.O.B.O.N.I.A.R.T. stands for "Central Mesopotamia Official Bureau of Noninformation And Red Tape."

NOAH: So it is the town office?

JABAL: Well, essentially. If you can call 20 sheep-herders, a couple of drunks, and a religious fanatic a town.

NOAH: Religious fanatic?

JABAL: Yeah, some kook named Noah lives up on Gopher Street. Now, *(pulls out a stack of forms)* what's your name?

NOAH: Noah.

JABAL: Noah? As in…

NOAH: Religious Fanatic. Yes.

JABAL: *(coughs and slides away, as though afraid of NOAH)* I see. Well, we'll get right to business. First name, Noah. Last name?

NOAH: What do you mean, last name?

JABAL: Last name, you know, surname?

NOAH: Oh, yes, I suppose you could call me Sir Noah if you wanted to.

JABAL: Yes, well, let's move on. Age?

NOAH: Ummmm. This would be the antediluvian age.

JABAL: Ante-what?

NOAH: Antediluvian. That means before the flood.

JABAL: Flood? What's that?

NOAH: Oh, never mind. You'll find out soon enough, I guess.

JABAL: Look, Mr. Noah…

NOAH: Sir Noah.

JABAL: Right. I just want to know how old you are.

NOAH: Three hundred and fifty.

JABAL: Oh, come on, you must be older than that.

NOAH: Look, son, when you get to be as old as I am, you won't be keeping track either.

JABAL: Okay, okay, 350. Occupation?

NOAH: That's a tricky one. I guess you could say I just do what God tells me.

JABAL: Hmmmm. I see. Religious Fanatic. And what is your permanent address?

NOAH: I don't have one.

JABAL: Of course you do. You live on Gopher Street, right?

NOAH: That's not permanent. I mean, Gopher Street isn't going to be there after the flood.

JABAL: Flood?

NOAH: Never mind.

JABAL: Right. Now, what exactly is it you want to build?

NOAH: I'm going to build an ark.

JABAL: A what?

NOAH: An *ark* .

JABAL: Ark of the Covenant?

NOAH: No, no, wrong ark. We don't even *have* a covenant yet.

JABAL: That's right. So, what is this ark you want to build?

NOAH: It's a boat.

JABAL: A *boat*? What do you want a boat for?

NOAH: The Lord told me to make one.

JABAL: Right. We're 50 miles from any body of water, and God wants you to build a boat?

NOAH: That's right.

JABAL: What're you going to do, Noah? Hook it up to your donkey and drag it to the Euphrates?

NOAH: I don't need the Euphrates for this boat.

JABAL: Oh, I get it. You're going sand surfing.

NOAH: No, no! God is going to bring the water to the boat.

JABAL: Well, I hope he's got a big bucket!

NOAH: *(chuckles)* He's not going to use a bucket. He's going to use a flood!

JABAL: Will you stop with this flood stuff already? Now, if we could get on with the permit application? How big is this boat of yours going to be?

NOAH: *(pulls out blueprints)* Uhh. Let's see. It's going to be 140 meters long.

JABAL: Wait. Stop there.

NOAH: What's the matter?

JABAL: I'm sorry, but Mesopotamia hasn't switched over to the metric system yet. How about giving it to me in units I can understand?

NOAH: Okay. Well, 140 meters. That would be… *(pulls out calculator)*

JABAL: Excuse me. But Mesopotamia doesn't have calculators yet either.

NOAH: Sorry. *(puts calculator away)* Well, let's see. Hummm. I guess that would be about 300.

JABAL: *(speaks slowly as he writes)* 300 spans.

NOAH: Excuse me, did you say 300 spans?

JABAL: That's right.

NOAH: No, that's wrong. It should be 300 cubits.

JABAL: *(falls off chair in surprise)* Three hundred *what*?

NOAH: Cubits.

JABAL: Are you crazy? Why in the world would you make a boat that big?

NOAH: God told me to.

JABAL: Uh-huh. And I suppose he told you why he wants this thing so big?

NOAH: Sure. We're going to put animals on it.

JABAL: Animals? What kind of animals?

NOAH: *All* kinds.

JABAL: When you say all kinds, what do you mean?

NOAH: *All* kinds. We have to make sure they don't all drown in the flood.

JABAL: Look, Noah, let's stop and think about this. Don't you suppose your neighbors are going to complain about a 300-cubit boat full of smelly, noisy animals in your back yard?

NOAH: So?

JABAL: Well, according to the Rural Development Code, section 13, paragraph 2C, no construction shall be approved that does not have the approval of the community.

NOAH: Wait a second. You're telling me I can't build an ark unless my neighbors say I can?

JABAL: That's right. I'm afraid you'll have to take your request to the C.M.R.D.B.A.C.C.

NOAH: Is that another one of those acrobats?

JABAL: Acronym. Yes. The Central Mesopotamia Rural Development, Building, And Construction Committee.

NOAH: And if they say I can build an ark?

JABAL: Then you can build an ark.

NOAH: Very well, I'll go to the C.M.R.-whatever. I need to start building next week.

JABAL: Uhh, not so fast, Noah.

NOAH: *(sigh)* What now?

JABAL: The committee is vacationing on the French Riviera. We're not expecting them back for another three months.

NOAH: Three months?

JABAL: Besides, I don't think your ark is going to fit in with the new look they have planned for this town.

NOAH: What new look?

JABAL: Oh, we're going to have a casino, a few bars, a pool hall, a couple of adult bookstores, and some movie theaters.

NOAH: What's a movie theater?

JABAL: Never mind. You'll find out soon enough.

NOAH: So, you're telling me I'm not going to get my permit?

JABAL: I'm afraid that's out of the question.

NOAH: Well, thanks anyway. *(stands up, shakes hands)* Have a nice day.

JABAL: Wait! Noah! What are you going to do now?

NOAH: Do? *(laughs)* I'm going to build an ark of course. Oh, and here's my business card, in case you want to join us for our cruise. *(starts to walk out)*

JABAL: But Noah, you didn't get a building permit.

NOAH: You don't think I'm going to let a bunch of bureaucrats get in the way of *God's* plans, do you? *(exit)*

JABAL: Wait! You can't build without a permit! *(pauses to look at card and reads it out loud)* "Noah's Last Chance Cruise Lines" Now I wonder what he means by that. *(shakes head)* These religious types are all the same. They're always making a big fuss about nothing. Oh well, we can always hope he doesn't come back from that cruise of his! *(exit)*

END

I'm Almost Ready

CAST
- Amy
- Man

PROPS
- Couch
- Magazine
- Flower

AMY *sits in her living room on a couch reading a magazine. When the doorbell rings, she slowly gets up from the couch to answer the door. She opens the door to find a MAN standing there. He wears nice clothes and holds a flower in his hand.*

AMY: Oh my gosh! You're here already?

MAN: It's time to go.

AMY: Can you come in for a second?

MAN: Thank you.

(The MAN steps in and looks around the room.)

MAN: Nice place. This is for you.

(The MAN holds out the flower, and AMY accepts it.)

AMY: Thanks. Look, as you can tell, I'm not quite ready, so why don't you sit down and watch some TV or read a magazine while I get cleaned up.

MAN: You look fine just like that.

AMY: No, really, I have to do a few things before we go. I've got to finish the laundry, pay the bills, and write several letters. I'm way behind on those. I've got a few people I need to call, I have to set the VCR for my favorite show, and I need to clean the house and put on my makeup and some nicer clothes. I wish you'd called before you came by because this is a really bad time.

MAN: I didn't know I was dropping by until right now. It's a surprise to me too.

AMY: How about this: why don't you pick up everybody else first and swing by here last? I could get the most important things done before you got back.

MAN: I can't do that.

AMY: *(starting to panic)* You don't understand! I've got so much to do. You showed up early, and I wasn't ready. I'm meeting Susan for lunch tomorrow.

MAN: Amy, calm down! None of those things matter. Right now, we're together, and we're going to have a great time. Isn't that what you've wanted?

(AMY *flops down on the couch, and the* MAN *sits down beside her.*)

AMY: Yes. I've been looking forward to this. I just lost track of the time, and I'm not exactly prepared right now.

MAN: Don't worry about it. You can finally relax. Come on. *(stands up and holds out his hand)* Let's go.

AMY: But what about my friends?

MAN: They'll be there too.

AMY: But not all of them! I didn't get a chance to tell everyone about you.

MAN: Didn't get the chance?

AMY: I thought I'd have more time! In fact, I was going to tell Susan about you at lunch tomorrow. Couldn't you come back for me after that?

MAN: I'm sorry, Amy, but I didn't plan to show up now. I was just told that now is the time.

AMY: I'm sorry. I should have done more.

MAN: Yes, you should have. Let's go.

AMY: Okay. I'm ready.

(The MAN takes AMY by the hand and leads her to the front door. AMY stops, looks at her room, turns off the light, and closes the door behind her.)

END

Community Kitchen

CAST

- Questioner, holds an imaginary microphone
- Bianca, homeless woman
- Hogan, male, wearing normal clothing
- Trevor, speaks in a thick surfer, valley, or rad accent and lingo
- Harold
- Lucia, wears an apron
- Sakura, a mother

PROPS

- Counter
- Trays
- Salt shaker
- Apron

Three community kitchen volunteers stand behind a counter. The three food recipients file through the line holding trays. They all chatter, and finally the three with full trays find seats.

The QUESTIONER wants to get personal stories about all of the people present. When he approaches an individual and begins to talk with them, everyone else freezes (mid-bite, mid-sentence, et cetera) All attention focuses on the QUESTIONER's conversation.

Part 1

QUESTIONER: *(to the audience)* So let's speak with some of these individuals and find out why they're here. Excuse me, ma'am. What are you doing?

BIANCA: Well, I'm presently looking for some salt.

QUESTIONER: Here. *(hands her the salt)*

BIANCA: Thanks. *(QUESTIONER stares at her as she eats)* Can I help you with something?

QUESTIONER: Oh, sorry. I was just wondering why you come here.

BIANCA: I ask myself that same question every day. *(pause)* Obviously I need the help. I need at least one meal a day.

QUESTIONER: The kitchen looks like it does a good job serving a decent lunch. Is a lunch all you need?

BIANCA: Not exactly. Living in a cardboard box is no thrill.

QUESTIONER: Don't you have someone who could help? A friend, a church, the Salvation Army?

BIANCA: I'm fresh out of friends. There was a time I went to church, but not any more. When life fell apart for me, I stopped going.

QUESTIONER: Why?

BIANCA: At first I was busy trying to get back on my feet. Then I couldn't stand the thought of anyone seeing me like this.

QUESTIONER: I thought churches weren't supposed to be judgmental.

BIANCA: They aren't...but I began to remember times when my friends turned their noses up at certain visitors who didn't dress right. I used to be like them. Before long, you get used to ignoring others. Now I can't stand the thought of them treating me like we used to treat other visitors.

QUESTIONER: Surely all churches aren't like that. Somebody cares.

BIANCA: Well, they aren't exactly knocking on my cardboard door.

QUESTIONER: *(turning to the next person)* Hello, sir. May I ask why you're here?

HOGAN: What does it look like? I'm having lunch.

QUESTIONER: Well I can see that, but why do you leave your job and come here for lunch? Certainly there are finer establishments for your dining pleasure.

HOGAN: What job? I'm looking for one.

QUESTIONER: You have no job?

HOGAN: That's right. I fell on hard times, and if I can just get a little assistance, then I think I can make it.

QUESTIONER: Hard times. What happened?

HOGAN: It's not as though I quit my job to come here or even got fired. I don't drink, smoke, or use any drugs. The factory where I was working just closed up. I worked there for 12 years—since I was old enough to drive. I'm not exactly qualified to run a business since I don't even have a high school diploma.

QUESTIONER: So this is a stepping-stone until you get back on your feet?

HOGAN: Exactly. I'll make it. I've already applied for two jobs, and one looks good.

QUESTIONER: Good luck.

HOGAN: Thanks.

QUESTIONER: Let's try one more. *(turning to the next person)* Hello, friend. How are you doing?

TREVOR: Well, Kimosabe, it's kind of a bad hair day.

QUESTIONER: You don't look so bad.

TREVOR: I'm talking about you, dude.

QUESTIONER: Oh, I'm just wondering why you come to this community kitchen.

TREVOR: No prob. The food is primo.

QUESTIONER: You think this food is good?

TREVOR: It's primo. Cuz cookin' for yourself is not too cool.

QUESTIONER: Others I talked to are here because they lost their jobs. How about you?

TREVOR: Job? Job! Don't say that word, compadre. It would take a serious bite out of my righteous life, as I know it.

QUESTIONER: I can only imagine.

TREVOR: Listen, your excellency, the less I do, the more others do. It makes for an ostentatious philosophy. If someone will do it for yours truly, then I can continue with life's ultimate mystery.

QUESTIONER: Which is?

TREVOR: Finding myself. Now that's real! At least it's supposed to be if I ever find it.

QUESTIONER: Thank you very much. I think I've found out enough about you. Have you ever considered the amount of time people spend preparing your meals, cleaning up, and generally taking care of you?

TREVOR: You're becoming a real drag on my life force. Besides, why should I think of others? I really couldn't say why they *(points to the servers)* bother. They must be weird.

QUESTIONER: Different from the rest of the world, maybe, but not weird. That gives me a good idea—I'll go talk to the servers. *(walks to the counter)*

(Read Matthew 20:20-28, Matthew 25:31-46 or John 13:1-17.)

Part 2

HAROLD: Hello! Would you like some meatloaf or soup today?

QUESTIONER: In a minute, thank you. I first want to ask you about the kitchen. Do you work here every day?

HAROLD: No, no, I'm a volunteer. I come once a week on Thursdays and do whatever they need me to do. Only Mrs. Phillips actually works full time. She finds the volunteers and arranges menus and food drives. She works hard.

QUESTIONER: So just about everyone who works here is a volunteer?

HAROLD: That's right! I admit that sometimes my week gets really busy. It's easy to find excuses for not showing up. But I believe this kitchen does a good job and serves a real need. If I don't help out, who will?

QUESTIONER: Thanks! *(turns to Lucia)*

LUCIA: May I help you? Beans, carrots, salad?

QUESTIONER: Thank you, but I was hoping to ask you a question.

LUCIA: Sorry, I can't help you then. I just work here.

QUESTIONER: I wanted to know why you're here today. Do you enjoy serving others?

LUCIA: Well, it's a job. Besides, my mom makes me come. She says it'll build character and look good on my resume, you know.

QUESTIONER: This isn't a job, though, right? You're a volunteer like the others.

LUCIA: You mean we're not getting a paycheck?

QUESTIONER: No.

LUCIA: Well, that explains it. I thought taxes were eating me alive.

QUESTIONER: But don't you enjoy helping others, even at the sacrifice of your own time and energy? That's what volunteerism is all about, right?

LUCIA: Are you kidding? I quit. *(takes off apron)* I've got better things to do...like my nails. Dishwashing is just too harsh.

QUESTIONER: You're not leaving, are you? Who will serve these folks?

LUCIA: They can help themselves. Pull themselves up by their own bootstraps like my granddaddy used to say, and get tough! If a person wanted to, really wanted to, they could look out for old number one. Hasta la vista, baby.

QUESTIONER: Well, so much for her. *(looks at Sakura)* Howdy, ma'am. Are you enjoying yourself?

SAKURA: *(nods in agreement)* You don't know how much!

QUESTIONER: What do you mean?

SAKURA: Well, it's a long story, but I used to be on the other side of this counter.

QUESTIONER: Please go on.

SAKURA: About 10 years ago I came here to get a hot meal for my two kids and me.

QUESTIONER: Let me get this straight. Ten years ago, you were being served, and now you're doing the serving?

SAKURA: That's right. My husband left me a long time ago. I was living out of my car with my two kids. This kitchen was a lifesaver—and I mean that literally. I wasn't any different from those people sitting down and eating out there.

QUESTIONER: You seem different now.

SAKURA: I am. I found Christ.

QUESTIONER: I thought you were going to say, "I found a job."

SAKURA: Well, that too, but it came later. You see, a stranger caught me going through his garbage can one day, so I just drove off. I was too embarrassed to apologize and too tired to care. But that same stranger happened to spot my car parked in an alley about three weeks later. He came up and started talking to me. I ignored him. He didn't know who I was—how could he understand what I was going through? He kept after me, though. He found me in the same place the next day, and eventually I accepted his offer to buy me a meal. I couldn't refuse because of my kids.

QUESTIONER: Wow! Why did he buy you a meal?

SAKURA: That's just it. He kept trying to help me, so I asked him why. That's when he told me about Jesus. He said he was praying for me, and then one day we prayed together. I've never been alone since. It took a long time, but I'm back on my feet. I know what it's like to be in need—physically and spiritually. You could say I'm returning the favor, but it's more than that. I never knew how much God truly loved me, and now I can't help but want to share that love with others.

QUESTIONER: Thanks for sharing it with me.

SAKURA: Like I said, I can't help it. God bless you.

QUESTIONER: *(turns away)* I think I understand.

END

Parable on Justice

CAST

• **Narrator** • **Judge** • **Widow**

NARRATOR: In a certain town there was a judge who neither feared God nor cared about men nor used deodorant.

JUDGE: *(steps forward next to Narrator and lifts elbow up high and flaps his arm)*

NARRATOR: *(faints and falls down)*

JUDGE: There was also a widow in town who came to me day after day.

WIDOW: *(sings to the tune of "You're Just Too Good to Be True")*

> I am upset, and I'm blue.
> I got ripped off; so will you.
> Please, give me justice, oh please,
> And punish my enemies.
> You need to give them the boot.
> I beg you please, persecute,
> I'm upset and I'm blue,
> I got ripped off—now I'll sue.
> Gimme a break! Gimme a break!
> Grant me justice with my enemy!

JUDGE: Take a hike. I don't fear God or care about men.

NARRATOR: *(revives and picks self up off the floor)* Or use deodorant!

JUDGE: I'm not going to lose any sleep over you or your Mickey Mouse problems.

NARRATOR: But the widow would not give up. She continually called out for justice.

WIDOW: *(sings)* Gimme a break! Gimme a break! Grant me justice with my enemy!

NARRATOR: Day after day after day, the widow would beg the judge.

WIDOW: *(sings)* Gimme a break! Gimme a break! Grant me justice with my enemy!

NARRATOR: Over and over and over.

WIDOW: *(sings)* Gimme a break! Gimme a break! Grant me justice with my enemy!

NARRATOR: On and on, day after day after.

JUDGE: *(steps forward, waving arms around)* All right! Okay! Enough already!

NARRATOR: *(faints and falls down)*

JUDGE: Listen, I don't fear God or care about men.

NARRATOR: *(revives and picks self up off the floor)* Or use deodorant!

JUDGE: But I'm going to grant you your motion, just to get you off my back. Hearing that song over and over is about to drive me crazy!

NARRATOR: Did you hear what the judge said? Now, if this disrespectful, uncaring, smelly judge will do that, how much more do you think our loving, heavenly Father is going to give his children who call out to him for justice, kindness, and love?

END

David and Jonathan

CAST

- David
- King Saul
- Herald, the paper boy
- A boy to fetch Jonathan's arrows
- Jonathan
- Abner, King Saul's assistant
- Four female dancers

PROPS

- Basic living room furniture
- Pillars (optional)
- One newspaper and a stack of newspapers
- Bow and arrows (or dart gun toy)
- Recording of "Love Is a Many Splendored Thing" or other sappy music (optional)
- Beverages and snacks
- Royal robe
- Sword
- Belt
- Table and chairs, with settings for a meal
- Cymbals and tambourines
- Bathrobe
- Shaving cream
- Towel
- Books
- Chef's hat and apron
- Spear or toy dart gun
- Sack, stuffed to look full (optional)

The scene opens in the residence of SAUL and his son, JONATHAN. SAUL paces back and fourth slowly while he talks to his assistant, ABNER. SAUL seems to be deep in thought. The street and outdoor scenes can be played out in front of the stage on a lower level or off to the side.

SAUL: Abner, did you see how that David lad fought today?

ABNER: Yes. I do believe it was a mighty victory. David is a striking young man.

SAUL: Yes, he was unusually impressive.

ABNER: *(enthusiastically)* Oh, you better believe he was! Did you see the way he hurled that stone? It was something else. *(mimics as if he is David battling Goliath)* But I come against you in the name of the God of the armies of Israel! Why, I wouldn't be surprised if it made the headlines in today's *Jerusalem Times.*

(The HERALD walks through the town. He is flashing the newspaper and chanting.)

HERALD: *(shouting and waving the newspaper)* Extra! Extra! Extra! Young shepherd boy slays Philistine giant! Extra! Extra! Extra! Read all about it!

(The HERALD exits. SAUL is deep in thought as he peers out the window and watches the HERALD depart. ABNER grins and shrugs his shoulders.)

SAUL: Abner, what sort of family does this young fellow come from?

ABNER: I really don't know, King Saul.

SAUL: *(angry)* Well find out!

ABNER: *(jumpy)* Yes, sir! Right away, sir! I'll have him here as soon as I can, sir.

(ABNER leaves. JONATHAN enters reading the Jerusalem Times.*)*

JONATHAN: Father, can you imagine that? Goliath was slain by a shepherd boy. I sure would love to meet this guy. *(hands the paper to Saul)* Here, read it for yourself, Father. It's astonishing.

SAUL: I heard about it already, thank you. I thought I told you to prepare your bow for target practice this afternoon.

JONATHAN: Yes, you did, father. I'm truly sorry. I'll take care of that right now.

(JONATHAN returns to the same place he entered. SAUL grudgingly picks up the paper, and glances at it.)

SAUL: *(sarcastically)* I can't believe it! Killed him with only a sling. Next thing you know he'll be battling Philistines with water pistols!

(King SAUL sits on his chair and thinks while clutching his fist. ABNER returns with DAVID.)

ABNER: Here he is, King Saul! I found him. I found him. I found him at the market purchasing a 12-pack of water pistols.

(King Saul immediately gets up, rolls his eyes, grins, and sighs in a disgusted manner.)

SAUL: Well, well, well, well, David. I do find this acquaintance stimulating. Would you care for a drink? Perhaps some cherry Kool-Aid?

DAVID: No, thank you, sir, I just had a Big Gulp before I came here.

SAUL: Well please, do have a seat.

(SAUL and DAVID sit down on the table, with ABNER standing at Saul's side.)

SAUL: So, tell me about your father, David.

DAVID: His name is Jesse, and we live in Bethlehem.

SAUL: Humm, herding country, huh?

DAVID: Yes, sir, I'm active in the sheep-herding business. It has been a family tradition for decades.

SAUL: Well, tell me something, if you would. How can a measly shepherd like yourself conquer such an enormous opposition?

DAVID: *(smiling)* Well, it's a secret.

ABNER: Oh boy, I love secrets.

SAUL: *(looks at ABNER disgustingly)* Shut up!

DAVID: I credit my physical attributes solely to my daily dosage of Flintstone vitamins. *(laughs continuously)* Yaba-daba-doo!

SAUL: *(stares at DAVID intently)* I'm not amused.

DAVID: I'm sorry. I don't know what got into me. Seriously, King Saul, all kidding aside. I credit my victory to none other than the God of Israel.

SAUL: Fascinating. Abner, will you go outside and prepare the chariot Benz. I would like to give David a little tour of the palace.

ABNER: Right away, sir.

(ABNER leaves, and JONATHAN enters the scene once again. He appears to be fiddling with his bow and arrow. He approaches the table.)

JONATHAN: *(not aware of DAVID's presence)* Father, can you help me? I can't seem to... Oh forgive me. I didn't know you had a guest.

(DAVID and JONATHAN instantly look at each other in splendid wonder. Play "Love Is a Many Splendored Thing" or other sappy music.)

SAUL: David, I would like you to meet my son, Jonathan.

(Music continues as DAVID and JONATHAN shake hands. Then music stops.)

JONATHAN: It is indeed a pleasure to have this acquaintance, David. I was just reading about you in the paper. I find this meeting truly an honor.

DAVID: The pleasure is all mine, Jonathan. Hey, listen, your father is going to give me a tour of the palace in your chariot Benz. Do you want to go with us?

JONATHAN: May I, Father?

SAUL: I suppose it would be harmless. Let's go. The Benz is waiting.

(They walk out.)

DAVID: Wow! I can't believe you guys actually have a chariot Benz. All we have is a Chariota.

JONATHAN: Yes, my father is very elaborate.

DAVID: Is there something wrong with your bow?

JONATHAN: Yes, I can't seem to keep it together.

DAVID: Well, let me see it. Maybe I can fix it. *(they exit)*

(Two hours later, JONATHAN and DAVID enter the living room. They are excited and happy. They each have a drink and some snacks.)

DAVID: At first I was afraid. I mean, Goliath is the biggest opponent I ever had to face. I did it for my people. And most of all, I did it for my Lord. It was by his strength and power that I was able to defeat Goliath.

JONATHAN: I can see why my father is so interested in you. You are truly a mighty warrior.

(They arrange themselves appropriately, and continue snacking and carrying on their conversation.)

JONATHAN: I'm glad that I had this time with you, David. I needed to have a good time. It's been a while since I was able to just go out and, well, forget who I am basically. You know it's hard sometimes, when you have the inheritance that I have. It's hard to tell who your real friends are.

DAVID: Yeah, I know what you mean. Hey, listen, Jonathan, I want you to know that I had a great time too. I mean, I can't remember the last time I was able to be with someone and just be myself. I haven't had many friends growing up. I was always busy tending to the sheep. But I know you are a true friend, a true blessing from the Lord.

JONATHAN: You're the first friend I ever had who accepted me for who I am and not for what I could give them. I promise you, David, to always be your friend. I want you to know that I am most grateful to have met a special friend such as you. From this day on, I promise with an oath before God to be your friend until the day I die, and I want to give you something as a seal of my word.

(JONATHAN takes off his robe and prepares to give it to DAVID, who appears to be distraught.)

JONATHAN: I want you to have this.

DAVID: Jonathan, I can't receive this. This is the robe of a king's son. It just wouldn't be right.

JONATHAN: But it will be right for a king to wear it.

DAVID: I don't understand.

JONATHAN: Please, my friend, receive this.

(DAVID receives the robe reluctantly but with honor. He puts the robe on and adjusts it.)

DAVID: Not bad. *(smiling)* Boy, if the guys around the block could see me in this!

JONATHAN: Now that my father has made you his special assistant and leader of his troops, I feel you should have this.

(JONATHAN gives DAVID his bow and sword.)

DAVID: Oh, Jonathan! This is too much. I don't know what to say. Why are you doing this?

JONATHAN: You will understand why in due time. As for now, whatever is mine is also yours.

DAVID: (confused, yet in awe) Wow! This is great! In that case, do you think I could have the chariot Benz?

JONATHAN: (smiles) That's my father's, and I don't think he's going to give that up for a long time. Now, there's one more thing I must give you. (JONATHAN takes off his belt and hands it to DAVID.) This belt represents our friendship. Wear it in battle. Let it hold you steadfast and upright.

(They give each other a handshake and then a hug.)

DAVID: Hey, isn't it great that your father is allowing me to stay here for a while? I mean, I was amazed that he actually made me commander of his troops.

JONATHAN: Yeah, and you can even stay in my room. I have a bunk bed with a TV and VCR. I've got so many things recorded on tape like the building of Noah's ark and when Moses parted the Red Sea. I've got it all on video.

DAVID: Wow, I can't wait to watch that! Did you get the Tower of Babel on video?

JONATHAN: No. I had it but my father accidentally erased it when he recorded the Samson and Delilah scandal.

DAVID: That's cool. I think I'm going to like it here.

JONATHAN: You know, my father really thinks highly of you. And I'm glad.

(SAUL enters the room with a serious expression on his face.)

SAUL: David, get your armor at once. We are going to battle!

DAVID: I'm ready, King Saul. Hey, listen, Jonathan, I have to go. I'll be back this evening.

JONATHAN: Be strong, David.

(DAVID looks at JONATHAN, grasps the robe and clinches it tightly, then winks at JONATHAN. DAVID and SAUL leave, and JONATHAN returns to his room.)

(The following morning, SAUL, DAVID, and JONATHAN are eating. DAVID and JONATHAN are dressed similarly.)

SAUL: I must commend you, David. You fought with great dignity. We had the Philistines conquered before they knew we had invaded their territory. Job well done. (Saul initiates a toast.)

JONATHAN: Father, may David and I be excused? I want to take him to town and show him around.

SAUL: Very well. Don't stay out past curfew.

JONATHAN: Thank you, Father.

(DAVID and JONATHAN leave. SAUL continues with his breakfast. HERALD passes by with a stack of papers, chanting.)

HERALD: Extra! Extra! Extra! Saul has killed his thousands, and David his ten thousands! Extra! Extra! Extra! Read all about it!

(The HERALD continues to chant until exiting. Suddenly FOUR WOMEN dancing with tambourines and cymbals dance across the stage singing, "Saul has slain his thousands, and David his ten thousands!" [Director or dancers can develop the tune.] They repeat the chorus until exiting. Saul suddenly becomes aggravated and disturbed.)

SAUL: (angry) What is this? They credit David with ten thousands and me with only thousands! Next, they'll be making David their king! That does it! I'm getting rid of him! He's history! Just wait until I get my hands on him. He's going to wish he was never born! Just wait and see. I'll get him. Abner!

(ABNER enters immediately in his bathrobe, face partially shaven.)

SAUL: Prepare the Jacuzzi! And this time make sure the four men blowing the bubbles have strong healthy lungs! I need a hot bath.

(SAUL grabs his towels and leaves. ABNER follows behind. Seconds later, DAVID and JONATHAN return from town.)

JONATHAN: Listen, David, I have to go to class right now. (gathers his books) So make yourself at home until I return.

DAVID: All right, Jonathan. Take care.

JONATHAN: I should be back in about two hours.

(JONATHAN leaves. DAVID sighs, approaches the table, pours himself a drink, and sits down against the wall next to the pillar. SAUL returns. He approaches the table and sits down on a chair. He appears to be bothered and deep in thought as he fiddles with his spear. DAVID takes out his harmonica and begins to play. After a few seconds, SAUL becomes irritated by the sounds of the harmonica. DAVID continues to play.)

SAUL: (angry) Will you shut up!

(SAUL takes out his bow and arrow—for comedy's sake the weapon could be a high-tech dart gun—fires a shot at DAVID, and barely misses him. DAVID is shocked that he was almost murdered.)

DAVID: (shocked) Holy cherubim wings! I believe I've been the victim of an attempted assassination. I'm outta here!

(DAVID runs away. SAUL continues in his rage.)

SAUL: Abner! Get over here now!

(ABNER enters immediately with a chef's hat and an apron. He appears to have been in the midst of preparing a meal.)

ABNER: Yes, what is it, King Saul? I'm in the middle of dinner.

SAUL: Tomorrow I want you to send David out to the battlefields and tell him I requested him to kill 100 Philistines.

ABNER: (stunned) That's impossible. He could be killed attempting that. He won't come out of it alive!

SAUL: That's the idea. Now do what you're told!

ABNER: (jumpy) Yes, sir! Right away, sir!

(ABNER leaves. SAUL enters his room. The HERALD enters again chanting. SAUL immediately comes out wearing his sleeping clothes.)

HERALD: Extra! Extra! Extra! David slays 200 Philistines! One hundred more than King Saul requests! Extra! Extra! Extra! Read all about it!

(The HERALD chants until exiting.)

SAUL: This is getting on my nerves. That's it! I've had it! If you want things done right, you have to do them yourself. Jonathan, Abner, get over here now!

(ABNER and JONATHAN enter at once.)

SAUL: Family meeting! Please have a seat.

(They sit around the table.)

SAUL: Where is David?

JONATHAN: He went home yesterday to visit his father. He returns this afternoon.

SAUL: David is no longer welcome here. And I want him dead!

JONATHAN: (shocked) What?

SAUL: I want him dead! He is making me look bad, and I don't like all the tension he's causing around here.

JONATHAN: Father, I ask you to spare David's life. He is the best friend I've ever had. I love him as if he were my own brother. He is the only friend who accepts me for who I am.

SAUL: I'm sorry. But he has to die.

JONATHAN: (confused) But why? He's never done anything to harm you. He's always helped you in any way he could. Have you forgotten the time he risked his life to kill Goliath and how the Lord brought a great victory to Israel as a result? You were certainly happy about it then. Why should you murder an innocent man? There is no reason for it!

(JONATHAN gets up and walks away.)

SAUL: (raising voice) So?!

(JONATHAN stops and faces SAUL.)

SAUL: As the Lord lives, David shall be killed.

(The following day DAVID sits against the wall playing his harmonica. He plays for several seconds. SAUL comes out from his room, sharpening his spear—or dart gun—and is aggravated. SAUL suddenly tosses his spear at DAVID. DAVID quickly moves, and the spear hits the wall right where DAVID was sitting. DAVID looks at the spear in shock.)

DAVID: (astonished) Déjà vu!

(DAVID gets up and immediately storms away. SAUL angrily goes back into his room. The focus turns to JONATHAN walking down the street with a full sack on his back. DAVID catches up to him.)

DAVID: (confused) Jonathan, what have I done? Why is your father so determined to kill me?

JONATHAN: I'm sure he's planning no such thing, for he always tells me everything he does. I know he wouldn't hide something like this from me.

DAVID: Can't you see, Jonathan? Of course you don't know about it. Your father knows perfectly well about our friendship. That's why he doesn't tell you—because he doesn't want to hurt you. But the truth is, Jonathan, I am but one step away from death. I swear it by the Lord and by your own soul.

(JONATHAN is in deep thought.)

JONATHAN: I believe you, my trusted friend. So tell me, what is it you want me to do?

DAVID: Okay, listen. Tomorrow is the beginning of the new moon. Always before I've been with your father for this occasion. But instead, tomorrow I'll hide in the fields and stay there until the evening of the third day. If your father asks you where I am, tell him that I asked for permission to go back to Bethlehem for a family reunion. If he says fine, then I'll know that everything is well. But if he gets angry, then I'll know that he is trying to kill me. Do this for me as my sworn brother and trusted friend. Or kill me yourself if I have sinned against your father. But don't betray me to him!

JONATHAN: (firmly) I'll never betray you.

DAVID: How will I know if your father does indeed want to kill me?

JONATHAN: My friend, I promise by the God of Israel, by no later than this time tomorrow, I'll talk to my father and let you know exactly how he feels. If he is angry and wants to kill you, then may the Lord God strike me dead if I don't warn you so you can escape. Come with me to the fields. (they walk a short distance away)

JONATHAN: They will miss you tomorrow at dinner when your chair is empty. And by the day after tomorrow, everyone will probably be asking about you, so hide in the fields where you did before. I'll come by and shoot three arrows as if I'm having target practice. Then I'll send a lad to bring the arrows back. If you hear me tell him that the arrows are on my side then you will know that all is fine. But if I tell him the arrows are still ahead of you then that will mean that you must leave immediately. And may the Lord make us keep our promise to each other, for he is our witness.

DAVID: So be it. I'd better go now. I'll be waiting for you.

(DAVID leaves. JONATHAN enters the house where SAUL is preparing to have dinner.)

SAUL: There you are, son. I've been waiting for you. Do have dinner with me.

(JONATHAN joins SAUL. It is quiet as they eat.)

SAUL: Son, why is it that David hasn't been here for dinner either yesterday or today?

JONATHAN: He asked me if he could return home to Bethlehem for a family reunion. His older brother demanded he be there. So I gave him permission.

(SAUL pounds the table with his fist, causing everything to rattle or spill.)

SAUL: (furious) You fool! Do you think I don't know that you want this son of a nobody to be king in your place, shaming yourself and your mother! As long as David is alive, you will never be king. Now go and get him so I can kill him!

JONATHAN: (boldly) Never! What has he done? Why must he be put to death? (gets up from the table and takes a few steps back) I beg you, Father, please don't kill him.

(SAUL continues his rage. He tosses his spear at JONATHAN and barely misses him. JONATHAN runs away.)

(The next day JONATHAN and a young lad enter the fields. JONATHAN has his bow and arrow with him.)

JONATHAN: (to BOY) I'm going to shoot the arrows now, so start running.

(JONATHAN fires the arrow far over the BOY's head.)

JONATHAN: (shouting) The arrow is still ahead of you. You must hurry!

(The BOY quickly gathers the arrow and returns them to JONATHAN. Then JONATHAN gives his bow and arrow to the BOY and tells him to return to the city. The BOY leaves. DAVID suddenly comes out from the fields shedding many tears. They're misty as they say good-bye to one another.)

JONATHAN: (close to tears) I'm so sorry, David. I wish I could do something. You must leave now, my friend. You can't waste any more time. I will always treasure your friendship.

DAVID: (weeping) My heart is grieving. Thank you, my true friend. You will never be forgotten.

JONATHAN: Cheer up. For we have trusted each other and each other's children into God's hands forever.

(They embrace meaningfully. JONATHAN breaks up the embrace.)

JONATHAN: Godspeed, my friend.

(DAVID returns to the fields. JONATHAN turns toward the fields and stares wonderingly into the distance. He appears to be deep in thought. Then he walks away sadly.)

END

THE WONDER YEARS

CAST

- Jesus
- John the Baptist, wearing fur vest

PROPS

- Two fishing poles
- One bucket full of fish
- One bucket with one fish
- Tackle box
- Fishing accessories
- Two backpacks
- Snack that can pass for locusts
- A jar of honey
- Rocks, plants, and trees for scenery

The scene opens in an outdoor campground with JESUS and JOHN THE BAPTIST sitting along a river bank fishing. A bucket full of fish sits beside Jesus, and an empty bucket sits next to John.

JESUS: *(teases)* Hey, John…Did you catch any fish yet?

(JOHN holds up one small fish. He frowns and JESUS laughs.)

JESUS: Thanks for coming with me, John. I really appreciate it.

JOHN: No problem, Jesus. It gives me a good reason to get out of the house for a while. I don't know, lately, my mom has been acting pretty strange.

JESUS: Really? That's funny. My mom too.

JOHN: What's with parents these days, you know? It's like my mom is watching every move I make. Then your mother comes over. Sometimes when I walk into a room it seems like they're talking about something important, but when they notice me, it's like they all of a sudden change the subject. Just like that. Why do parents act so weird sometimes?

JESUS: I don't know. They just do. You're an only child. I know they're really proud of you.

JOHN: *(chuckles)* I don't think so. I'm too much of a rebel.

JESUS: That you are. By the way, did your mom pack you a lunch?

JOHN: *(frowns)* Yeah, she did, but I forgot to bring it 'cause I was getting my pole together. So, I just picked up something on the way here.

JESUS: Well I brought plenty of fish and loaves of bread. You can just have some of mine.

(They position themselves a little more comfortably. JOHN opens his knapsack and tries to conceal it from JESUS as he takes out some locusts and eats them one by one. JESUS notices and appears to be upset.)

JESUS: Man, John! How many times do I have to tell you? I hate it when you eat locusts around me. They're so disgusting! How can you eat those things?

JOHN: *(with mouth full)* I can't help it, Jesus. I like 'em.

JESUS: Yuck! *(JESUS opens his knapsack, takes out a jar, and hands it to JOHN.)* Here, try some of this with it. It might make it better.

JOHN: *(looks at jar)* What is it?

JESUS: It's wild honey. It's a new brand. My mom got it from the market yesterday.

(JOHN opens the jar of honey, dips one of the locusts in, and stuffs it in his mouth. He seems to like it a lot.)

JOHN: This stuff is great! Awesome! *(JOHN dips more locusts into the honey and continues to stuff his mouth.)*

JOHN: Delicious! Absolutely delicious! Man, I could live off this stuff!

(JESUS smiles, then grins.)

JESUS: My cousin, you better be glad we're family.

JOHN: Thanks for the honey, Jesus. I could never find a cousin like you. You're always doing things for me.

JESUS: Well you do things for me too, John. Like at my birthday last year when you announced my name to everybody in the room—that made me feel much better about the party.

JOHN: Well that's nothing compared to what you do for me. How about that time when we had the ball game at the beach last summer? I sprained my ankle real bad, we ended up getting lost, and you had to carry me all the way home. And I remember at that particular time, I was feeling messed up. *(chuckles)* But it was kinda funny, because nobody could find us, cause we only left one set of footprints in the sand. Nobody knew you carried me. How did you carry me all the way home? It was far!

JESUS: *(smiles)* Wheaties.

JOHN: Well I've been eating Wheaties just as long as you have, and it doesn't do me any good.

JESUS: We're all different, I guess. *(JESUS looks at JOHN's vest.)* John, where did you get that vest? I really like it.

JOHN: *(looks at vest)* Oh this? I picked it up at a village yard sale last week. It's pretty cool, huh? It even came with a matching leather belt. You know, this vest was made from an ancient camel.

JESUS: Yeah.

JOHN: How did you know?

JESUS: I mean, yeah? I mean, like *really*?

JOHN: It sure did. From now on this vest is going to be my trademark. And Drusila thinks I look great in it too.

JESUS: So what's going on with you two, nowadays?

JOHN: Eh, we're just keeping a low profile right now. She's got an older brother who's bigger and uglier than Goliath. He'll break every bone in my body if I get near her.

JESUS: Drusila is very pretty. I really like her for you, John.

JOHN: Say, Jesus, do you, like, kinda like anyone at the temple? I mean, you don't talk about the girls much.

JESUS: No, not really. It seems like none of the girls at the temple are my type. Actually, I'm not interested in a relationship right now.

JOHN: Is that right? Well, since you've mentioned it, I've never seen you show any interest in anyone at all. Jesus, you're not...

(JOHN flips his hand back and forth in suggestion.)

JESUS: No, of course not. You don't understand.

JOHN: What's with you, Jesus? You sure are trippin' out these days.

(They become a little more serious.)

JESUS: Listen, John, I need to talk to you about something.

JOHN: What about?

JESUS: Well, it's extremely important and totally confidential.

JOHN: *(persuasively)* Well, come on, Jesus, you know me.

JESUS: Yeah, and that's what worries me. But I need to tell someone or I'll bust. And you are my best and favorite cousin.

JOHN: Well, what is it? Stop beating around the bush and just come out with it straight up.

JESUS: All right. Do you remember when I was 12 years old, when everyone thought I was lost, when actually I was at the temple talking to the chief priest and teachers of the law?

JOHN: Boy, do I!

JESUS: It was kind of an unforgettable experience, wasn't it?

JOHN: I'll say it was. I remember that day so clearly. You had us all worried. Your mom thought you were kidnapped or something. And I almost got in big trouble that day because everyone thought you were spending the night at my house.

JESUS: Yeah, I know.

JOHN: What's that got to do with what you want to tell me?

JESUS: Well, do you remember what I said to my parents?

JOHN: I think so. You said something about having to be at your father's house or something like that.

JESUS: Listen to me, John. Haven't you noticed anything peculiar about me these past couple of years?

JOHN: You mean besides the fact that you're shaving twice a week, and I don't even have peach fuzz?

(JESUS smiles warmly.)

JESUS: How about when I aced my synagogue test in Greek every week for a whole year. Didn't you think anything about me then?

JOHN: *(casually)* No. I mean, you deserve those grades. You're always studying. Every time I come over you always have your head buried in the Old Testament manuscripts. I can't even get you to come out and play ball with the guys for a couple of hours, you're so busy studying.

JESUS: Well how about the time we hiked up Golgotha Hill and that huge boulder fell off the top and barely missed crushing us like pancakes. I mean, how could that big rock, coming down with that much momentum, suddenly just miss us at the last second?

JOHN: It must have been a miracle. *(JOHN appears to be in deep thought.)* It only makes me realize one thing.

JESUS: *(smiles)* Yes.

JOHN: *(proudly)* That God must definitely have a purpose for *my* life.

JESUS: What about all those times we went fishing—like right now? Didn't you ever get suspicious or even wonder why I always catch gobs of fish, and you almost always only catch *one*?

JOHN: Jesus, you've been fishing all your life. And if you're not fishing you're always building tree houses. Me on the other hand—my mom hardly ever lets me do anything adventurous. I'm surprised she lets me go fishing with you this far away from the village. But, hey, being out in the wild should do me some good. It will be a great experience for me. *(sarcastically)* With my luck, I'll probably get stranded in the desert someday, and the only thing I'm going to have to eat is locust and wild honey. *(He chuckles lightly, and JESUS appears to be in deep thought.)* Can you imagine that?

JESUS: Yes, I can.

JOHN: What?

JESUS: I mean, yes, I can. You, you, you just seem to run into so much misfortune. *(JESUS comes to his senses.)* This isn't getting anywhere. Listen, John, I have something to tell you that will probably blow you away, but it's the truth. You may not understand everything right now, but in time you will.

JOHN: Wow, now it's beginning to sound really important. What happened?

JESUS: First, you must promise me that you will never tell a single soul about what I'm about to tell you. Well, at least until it's time.

JOHN: *(confused)* Huh? What are you…? Okay—I promise. So come out with it already!

JESUS: Do you remember in the manuscripts when the prophet Isaiah told how a child will be born unto us, and how the government will be upon his shoulder, and that his name shall be Wonderful Counselor, Prince of Peace, Mighty God, and so forth?

JOHN: Yes. He was describing the coming of the Messiah.

JESUS: Exactly. *(JESUS points to himself and whispers.)* That's me.

(JOHN stares at JESUS with a weary expression. They're silent. JOHN slowly shakes his head in disbelief. And in return, JESUS slowly nods his head in assurance. They repeat this gesture several times until JOHN finally nods his head slowly in acceptance, and then JESUS nods his head for the last time and smiles.)

JOHN: *(astonished)* No way!

JESUS: I am the Messiah.

JOHN: Yeah, right! And I'm Moses! You, the Messiah? Oh man! Jesus, this is too much. I mean, you've come up with some good ones before, but this time I think it's a little… *(JOHN points his finger at JESUS.)* You, the Messiah? *(JOHN begins to laugh hysterically. JESUS isn't amused. After a brief moment, JESUS stares intently at JOHN. Then JOHN suddenly grasps his head and begins to cry out in pain.)*

JOHN: Ugh! It hurts! Ugh, oww, make it stop! It hurts! Ughh! Somebody make it stop!

(JESUS smiles within himself and chuckles lightly. He stretches out his arm and lays his hand on top of JOHN's head, making the pain go away. JOHN instantly stops screaming and is overwhelmed with shock.)

JOHN: How did you do that?

(JOHN begins to pace aimlessly. He points his finger at JESUS, looks at him, and breathes heavily.)

JOHN: You, you, you're…you're, the, the Messiah? The Messiah? You're the Messiah? My cousin is the Messiah? *(JOHN continues to be in shock. He rubs his head and then realizes what he's just discovered.)* Yeah! My cousin, the Messiah! Boy, I could get used to this. Yo, everyone, listen up! My cousin is the Messiah! Great! This is awesome! *(JOHN calms down.)* How come you waited this long to tell me?

JESUS: I was just waiting for the right time.

JOHN: *(in awe)* The Messiah. Do James and John know about this?

JESUS: Yes. My whole family knows. But that's just it. We don't want word to get around yet.

JOHN: This is heavy, man.

JESUS: Yeah, you ain't kidding.

JOHN: So is this what this whole fishing trip was about?

JESUS: Yeah.

JOHN: Why you, Jesus? I don't understand. Why you?

JESUS: I know it's the Heavenly Father's plan. Ever since I was 12 years old, the Father has been preparing me for the day when I will redeem mankind.

JOHN: How are you going to do that?

JESUS: I'm going to lay down my life for my friends.

JOHN: *(confused)* Well, I don't…how…I mean, I don't understand. How?

JESUS: I'm going to bear the sins of the entire world and be crucified between two thieves. The Father sent me here to be the ultimate sacrifice for all of mankind. My sole purpose for coming into this world is to do the will of God. And nothing else.

(They are quiet. JOHN thinks deeply and tries to gather his emotions.)

JESUS: You're going to have a part in this too.

JOHN: *(bewildered)* Me? How?

JESUS: You're going to baptize me.

JOHN: Baptize you? Me? Jesus, I'm not even worthy enough to unbuckle your sandals.

JESUS: You're going to baptize me in the Jordan River.

JOHN: *(seriously)* But Jesus, I don't even know how to swim. *(JESUS looks at JOHN witheringly.)* I'll learn. I'll learn.

JESUS: John, I need you to pull through with me on this.

(JOHN takes a few steps, thinking. Then he turns and faces Jesus.)

JOHN: *(proudly)* You can count on me, Jesus.

JESUS: *(smiles)* Thanks, John. I knew I could.

(They sit close to each other. JOHN puts his arm around JESUS.)

JOHN: You know, Jesus, ever since we were kids, I've always known you were special in some way. I mean, I didn't expect it to be this special, but…Listen, Jesus, I totally believe you and everything, and I'm behind you 100 percent. But what's the plan? If you're going to be the Messiah, how are the people of Israel going to respond to that? I mean, I'm sure they're going to be expecting the Messiah to be born of a wealthy family with political background…You were born in a stable, Jesus. You walked every place you ever went to. You only own one pair of sandals. How are the people going to accept that?

(They're both deep in thought.)

JESUS: We're just going to have to make sure the people are prepared.

JOHN: How?

JESUS: Well, before the Heavenly Father instructs me to begin my mission, maybe you could make a way for me, by preparing the way for them. Like you did at my birthday party last year. Let the people know I'm coming.

JOHN: Yeah, good idea, Jesus. I could be a voice.

(They reel in their fishing lines and begin to gather their things to leave.)

JOHN: Well at least now I know why you always beat me at everything…and how you carried me from the beach…and how you always passed your tests…and how you made the big rock miss us.

(They exit.)

JESUS: You know, John, I'm kinda glad you like eating locusts after all.

JOHN: Why?

JESUS: Well, let's just say you'll have plenty of locust in the next few years.

JOHN: As long as I've got that honey. Oh, that reminds me, Jesus, there are a couple of Philistines I want you to beat up for me. One's over six feet tall.

JESUS: Well that isn't so unusual.

JOHN: I know but this guy is only five years old.

(JESUS begins to laugh.)

JESUS: That's my cousin.

(They exit the stage.)

END

 Trust

CAST

• Ivy   • Mort   • April

IVY: You know, if there's one thing you can trust, it's a well-built car. You get into it, it starts, and you can depend on it to take you anywhere you want to go.

MORT: I can trust a fishing trip to take me away from it all. Whether it's one day or a week, I can depend on a trip out on the water to relax me as if I've been away for a month. There's nothing like throwing those lines overboard to help me forget whatever's on my mind.

IVY: I trust my credit card to be there when I don't have cash. When I see something I want, I just flash my plastic card, and I know I'll get what I want. I get a great a sense of satisfaction and contentment knowing I can use my card to buy food, shelter, and clothing.

MORT: I trust the radio to bring me all the news I need.

IVY: I get the sports and weather.

MORT: And music. Twenty-four hours a day, every day of the year, I can turn on the radio to fulfill my listening needs.

IVY: And when I'm not listening to the radio, I put my trust in a good book to keep me occupied. I can go anywhere in the world on the pages of a book from the library.

I remember when I was small my sisters read to me, and I couldn't wait to be able to understand the words on the paper by myself so I could enjoy the stories without someone's help.

MORT: Books are our trustworthy friends.

(APRIL enters.)

APRIL: Psalm 33:20-21: "We wait in hope for the Lord; he is our help and our shield. In him our hearts rejoice, for we trust in his holy name."

MORT: What?

APRIL: Psalm 119:42: "Then I will answer for the one who taunts me, for I trust in your word."

IVY: Huh?

APRIL: Trust in God's name; trust in the Word; trust in Christ.

MORT: But what about a nice automobile, a fishing trip...

IVY: A good book...?

APRIL: Those are fine such as they are, but they must not be taken out of their place. Man must not put undue trust in riches, weapons, leaders, or other men and their works.

MORT: I just listen to the radio four or five hours a day. I trust that's not too much.

IVY: And I just read three or four hours a day. I trust that's not too much either. I'll find time for all that other trusting some other time.

APRIL: Trusting in the Lord has many benefits...joy... Psalm 5:11: "But let all who take refuge in you be glad; let them ever sing for joy." Psalm 22:4-5 describes the benefit of deliverance. Some of the other benefits are triumph, safety, guidance, inheritance of the kingdom and more.

MORT: But I can't really put my hands on all that.

IVY: That's right; it's all so nebulous.

APRIL: These are some of the things that are the most real—even though you may not be able to see them or grasp them immediately, they are realities greater than all you've mentioned and probably ever experienced so far.

MORT: Well, I'm not so sure. Maybe I'll think about some of this on my next fishing trip.

IVY: And maybe I'll read a book about it.

END

NEW TESTAMENT NEWS

Good News, All the Time

CAST, IN ORDER OF APPEARANCE

- **Scripture Cue Card Holder:** (In studio) Sits or stands in studio and holds up large, numbered cue cards with Scripture references or messages on them. Use the cues in parentheses throughout the script to create the cue cards.
- **Ava Acts:** (In studio) Professional news anchor who recaps weekend events, reports on news items, and announces breaking news stories.
- **Delah Shmee:** (In studio) Professional news coanchor who recaps the weekend events and reports on news items.
- **Ronda Maloski:** (In studio) Professional weather forecaster who reports strange, weather-related events.
- **Dodge Viper:** (In studio) Professional traffic reporter who reports on detours, accidents, and roadwork.
- **Advertiser:** (On video) Have students create their own video commercials to run between segments. Make them humorous. Wear current clothing, but use items or products available during New Testament times.
- **Kent Brackman:** (In studio) Professional sportscaster who reports on the weekend sports events.
- **Assyria Mahershalahashbaz:** (On video, in a park or street setting) On-site reporter who reports from the streets of Jerusalem. Interviews an angry Pharisee and many people who have been healed by Jesus.
- **Moe:** (On video, in a park or street setting) Blind man, healed by Jesus and excited that he can see, who Assyria interviews on the streets of Jerusalem.
- **Zerah:** (On video, in a park or street setting) Woman crippled for 18 years by a demon and then healed by Jesus. She shows her happiness by bending and standing up. Assyria interviews her on the streets of Jerusalem.
- **Angel Faith:** (On video, in a park or street setting) Jairus' daughter who Jesus raised from the dead. She loves Jesus more than anything, and Assyria interviews her on the streets of Jerusalem.
- **Ralph:** (On video, in a park or street setting) A snobby Pharisee who thinks he's holier than anyone. He's convinced that Jesus and his followers are crazy. Assyria interviews him on the streets of Jerusalem.
- **Steve:** (On video, in a park or street setting) Young man raised from the dead by Jesus and excited to be alive. He doesn't like the Pharisee, Ralph, at all. Assyria interviews him on the streets of Jerusalem.
- **Selena:** (On video, in a park or street setting) Leper for 10 years, healed by Jesus, and happy to be able to touch her kids. Assyria interviews her on the streets of Jerusalem.
- **Seba Jackels:** (In studio) Professional interviewer who wants to get to the truth and interviews Governor Pontius Pilate and the apostle John. Breaking news from the tomb interrupts him.
- **Governor Pontius Pilate:** (In studio) Governor of Judea. Interviewed by Seba Jackels in same studio as the apostle John. Pilate gave in to pressures from the religious community and the people of Judea and sentenced Jesus to death. He's a weak, very defensive, and nervous man who gets angry and frightened during breaking news and leaves the set.
- **John:** (In studio) Seba Jackels interviews the apostle John, disciple of Jesus Christ, in the same studio as Pilate. He is sad, upset, and confused and tells eyewitness accounts of Jesus' power

and love. Breaking news from on-site reporter at the tomb interrupts the interview, and John is so excited when he hears the breaking news that he can't sit still.

- **T.J. Thomason:** (On video, in a park or garden setting) On-site reporter who reports live from Jesus' empty tomb. She is excited and confused as she interviews a Roman guard named Russell, the apostle Peter, and witnesses: Mary (Mother of Jesus), Mary Magdalene, and Joanna.
- **Russell:** (On video, in a park or garden setting) Roman guard, hired by Pilate to guard Jesus' tomb. He now fears that Pilate will have him killed because the tomb is empty. T.J. interviews him.
- **Peter:** (On video, in a park or garden setting) T.J. interviews the apostle Peter live at the empty tomb. He jumps with joy that Jesus has risen, gives his account, and runs off to Galilee to see Jesus for himself.

- **Mary:** (On video, in a park or garden setting). T.J. interviews Mary, Mother of Jesus live at the empty tomb. Mary is excited and shaken because she just saw Jesus alive.
- **Mary Magdalene:** (On video, in a park or garden setting) This follower of Jesus was with Mary and Joanna when they saw the empty tomb and Jesus. T.J. interviews her live at the empty tomb.
- **Joanna:** (On video, in a park or garden setting) This follower of Jesus is excited and shaking because she was with the other women and saw Jesus too.
- **Chi-Chi Rosita Conchita Smith:** (In studio) Begins with a commercial but gives the audience an invitation to ask Jesus into their hearts. Her name is funny, but the rest is truly serious.

PROPS

- **Long desk**

The scene opens with Ava Acts, Delah Shmee, and Seba Jackels sitting at a long desk. Ronda Maloski, Dodge Viper, and Kent Brackman stand behind them, smiling. Music plays.

Cue card holder displays card 1 (NTTV PRESENTS), then 2 (NEW TESTAMENT NEWS—GOOD NEWS ALL THE TIME), then 3 (WEEKEND EDITION).

Music stops.

AVA ACTS: Hello, I'm Ava Acts, and thank you for joining us on this beautiful Sunday morning.

DELAH SHMEE: Good morning. I'm Delah Shmee, and welcome to the weekend edition of New Testament News—Good News All the Time.

SEBA JACKELS: Hi. I'm Seba Jackels, and later this morning I'll speak with two interesting gentlemen, Governor Pilate and John the Apostle.

RONDA MALOSKI: Good morning. I'm Ronda Maloski, and I'll try to explain the wild weather that took place over the weekend.

DODGE VIPER: Hello. I'm Dodge Viper, and I'll let you know where the traffic problems are this morning.

KENT BRACKMAN: And I'm Kent Brackman. I'll let you know how your favorite teams did this weekend.

AVA: Thank you, Kent, and thank *you* for tuning in this morning. We'll give you a recap of the weekend's news when we return.

Play first commercial.

AVA: Some strange things happened this past week here in Jerusalem. Topping the news today, a man identified as Judas Iscariot was found hanging from a tree. An investigation is still underway, but sources say it was an apparent suicide. Delah, do we have any information on Mr. Iscariot?

DELAH: Well Ava, it seems this Judas was a follower of a man who was put to death Friday. Sources say, however, that Judas was a traitor. They claim Judas was paid 30 pieces of silver to lead authorities to Jesus of Nazareth's location. By the way, the silver pieces were not found on the body. Also topping the news list, known murderer and local hit man, Barabbas, was released from prison this week. Governor Pilate will tell us more about this bizarre release when he joins us later in the newscast. Just a warning to our viewers, Barabbas is a convicted murdered and extremely dangerous, so be careful out there.

AVA: Thank you, Delah, and speaking of silver, we learned this weekend that the Chief Priests of our city paid *exactly* 30 pieces of silver for a plot of land. It is reported that these officials bought the land for a cemetery. Our sources tell us they plan to use it to bury strangers when the need arises. We're not sure yet how all these things tie together, but we'll keep you posted.

DELAH: In other news, two earthquakes shook Jerusalem this week. The first one was reported around 3:00 p.m. Friday. Strangely enough, the only reported damage was to the city's cemeteries. Many graves were broken open, and bodies are mysteriously missing. We should have more information on this later. The second earthquake was reported—and felt—early this morning before sunrise. Damage reports are not yet in. It's as if an unseen force moved the mountains.

AVA: It seems that many odd things happened Friday afternoon. Jerusalem priests reported that at *exactly* 3:00 p.m. on Friday the beautiful, ornate curtain in the Temple was torn in half—from top to bottom. Eyewitnesses claim the curtain tore *itself* in half!

DELAH: That's some report, Ava, but more shocking than that was the unexplained darkness that reportedly covered the whole earth from noon to three this past Friday. Witnesses first noticed this darkness while watching a triple crucifixion on Golgotha. They reported that the air stood still, and then the sun disappeared. The air seemed to be swallowed in the darkness.

AVA: The religious community has no explanation for these bizarre events. They claim they are natural events and that the timing is purely coincidental. A small group of heretics however, claim the events happened because the Son of God was put to death on a cross on Friday. Later in the newscast, Seba Jackels brings us an interview with Governor Pontius Pilate and a man named John, a follower of Jesus of Nazareth, the alleged Messiah.

DELAH: Yes, Ava, Jesus of Nazareth made quite a stir here in Jerusalem this past week. He was nearly arrested last week for destroying the flea market inside the Temple. Other reports however, claim thousands of people follow him and listen to him teach about God. Let's check in with Ronda Maloski to see how hot it's going to be today. Ronda?

RONDA: Thank you, Delah. Boy, it's going to be a hot one! Our morning temperature is already 87 degrees! We could reach 105 this afternoon! We're hoping for some afternoon showers later with a 30 percent chance of

thunderstorms. The current temperature of the Jordan River is a record 81 degrees. Even the fish are feeling the heat! As for the darkness that covered the earth Friday for three hours and the two earthquakes felt everywhere, we can only guess that El Niño was responsible. How are the roads looking out there, Dodge?

DODGE: Not too bad, Ronda, but we do have some possible delays—nothing compared to the traffic jam reported Friday, though. The road to Golgotha was like a parking lot during the crucifixions. Many accidents occurred when the air turned black. Visibility was zero within seconds and horses and wheels were everywhere. The cleanup took hours! This morning crews are doing roadwork on Emmaus Road, so a detour leads travelers off the beaten track. A serious chariot collision is reported on the Jerusalem Highway and is causing quite a backup. More roadwork is reported on the road adjacent to Herod's palace. A large sinkhole that appeared Friday just after the first earthquake is being repaired. If you must take these roads, give yourself extra time or take another route. Drive safely out there!

AVA: We'll be right back.

Play second commercial.

AVA: Welcome back, and thank you for joining us for the weekend edition of New Testament News. Good News all the time. Speaking of good news, Kent, tell us good news in sports this weekend.

KENT: Thank you, Ava. We had good news and bad news in the sporting arena over the weekend. The good news was no one was killed during the Chariot Race Finals. A vicious crash occurred when the Golden Warrior's chariot broke a spoke and sideswiped a chariot owned by the Silver Riders. Both drivers are okay, but their chariots will be in the shop for at least a week.

Later today, the Sadducees will meet the Pharisees in the International Championship Fight of the Century. This volatile rivalry has been going on for years and promises to be a real battle. You can catch this exciting boxing match on pay-per-view for the low price of five goats.

Roman guards were scheduled to compete in the Annual Crocodile Run last night. Unfortunately, many of the guards had to pull special duty in the cemetery—of all places—reportedly to guard the dead body of a man from Nazareth. What will they think of next? Sadly, during the Crocodile Run, a local man replaced one of the guards and was killed. During the run, three large crocs came from all directions and attacked him. Please remember folks, these crocodile runs are for professionals only. Do not try this at home.

The good news is the Annual Run will complete the final eliminations next Saturday as scheduled. Delah, back to you.

DELAH: Kent, it sure sounds like you had a busy weekend, and this man from Nazareth was a popular news item this week. For more information on this man named Jesus, we go now to an interview prerecorded on the streets of Jerusalem. Our on-site reporter, Assyria Mahershalahashbaz, asked people who this Jesus person is.

Play video of street interview.

ASSYRIA: Hi. I'm Assyria Mahershalahashbaz, and I'm here on the streets of Jerusalem talking with a large crowd of people who follow a Man named Jesus of Nazareth. I've heard some amazing stories about this Man, and we're all seeking the truth. Excuse me, sir, you told me you know Jesus and he helped you in some way. Can you tell us how?

MOE (BLIND MAN): *Helped* me? This Man is the Son of God! He *healed* me! I'm Moe, and I was born blind! Well, there I was, sitting on the street begging, as usual, when I *felt* him come up to me. At first, I wasn't *sure* who he was, but after he started speaking to me, I knew! I just knew! I never thought anyone could ever help me with my eyes, but I was wrong! I heard him doing something. I didn't know what. Then he smeared some stuff on my eyelids—I think it was clay—but it burned. He told me to go to the pool and wash it away. I did and as I picked my head up I began to see lights! Then faces! Then I saw *his* face! It was a miracle! I know he is the Messiah, and I will worship him forever! I once was blind, but now I see! **(puts hands on Assyria's shoulders, looks in her eyes, and smiles real big)**

ASSYRIA: Thank you Moe. Ma'am? You claim that Jesus healed you, too. Is that right?

ZARAH (HANDICAPPED WOMAN): Oh, yes! My name is Zarah, and Jesus, the Son of God, said I had a demon living in me and he cast that old demon out! For the last 18 *years* I have been bent nearly in half! I looked like this. **(bends over)** I was so crippled **(eyes tear up)** I couldn't even pick up my own children. But now look at me! **(twists, dances, hugs someone)** Some Pharisees got mad because he healed me on the Sabbath, but I didn't care about that and neither did my kids! I've been

touched by the Master's hand. I and everyone who knows me will worship and thank our Lord all our lives!

ASSYRIA: Wow! These stories are truly amazing! Standing right here, living, talking, and breathing, is a young lady with an even more incredible story about this man, Jesus. Would you tell us what happened to you?

ANGEL FAITH: Well, I was asked not to tell anyone, but I just have to! My name is Angel Faith, and I'm 12 years old. I started getting sick, and I just got worse. I was at death's door. My father, Jairus, is the head pastor at the synagogue, and he'd heard about Jesus. Dad believed that the only way I could be healed was through Jesus. Dad went to ask Jesus to heal me, but on his way to find him, somehow Dad knew that I died. I really did, but I don't remember anything. Dad kept going and asked Jesus to come to our house anyway. When they came back Jesus brought some of his friends with him. As I lay there dead on my bed, the people standing outside my house were very upset and told the men that they were too late and that nothing could be done for me. But Jesus said, "She's not dead; she's only asleep." Of course no one believed Him, except my dad. Jesus allowed only my parents and his friends Peter, John, and James in the room with me. They *all* believed as Jesus took my hand and told me to get up. Dad says my spirit filled me, and I stood up! I remember looking into Jesus' face, and I'll never forget the love I saw in his eyes. Jesus is my savior, and I'll love Him forever!

ASSYRIA: As shocking as these reports of miracles are, someone here doesn't believe any of them. Sir, you said earlier that these stories are fairytales. Can you tell us why you feel this way?

RALPH (PHARISEE): Yeah, I can. I'm Ralph, and I'm a Pharisee. I'm not buying any of this. This guy named Jesus is crazy. These people are crazy. He has a group of i followers, and they believe everything he says! It's sick! Only God can raise someone from the dead. Everybody knows that. All of us religious leaders in the community think he should be put to death. He's a blasphemer. He claims to be the Son of God, and yet he breaks the holy, sacred Sabbath laws. God created those laws, and he breaks them by doing his healing tricks on the Sabbath. Did you know he actually claims to be *the* Messiah? *The* Messiah is supposed to come and rule the world on a throne. *This* man has no money, no throne, no kingdom, and he's homeless! He's a freak and causes mass hysteria. He's dangerous. That's all I have to say.

STEVE (LIVE BOY): *(grabs Ralph's arm and Assyria holds the microphone for them)* Hey! Wait a minute, mister! Jesus is no freak! *(gets in Ralph's face)* He *is* the Messiah!

ASSYRIA: Can you tell me your story?

STEVE: Yes, and I want to make sure *he* hears it because it's true! My name is Steve, and my mom is around here somewhere—anyway, last month I got really sick. I couldn't eat or anything. One day things got dark, and then I don't remember anything. My mom says I died. She was really sad. She says while our family was walking down this very road—taking *me* to *my funeral*—Jesus saw my mom and felt sorry for her. He came over to my body, and the next thing I know, I hear a voice saying, "Young man, I say arise!" I opened my eyes, and Jesus was smiling at me. I woke up in a *coffin*! I was at a funeral! My funeral! Man, my mom was crying and hugging me—even though I smelled bad. Mom was yelling that Jesus saved me! I thank him every day, and that's how I know he's *the* Messiah! And…

SELENA (LEPER): *(interrupts)* Hey, wait! I have to tell you *my* story! I'm Selena, and I heard about Jesus. Many people were following him because he taught the truth about God. I knew he was the Son of God and that if he wanted to, he could heal *me*! I have been forced to live outside the city walls for 10 years. I had leprosy. My kids were very young when the terrible white spots started spreading on my arms. I had to leave my family, and I didn't even get to hug and kiss them good-bye. I wasn't allowed to touch anyone ever again. Ten years without a hug or even a touch from *anyone*! Jesus was teaching on a mountain, and I saw him and all the people following him. They were coming toward me. When he came close, I fell on the ground worshiping him. I said, "Lord, if you will, you can heal me." Jesus stopped, reached out his hand and *touched* me! He said, "I am willing; be clean." *Instantly*, I was healed! This man is Lord of all and I love him!

ASSYRIA: Wow! These accounts speak for themselves! I'm *convinced* this is no mass hysteria. These people are *real*, and I *believe*! This Jesus doesn't sound dangerous to me—he sounds like the true Messiah!

Stop video.

AVA: Well! What a stunning report from the streets of Jerusalem! This information definitely adds to the mystery of this man Jesus. Seba, can you shed some light on Jesus of Nazareth?

SEBA: I hope so. I'm Seba Jackels and with me this morning is the Governor of Judea, Pontius Pilate. Good morning, Governor.

PILATE: *(nervous)* Good morning.

SEBA: Also with us for this interview is John the Apostle. Good morning, John.

JOHN: *(sad and angry)* Good morning, Seba.

SEBA: Now both of you gentlemen have been involved with Jesus of Nazareth recently. Governor Pilate, I understand you ordered this man's death. Is that right?

PILATE: *(nervously)* Yes.

SEBA: Well, Governor, we just heard some remarkable stories of how Jesus healed all these people. Can you tell us what crime he committed that led to you to give him the death sentence?

PILATE: *(agitated, angry, defensive)* Let me set the record straight right now! As far as I'm concerned, his blood is not on my hands! I found him totally innocent of any crime. I only did what the people *demanded* of me!

SEBA: What do you mean?

PILATE: I gave the people the choice. I was being pressured by the religious leaders to put him to death. I even allowed the crowd to choose a prisoner to release. They could either release Barabbas, the murderer, or Jesus of Nazareth. *They* chose to release Barabbas! Not me. It's as simple as that.

SEBA: John, they say you're a disciple. Were you a disciple of Jesus of Nazareth?

JOHN: Yes. I was. I served him for close to three years.

SEBA: What can you tell us about him?

JOHN: I can tell you that his claims were true, and I was with him when he healed the people we just saw in the interview. I have seen him heal *multitudes* of people. But that was not his real mission. He didn't just heal people physically; he healed their *souls*. He is the promised Messiah (Isaiah 53) and can forgive our sins, if only we ask. He taught us all to love each other and to serve the only Holy God. By simply believing in him—putting all our faith in him—believing he is the promised Son of

God and that he and the Father are One, he promises life everlasting. Jesus fulfilled the prophecies of the scriptures and is God sent in the flesh! The only way to the Father is through him.

SEBA: But, he was crucified Friday. Are you saying the people killed God?

JOHN: I'm kind of confused about a lot of stuff right now, because he taught us so many things. He told us he was coming into his kingdom to reign forever. We had a dinner the night he was arrested, and he told us he wouldn't be with us for long. We didn't understand what he meant. Judas Iscariot betrayed him. Then he was arrested, tried at midnight, convicted of who-knows-what, and sentenced to death by *(point to Pilate) this man!* Now he's dead! The scriptures in Isaiah described his death. But we don't know what to do now. I just can't believe this has happened. My Lord and savior was *crucified!*

SEBA: *(to audience)* We have to go to a commercial now, but when we come back, we'll ask Governor Pilate what he thinks of these Messiah claims.

Play third commerical.

SEBA: Welcome back. In case you just joined us, I'm speaking with Governor Pilate and…

AVA: *(interrupts Seba)* Excuse me, Seba, but we have some breaking news about Jesus of Nazareth's body. We go now live to T.J. Thomason at the cemetery.

Play video of tomb scene.

AVA: T.J., what's happening there?

T.J.: Ava, Friday night, the body of Jesus of Nazareth was placed here, inside a tomb owned by Joseph of Arimathea. Joseph and a small group of women brought the body here and sealed the tomb with a huge stone set in a sloping track. Joseph is apparently a respected member of the Sanhedrin that found Jesus guilty of blasphemy. We know that Governor Pontius Pilate then ordered a large group of Roman guards to seal the tomb with the royal seal and watch for anything unusual. This morning the tomb was found open and the body gone. The death shroud is still where the body was, undisturbed. We also have reports that a man with brightly shining clothes was sitting inside and spoke to some woman who came here this morning to tend to the body. Standing here with me is Russell, one of the Roman guards on duty this weekend. Russell, can you tell us what you know?

RUSSELL (ROMAN GUARD): I'll try, T.J. *(nervously)*

(John seems excited, and Pilate gets nervous in the studio.)

RUSSELL (ROMAN GUARD): Um, we were all standing there guarding the tomb—like Pilate said—and the earth started to tremble. We saw a bright light, and then we *all* passed out! When we woke up, the stone was rolled away and the body was gone! We were terrified! Pilate is going to *kill* us! Maybe his followers stole his body *(looks scared)*. Yeah, that's what we'll tell Pilate—they stole it so it would look like he rose from the dead. You know, that's why Pilate stationed all of us here in the first place. He was afraid Jesus would rise from the dead. Oh, man. I shouldn't have told you that—I gotta get outta here! *(runs away)*

(Pilate walks off stage scared, looking over his shoulder.)

PETER: *(grabs the microphone)* He's alive! *(does a little dance)* He is alive!

T.J.: Sir, who are you, and what do you know about all this?

PETER: I'm Peter. *(dances)* He did it! He told us he would be given over to sinful men, crucified, and rise from the dead on the third day! None of us knew what he meant when he said it, but this is it! It's the third *day!* He's *alive!* He has beaten death! *(falls on his knees in worship)* Now through him we can all have life eternal. It's a *gift alive!* He died on that cross to pay for *our* sins! He *bought* us! All we have to do is believe! Do you believe, T.J.?

T.J.: Well, um.

PETER: We must tell everyone! He *is* the Messiah, and he's *alive!* I've got to get to Galilee right now! We're supposed to find him there!

T.J.: Okay, as I said earlier, some women found the empty tomb. Let's ask them what they know. Excuse me, ladies? What do you know about the missing body?

MARY (MOTHER): I'm Mary, Jesus' mother. We came here early this morning to put spices on Jesus' body.

MARY MAGDALENE: And that big rock was rolled away!

JOANNA: We looked inside, and there was a man in glowing clothes who spoke to us. It wasn't Jesus, though.

MARY (MOTHER): And he asked us why we were looking for the living among the dead!

MARY MAGDALENE: He told us Jesus had risen from the dead just like Jesus said he would!

JOANNA: Then we all went running to tell his disciples, and we *saw* him! We were running in the woods, and there he was!

MARY (MOTHER): We fell at his feet and grabbed them to kiss them. We were afraid but bursting with joy at the same time!

MARY MAGDALENE: He told us not to be afraid, and to go tell his disciples what we had seen and tell them to go to Galilee and they would *see* him there!

T.J.: Wow! This is truly a miracle! I guess we're headed for Galilee too, and we'll see what we find when we get there. Back to you. Ava.

Stop video.

AVA: I've been praying to see the Messiah before I die all my life! This sounds like the *true* Messiah has finally come! Speaking from personal knowledge, I know the scriptures, and the words of the prophets prove he is the one!

DELAH: I'm with you, Ava! He must be the Christ! **(raises hands to God)** Thank you, Father!

AVA: Well, that's all the time we have but tune in tomorrow as we learn more about this miraculous story. Thank you for watching NTTV's New Testament News—Good News *all* the Time!

Music plays. Chi-Chi takes center stage. Wait for applause then hold up hand to quiet applause.

CHI-CHI: Hi, I'm Chi-Chi Rosita Conchita Smith **(big smile)**. I'm from Teen Ministries. I'm a believer and you can be one too! You have just heard some strong evidence taken from scripture that Jesus *is* the promised Messiah. This newscast was taken from true, eyewitness accounts found in the Bible. God promises eternal life to *all* who believe in Jesus. We can never be good enough on our own or earn our way to heaven. You don't need to. Jesus paid the price for your sins. It takes only one step of faith to ask Jesus into your heart. If you've never asked Jesus into your heart and life, you can do it right now. Right where you sit! He will absolutely change your life—and your eternity. He was crucified on that cross and shed his blood for *you*! That's right, *you*! The Good News is that Jesus didn't stay dead on that cross. Three days after his death he arose from the dead, just as he said he would. This very same Jesus wants a relationship with *you*—free of charge. Are you ready for one? None of us deserve his sacrifice, but God loves you so much that he allowed his only son to die for you. He only asks that you believe in him. His son is the promised savior! Let's bow our heads now. **(pause)**

If you want Jesus to be forever in your heart and life, please pray this simple prayer with me right now:

Dear Jesus, I know who you are, and I know that you died for me. I know I am a sinner, and I know only you can save me. Please forgive my sins, and come into my life. I want you to be *my* personal Savior. Thank you, Jesus, for loving me enough to die for me. I love you. Amen.

If you prayed that prayer tonight, welcome to the family! We have people here that would like to welcome you and pray for you, so join us up front. Thank you and good night.

Cue card holder displays the final card: GOD BLESS YOU AND JESUS LOVES YOU

END

Running from GOD

CAST

- Narrator
- Ticket Agent
- Kaleb, shipmate 1
- God, voice only
- Captain
- Bart, shipmate 2
- Jonah
- King
- Shipmates, extras
- People of Nineveh

NARRATOR: The word of the Lord to Jonah.

GOD: Jonah! *(JONAH sits up, looking around.)* Jonah! *(shakes his head, with a confused look on his face)* Jonah, turn off the TV, Jonah!

JONAH: God, is that you?

GOD: Yes, Jonah, it is!

JONAH: Lord, I haven't heard from you in awhile, is everything okay? What do you want of me this time, Lord?

GOD: Pack your bags, Jonah, and get on a flight to Nineveh. I want you to go and warn the people of my coming judgment upon them. They have been very wicked.

JONAH: *(in fear)* O Lord, not them. I've heard about the Ninevites and all the wicked things they do. Please, I don't want to go there. Remember the last place you sent me? I came back home with a broken leg and a black eye, and I smelled like a llama for three weeks. Isn't there anyone else?

GOD: I have chosen you, Jonah.

JONAH: *(stands up and walks around worried)* But, what difference can I make? It's a huge city. They'll kill me if I speak out against their gods. *(pause)* Hey, why don't you send that *(pick the name of the senior pastor, youth pastor, or someone you can tease)* fella? Maybe he can do it. *(pauses and looks up like he's thinking, then gets a big smile)* Oh, wait, I forgot. He's still recovering from his last sermon. It was messy; at least that's what everyone is saying. Sorry, God, but I've gotta get out of here. *(JONAH quickly exits and heads for the shipyard.)*

JONAH: *(impatiently)* Any boats going east?

AGENT: Yep, one is leaving in *(looks at his watch)* two minutes to be exact. You in a hurry?

JONAH: *(sarcastic)* No, I talk this fast all the time. Of course I'm in a hurry, and I need to be on that boat.

AGENT: *(jokingly)* Why are you in a hurry? Are you running from God or something? We get a couple of them comin' through here every year.

JONAH: *(looks up surprised)* Uhh, uhh. No, I'm going umm, to see my aunt Ruth's new, uhh, *(pause)* pig. Yeah that's it, her new pig.

(JONAH *grabs his ticket and runs off.*)

AGENT: *(after JONAH leaves, agent talks to himself)* Yep, he's running from God. I can spot 'em every time. Excuses seem to follow them everywhere they go.

NARRATOR: So Jonah ran from God. And the Lord caused a mighty wind on the sea, and there was a great storm. Jonah's ship was in serious trouble, and it began to break up.

MATES: *(with fear)* Captain, Captain, the ship is breaking up. *(Some SHIPMATES begin falling on their knees in prayer.)* Each man is crying out to his god, and some are throwing the cargo over board. What are we going to do?

CAPTAIN: *(approaches JONAH who is asleep)* How can you sleep in this storm? *(shakes JONAH)* Get up! Get up, man! *(JONAH wakes up.)* Call on our—hurry, there's trouble with the ship.

JONAH: What is it?

CAPTAIN: The storm is breaking the ship apart. We think that someone's god is a little upset.

KALEB: Let's cast lots to see who brought this calamity upon us. *(They use the "Eeanie, meanie, mynie, mo" routine to decide. The lot falls to JONAH.)*

CAPTAIN: *(to JONAH)* Where are you from? Why is your God trying to kill us?

JONAH: *(unenthusiastic)* My name is Jonah, and I'm a holy rolling, devil stompin', law abiding, prophet of God, who happens to be running scared.

BART: What have you done, and how can we stop this storm?

JONAH: You see, fellas, I'm scared because I'm supposed to go see my aunt Ruth because she just got a new pi… *(pauses with worried look on his face)* I can't do this. I can't keep running.

KALEB: *(angry)* What, what is going on, man? Hurry, we're all about to die. What did you do to your God?

JONAH: I, I, was not obedient. I'm running from God. The only way to save the ship is to throw me overboard. Then the sea will become calm again.

MATES: *(They don't waste any time. They grab JONAH by his hands and feet and shout.)* Red rover, red rover, throw Jonah right over! *(make sure JONAH lands on something soft)*

CAPTAIN: *(amazed)* Cool! *(points)* Look, the sea is totally calm!

BART: Even the wind is gone! Let's offer a sacrifice to Jonah's God. *(The men bow down to pray.)*

NARRATOR: So the Lord sent an absolutely, humongous fish with the most gargantuan mouth you have ever seen to ingest Jonah.

JONAH: *(depressed, from inside the fish. He could be off stage, with the lights off.)* God, I'm calling to you from the belly of this absolutely humongous fish with the most gargantuan mouth I've ever seen. You hurled me into the sea, and I was tossed from your sight, but I hope to return to you again. I was in the sea until I almost died and was mummified by seaweed. Lord, when I had almost drowned and couldn't hold my breath for one more second, you rescued me. While I was fading away, I remembered you and you heard my prayer. People who worship idols forfeit the thanksgiving, and I will be what I have vowed to be. I will be the prophet of the Living God. I will be what you have called me to be. *(loud and begging)* Now get me out of this stink'n fish!

NARRATOR: Then God commanded the absolutely humongous fish with the most gargantuan mouth you have ever seen to vomit Jonah onto the dry land. Once again the word of the Lord came to Jonah.

GOD: Jonah! Get up! Go to Nineveh, and tell the people of the city to repent.

NARRATOR: So Jonah went to the great city of Nineveh, which was a hop, skip, and a trip *(hops, skips, and trips)* away. Basically, a three-day journey.

JONAH: In forty days the city of Nineveh will be terminated, wiped out, obliterated, smashed, cleared away, destroyed, devastated, thrashed, annihilated, butchered, consumed, crushed.

PEOPLE: *(in unison)* We get the idea!

JONAH: Oh, I'm sorry. Where was I before *(pause)* Oh, yes, in forty days the city of Nineveh will be destroyed because of your wickedness, sin, hate, immorality, evilness, corruption *(The people all react with rolling eyes and disgust.)* perversion, treachery, vileness, deception, mockery, lust, darkness…

GOD: *(interrupting)* Jonah. *(JONAH stops and looks up.)*

JONAH: Yes, God?

GOD: I think they get the idea!

NARRATOR: And the Ninevites believed God and declared a fast and put on potato sacks. And the king did the same and gave a command to the people saying… *(pause)*

KING: By my command, no person or beast may eat or drink. All of us must pray and turn from our wickedness so the Lord may have compassion on us and not destroy our city.

NARRATOR: When God saw the people fast and pray and turn from their wicked ways, he had compassion on the city and did not destroy it. What kind of lesson do we learn from Jonah? First of all, running from God doesn't pay. Someone once said, "It doesn't make much sense to run from God, because when he catches you, he's just going to love you. Secondly, living in wickedness and sin doesn't pay either. If you are, don't wait for the giant fish of life to swallow you, just turn to God today. He will rescue you and change your life."

END

Hell's Barbershop

CAST

• Barber • Satan • Larry • Oscar

PROPS

• Chair • Sheet • Pair of scissors • Comb
• Lock of hair • Red shirt or blouse

As the lights come up, LARRY sits in a chair with a sheet wrapped around him. The BARBER works on LARRY's head with a pair of scissors in one hand and a comb in the other hand. When the lights come up LARRY begins to speak.

LARRY: And another thing—I had to wait for what seemed like 1000 years to get a haircut. And you didn't have anything interesting for me to read while I waited. You've only got three things to pick from. Dante's *Inferno* if you're in the mood for fiction and those copies of the Bible in the bookshelves and magazine rack near the door. What are those doing here?

BARBER: Those Gideons even came to Hell's Barbershop.

LARRY: And what about all those glossy vacation brochures in that little cardboard stand that say "Visit New Jerusalem" on the cover. Since we can't go there and they're in your shop, that's false advertising. I'm thinkin' about suing you. We can still do that, you know. We have lots of attorneys here.

BARBER: *(interrupts)* You're done.

(Without another word LARRY stands and exits left. The BARBER cleans up around the chair and talks to himself.)

BARBER: This is ridiculous. Since my placement here, I bet I've cut over 16 million heads without taking as much as a good stretch. I've got shoes that are half a size too small, and I've been standing for as long as I can remember. This is hell. *(pauses shortly, shakes his head, and walks over to stage left, points offstage and yells)*

BARBER: Next, you in the red.

(The BARBER quickly walks to the right and stands behind the chair with the sheet folded over his right arm. The next customer walks in from stage left in a red shirt with a confident stride, walking tall. The customer stops before he arrives at the chair. He turns to the audience. His confidence evaporates, his physical stature deflates, and he begins to speak.)

SATAN: Next, you in the red. *(sarcastically)* I'll never get used to not being recognized. I should be addressed properly. But on that fateful day it was decreed that the appropriate price for supreme arrogance is utter anonymity. Part of my punishment is not being recognized as the former prince of darkness. For the past five eons everyone around me has treated me like a nobody. This is hell.

(SATAN pauses, walks to the chair, and sits down. As the BARBER puts the cloth under SATAN's chin, the BARBER speaks.)

BARBER: How's it goin'?

SATAN: This is not my best day.

BARBER: Mmm. *(uninterested)*

(The two people are quiet for 30 to 40 seconds. SATAN appears more and more uncomfortable and finally blurts out.)

SATAN: You know it didn't have to be like this.

(BARBER rolls his eyes.)

SATAN: I heard there was a short period of time when things could have changed so we would have servants and praise and our beings filled with contentment, but we exist here, hot, hurt, and unfulfilled.

(BARBER *briskly clips a strand of hair with each word he repeats.*)

BARBER: Hot, hurt, unfulfilled.

SATAN: We were so, so close; I'm sure of it.

BARBER: Yeah. (*forcefully, trying to end the conversation*)

(SATAN *pauses for 5 to 10 seconds and sits up straight gaining some of the confidence he entered the room with. A calm distant stare enters SATAN's eyes, and he begins to speak in a calm voice, which intensifies as his story progresses.*)

SATAN: I remember. It had been a long time since Yahweh walked the planet. The earth had become a different place. The soul count had grown from two to hundreds of thousands. The thought of animal skin as one's entire wardrobe was in the past. People cherished gods for every occasion. Gold was being smelted and humans owned other humans. Our work was going well.

Then it became known that a Man like no other was living. If the Special Man could have been swayed to be like us, we could have lived the life we were supposed to. A plan was set in place. (SATAN *points to himself and mouths as if he is about to say the word "I" when his face shows pain. Instead he says...*) The leader of the plan thought a personal tour of the possibilities of a darker life would break his iron will.

This Man was shown all there was at that time. Money, monuments, physical desires, personal powers were all offered to him. He was shown power! Nothing affected him.

(SATAN *pauses shortly and wets his lips.*)

SATAN: It could have all changed there. He could have succumbed to the pressure. He was content to decline the offers and quote scriptures. A different tactic was in order. We thought people with souls could sway things to our side where a direct attack had failed. So we used people to shake things up. Some of my friends visited individuals. My friends would make

their hosts run errands for them. My friends used people like puppets. Run here. Scurry there. Sometimes they made people just shake around and fall to the ground. Some people caught on and claimed demons were to blame. Well, the Man would go to the hosts and make it (*pause, searching for the right word*) uncomfortable for my friends. My friends would leave the people. But that (SATAN *emphasizes the word "that"*)... that was the action that sprang the trap! People suggested the Man was the prince of demons and that was how he was making the demons flee. Here he was doing what he was doing and people were calling him (*with emphasis*) Beelzebub. It was genius! (*triumphantly*)

(SATAN *pauses and continues sarcastically.*)

SATAN: Did he make himself known? Did he peel back the sky? Did he strike down his accusers? *Noooo!*

(SATAN *turns his head and speaks directly to the BARBER.*)

SATAN: Wouldn't you have at least made someone burst into flame?

(BARBER *looks surprised.*)

BARBER: Huh? I'm sorry, Bud, but I've only been half listening. This has turned out to be another Jesus story, hasn't it? I bet I've heard them all. Sure, every story starts differently. They have different times, different characters, and different names. Some start out "I saw him speak once, but..." "I felt he could be the one, but..." "I had a friend who knew him but..." "I thought I knew him but..." But all the stories end the same way. "If I had it to do over again, I'd make a different decision." Hindsight is 20/20, even in hell.

SATAN: Well, my story is different. (*pointedly*) Let me repeat myself. If you had the power and someone was not addressing you properly, wouldn't you want to make them just burn to a cinder?

BARBER: Yeah. Sure, Bud. (*goes back to work*)

SATAN: Well, it became quite clear to the leader that he couldn't stop the Man's ministry while he was living, so the stakes were raised. With the help of some of my other friends, the people in power at the time began to kill anyone who did not see things the way they did. This simple fact set the stage for the final showdown. The Man was going around talking about his new kingdom. He was saying the temple was going to be torn down.

(SATAN *begins to speak with more force.*)

SATAN: The right people heard this, and his own words were going to bring him down! Once the leaders (with the help of another of my friends) found his whereabouts, they prepared to execute him. This new plan worked like clockwork. His friends began to scatter. Only his enemies rushed to his side.

(SATAN *begins yelling almost in a frenzy. The BARBER stops clipping and moves backwards.*)

SATAN: Kill, Kill, Kill! They requested. And it was done!

(SATAN *pauses and nods his head. The BARBER resumes his clipping.*)

SATAN: It was my best day. With the Man out of the way, things would be different. Imagine having everything you want forever, rather than this. Imagine being addressed as "Sire" rather than "Hey, you." Imagine me having a regal place in the hierarchy rather than coming to a common *barber*.

(*The BARBER's face shows anger, and he makes a strong clip to the back of SATAN's head, out of view of the audience. The BARBER produces a long strand of hair in his hand, raising it above his head. The BARBER lets go of the hair and it falls slowly to the floor behind SATAN.*)

SATAN: It could have all been ours, my friend.

BARBER: We're here, though.

(SATAN *becomes very animated as he speaks.*)

SATAN: You'll get no argument with that. When it was revealed to me that the Man was alive again, I knew this would be the outcome. The clock was ticking toward the end. I got out and lived like there was no tomorrow. I visited the earth so often you'd have thought it was my home. Then *bam!*

(SATAN *pauses shortly and speaks calmly once again.*)

SATAN: It was all over. Yahweh called his entire people home, and we were left. We're now in this place without life, and I'm nameless, faceless, and here forever. (*visibly shaken and near tears*)

BARBER: You're done.

(*Without a word SATAN jumps out of the chair, takes off the sheet, and hands it to the BARBER. SATAN takes a few steps to the left. SATAN stops, turns to the BARBER, and scratches the back of his neck. SATAN turns and walks off the stage to the left. The BARBER's eyes follow SATAN off the stage. The BARBER cleans his chair and talks to himself.*)

BARBER: Almost everyone cries in my chair. They begin talking. They talk about how things *were* and how things *are*, and they cry like babies.

(BARBER *looks to the left and yells.*)

BARBER: Next!

(*A small man, OSCAR, with disheveled hair, walks in from the left and sits in the chair. The BARBER puts the sheet on OSCAR.*)

BARBER: How's it goin'?

OSCAR: Nobody told me there would be days like these.

BARBER: Sure, Bud.

(*Lights fade*)

END

Bible Walk Through

CAST

- **Guides, shepherd costumes**
- **Pharisee, Pharisee costume**
- **Tax Collector, tax collector costume**
- **Peter, shepherd costume**
- **Martha, shepherd costume**
- **David, Israelite soldier costume**
- **John, shepherd costume**
- **2 shepherds, shepherd costumes**

PROPS

- **Live rooster in a cage (optional)**
- **Snacks**
- **Tape of the Sermon on the Mount and Jesus' dialogue with Martha and tape player**
- **Tent or sheets over a table**
- **Small bonfire**
- **Marshmallows and sticks (cut from bushes)**
- **Small oil lamp**
- **Bucket of sand**
- **Bucket of rocks**
- **Soft balls**
- **Loaf of bread**
- **Big spear**

Set up eight stations to give the kids a walk through Jesus' Sermon on the Mount. This is a great way to wind up a lesson series on the Beatitudes. Use adults, senior high, and junior high students as your performers. This also is good as an evangelistic tool or Halloween alternative—primarily for elementary kids and their families.

STATIONS

1. Blessed are the poor in spirit
Possible location: narthex

The children enter the narthex and a pompous Pharisee tries to usher them out saying, "The temple is no place for children, this is not a place to play, but to worship." The guide gets the attention of the Pharisee and lets the kids sneak in. They sit down up front to see a tax collector praying. Pharisee enters sneering and pointing a finger at the kids as

the two begin their dialogue. (See Luke 18:9-11.)

2. Blessed are those who mourn
Possible location: **rear of the sanctuary**

Kids meet Peter, and he tells them the story of how God comforted him after he denied Jesus. Have a question and answer session. (See John 21:15-19.)

3. Blessed are the meek
Possible location: **front of the sanctuary**

A guide leads kids to dig their hands in a container of sand. Then the group discusses how people would get their feet dirty and need washing in Bible times. Then wash each child's hands and discuss being humble. Compare this to Christ washing away our sins. (See John 13:3-12.)

4. Blessed are those who hunger and thirst for righteousness
Possible location: area outside kitchen door

Martha is busy getting supper ready for the kids, but she stops to complain to them about her sister Mary. Have the kids go to the kitchen door and eavesdrop on Jesus talking to Mary. (Use a Bible tape of the Sermon on the Mount, followed by Mary and Martha.) Then have Martha come out and serve the kids a snack while telling them how she was wrong in assuming Mary ought to help instead of sit at the feet of Jesus. (See Luke 10:38-42.)

5. Blessed are the merciful
Possible location: outside

Visit David's camp and roast some marshmallows. Listen to him tell about being chased by King Saul and having his life spared. Have David act the story out using some of the kids and a big spear. (See 1 Samuel 18:10-12, 1 Samuel 19:9-10.

6. Blessed are the pure in heart
Possible location: classroom

Visit John as he talks about having wrong motives and the apostles' argument about being first. (See Mark 10:35-45.)

7. Blessed are the peacemakers
Possible location: playground

The two shepherds argue over a loaf of bread and try to get the kids to take sides. The idea is to get the kids to propose sharing the bread by breaking it in two, so they become peacemakers. After the kids propose the solution, have the shepherds become best friends and thank the kids.

8. Blessed are those who are persecuted because of righteousness
Possible location: fellowship hall

The guide talks about Stephen being stoned for preaching about Jesus. Introduce a game of dodge ball with rocks. Show them a bucket of rocks. At the last moment pull out some soft balls and use those for a game of dodge ball. (See Acts: 6:8-7:60.)

END

Genesis 1-3

CAST

• Tree   • Bush

TREE: This is some place—this Garden of Eden, huh, Bush?

BUSH: Oh, yeah, Tree. Lots of warm sunshine, plenty of water, nice breezes, all the beautiful plush neighbors you could want. You're looking particularly green today.

TREE: Thanks! You too. Yes, the Lord did a fine, fine job creating this place. Why, I wouldn't be surprised if it went down in history someday, "The Garden of Eden, Where It All Began."

BUSH: Where it all began was with the Lord. We must always remember that. We shrubs and other plants and all of creation were made to glorify Him.

TREE: That is first and foremost.

BUSH: Any gossip lately?

TREE: Some birds weren't watching where they were going and crashed right into the cliff by the pond.

BUSH: Anybody hurt?

TREE: They were a little stunned but came out of it okay.

BUSH: But, of course, the big news is about those people creatures who were walking around here.

TREE: Did you hear that story? Can you believe it?

BUSH: What were their names? Something like Arnold and Elsie.

TREE: Alice and Ace.

BUSH: Adam and Ethel...Adam and Eve...that's it...Adam and Eve...two losers.

TREE: That's not nice.

BUSH: Well, it's true. They lost all this *(looks around while stretching arms out wide)* beautiful place. All this scenery, this climate, these animals, the plants like you and me.

TREE: They did lose.

BUSH: Something told me these human creatures were a little inferior when the Lord created them last.

TREE: What do you mean?

BUSH: I mean, the Lord worked day after day creating the heavens, light, dark, sky, dry ground, us vegetation, stars, fish, birds, land animals. If the Lord was in such a hurry for man, he could have made him first and adapted him to no air and all, if necessary. Instead, the Lord created man last because he knew man would turn things upside down.

TREE: I never thought of that.

BUSH: I heard those people creatures had dominion over all the eye could see. They even got to name the animals! Their only restriction was not to eat the fruit of that tree over there.

TREE: That would give the normal creature about all he could ever want.

BUSH: But a crafty serpent caught the woman's attention and tricked her into eating the fruit by saying that she would receive knowledge of wonders.

TREE: She handled the fruit for a while and was impressed with its good looks. Before you knew it, she had bitten off a piece and eaten it because she thought she would obtain wisdom.

BUSH: Adam came along and with little prompting, he chomped down a piece of the fruit too. Right away they realized their error and were ashamed and hid from the Lord who was in the Garden.

TREE: The Lord asked them if they had eaten from the forbidden tree. Each of them tried to blame somebody else, but it boiled down to each being responsible for his own actions. The Lord cursed the serpent and told the man and woman that, because of their actions, they would have much pain and toiling in their lives.

BUSH: Adam and Eve were very ashamed. And the Lord wanted to make sure they never had the chance to enjoy the pleasure of this paradise, so he banished them from the garden. Now they're on the outside.

TREE: And I've heard that there is an angel at the east side of the garden to protect us here. I sure hope those humans do all right in the world.

END

Walking on Water

CAST

- Peter
- Disciple 1
- Disciple 2
- Disciple 3
- Jesus

PROPS

- Flashlight
- Bucket of water
- Chairs arranged like seats in a boat

The disciples are out in boat on rough water, without Jesus, in the dark.

PETER: Hey, it's been hours since we left the shore. Where the heck is Jesus?

DISCIPLE 1: Who knows? The guy always gets himself into trouble.

DISCIPLE 2: Not just himself, either. John the Baptist just lost his head, and I'm afraid we're all going to get arrested!

DISCIPLE 3: Oh man, I gotta hurl! *(makes hurling noises)*

DISCIPLE 2: C'mon buddy, we're almost there!

DISCIPLE 3: *(weakly)* Whaddya mean? I can't even see the shore yet! *(hurls again)*

(Suddenly a flashlight shines on Jesus.)

PETER: Hey, look! What's that? I see lights!

DISCIPLE 2: Yeah, but they're coming from the wrong side of the boat. That's where we came from!

DISCIPLE 3: *(begins to hurl again, then pauses)* That's not shore! It's...

DISCIPLE 1: It's a ghost! *(all scream)*

JESUS: Take courage! It is I. Don't be afraid. *(screaming continues)* I said, don't be afraid! *(still screaming)* C'mon, guys, knock it off!

(All cease screaming except PETER.)

JESUS: *Peter!*

PETER: Oh, sorry.

DISCIPLE 3: I think I'm gonna hurl again...

JESUS: *(forcefully)* No, you're not. I command you not to hurl.

DISCIPLE 3: *(looks and sounds 100 percent better)* Hey, I feel pretty good.

DISCIPLE 1: What a chicken, Peter. All that screaming *(others chime in with "Yeah, what a wimp," etc.)*

PETER: *(to Disciple 1)* Dude, you started it all with that it's-a-ghost stuff.

DISCIPLE 1: Well, if you're such a big man, why don't you walk out there too?

PETER: Out where?

DISCIPLE 1: Out of the boat, man. Walk out there where Jesus is.

DISCIPLE 2: Yeah, let's see it!

PETER: No way! I can't do that. I'd fall in! Besides, he's the magic man, not me! *(all chant PE-TER! PE-TER!)* C'mon, you guys. Who do you think I am? *(chanting continues)* All right. *(Chanting stops as PETER pauses and gathers courage.)* Lord, if it's you, tell me to come to you on the water.

JESUS: Come.

PETER: Oh, boy. *(PE-TER! chanting starts up again)* Knock it off, guys! *(All stop and watch intensely as PETER climbs out of the boat toward JESUS, whose arms are outstretched to him.)*

DISCIPLE 3: Look out for that wave! *(Bucket of water hits Peter, and he begins to sink.)*

DISCIPLE 1: Ha, ha. I knew you'd blow it.

PETER: *(terrified, looks at Jesus)* Lord, save me!

JESUS: *(walks over quickly, and pulls Peter back up)* You of little faith. Why did you doubt?

PETER: I didn't think I could do it. And they were laughing at me.

JESUS: They will always be laughing at you. But you can do even greater things than this, as long as you have faith in me. Now let's get back into the boat. We've got places to go and people to save.

END

Love That Will Not Let Me Go

CAST

- Jesus, white robe
- Guy, in black robe
- Alma

PROPS

- "Love That Will Not Let Me Go" by Steve Camp (on the *Justice* or *Doing My Best, Vol. 1* releases)
- Several signs with string attached. Signs can name a variety of sins, such as lying, cheating, rebelling, overcommitment, anxiety)
- Large rope
- Large red poster-type marker

As the music begins, scriptures and quotes about God's love for us can be shown on the screen if you have one or have two different actors read them. Some to choose from include—1 John 4:10, Zephaniah. 3:17, Romans 5:8, Psalm 51:1, Psalm 103:4, Proverbs 17:9.

When the singing on the tape begins, fade lights up. Alma crouches at center stage and begins to rise up as lights come up. Alma has the rope tied around her waist; and the other end is attached to Jesus, standing offstage left. Alma and Jesus remain connected by the rope for the duration of the skit, to symbolize that Jesus never lets go, even when we wander and stray. His love is constant.

Alma goes to Jesus, and they embrace. They do a short dance step—she's obviously in love with Jesus. Her hand slips from his, and she stumbles to the other side of the stage. Guy appears in a black robe, with signs around his neck (**backwards, so the audience can't see what they say yet**).

Alma looks curious, glances back at Jesus, then takes one of the signs off Guy's neck and places it around her neck.

Looking confident, she takes a couple of steps toward front center, proud of her new sign.

Guy walks over and gives her a shove. She starts to fall but catches herself.

She goes over to Guy, removes another sign, and places it around her neck.

Again, she's confident and striding toward front center. Guy shoves her harder and she falls to the ground.

Jesus comes over (**the song's chorus should be playing at this point**), and picks her up. He comforts her, fixes her hair, wipes a tear from her eye, and removes the signs from her neck. With the big marker, Jesus places a large "X" over the word and places the signs around his own neck. They embrace, do the little dance, and again she breaks free and wanders to the other side of the stage.

Repeat the above episode, with Alma taking signs from Guy, placing them around her neck, and getting pushed by Guy. Take off as many signs as there is time in the song.

Right before the chorus, the final shove should send Alma to the ground violently. Jesus then picks her up, comforts her, and repeats the actions from above.

After the last embrace, Alma looks back at Guy, as though she's going to go to him again. This time, she slowly walks over, grabs him by the shoulders, and turns him around to face the other way.

Alma returns to Jesus, and instead of embracing, he puts his arms out and his head down, then she kneels in front of him, looking up as the lights and music fades.

END

In the News This Week

CAST

- Orpah, anchor
- Baz, anchor 2
- James, reporter 1
- Simeon

- Nathan, reporter 2
- Joseph, boy
- Messenger
- Announcer

- Micah, reporter 3
- Melchior, wise man
- Rachel, reporter 4

Use music, such as the opening instrumental from Steven Curtis Chapman's Great Adventure, *to introduce and close each segment of the news broadcast. Except for Simeon and the wise man, the character names and genders may be changed to suit the actor's gender. The first scene opens with TV broadcasters on location at the temple.*

ORPAH: Good evening and welcome to Channel 14 weekly news, broadcasting live from Jerusalem. I'm Orpah.

BAZ: And I'm Maher-Shalal-Hash-Baz.

ORPAH: This week in the news: a Publican from Bethsaida was allegedly torn apart by a pack of wolves.

BAZ: The town council declared the day an official day of remembrance in honor of the wolves.

ORPAH: In Jericho, the Board of Education stands hopelessly divided on many issues.

BAZ: They were, however unanimously agreed that prayer in the schools is a *good* thing!

ORPAH: In the town of Capernaum, the Sanitary Engineers have gone on strike.

BAZ: They're demanding a pay raise and something they called a *garbage truck.*

ORPAH: In the little town of Bethlehem a bunch of shepherds had a group delusion about some angels.

BAZ: And in our own city of Jerusalem, an old man in the temple reports seeing the long awaited Messiah.

ORPAH: We go now to James on location with that story.

BAZ: James? Are you there?

JAMES: Hi! Yes, I'm here, standing in the court of the temple and next to me is a man named Simeon. Simeon claims that he has seen the Messiah right here in the temple. Is that right, Simeon?

SIMEON: *What?*

JAMES: I said, "Is that right, Simeon?"

SIMEON: Is *what* right?

JAMES: That you saw the Messiah?

SIMEON: Yes, I did. Right here in this very temple. It was the moment I'd been waiting for all my life.

JAMES: All your life?

SIMEON: *Huh?*

JAMES: I said, "*All your life?*"

SIMEON: That's right. All my life!

JAMES: Did he say anything to you?

SIMEON: *What?*

JAMES: I said, "Did he say anything to you?"

SIMEON: Did *who* say anything to me?

JAMES: The Messiah, of course.

SIMEON: Of course not. Are you crazy?

JAMES: I don't think so. Why didn't he say anything to you?

SIMEON: Because he's just a baby.

JAMES: A *what?*

SIMEON: I said *a baby*. What's the matter, are you deaf or something?

JAMES: Wait a second! I thought the Messiah was supposed to rescue the people of Israel.

SIMEON: That's right.

JAMES: How is a baby going to do that?

SIMEON: *(looks disgusted)* Babies do grow up, you know.

JAMES: Well, that's true, I suppose. What's this baby's name?

SIMEON: Jesus.

JAMES: Well, that's a good name for a Messiah, I guess. How did you know this baby was the Messiah?

SIMEON: The spirit of God told me.

JAMES: You mean, God *talked* to you?

SIMEON: That's the general idea, yes.

JAMES: Extraordinary! What did you say when you saw this…uh…Messiah?

SIMEON: Do you want the exact words?

JAMES: Is, ahh, umm, is your memory that good?

SIMEON: Son, I can't remember anything *except* those precious moments.

JAMES: All right then, what did you say?

SIMEON: I said, "Lord, as you have promised, now dismiss your servant in peace, for my eyes have seen your salvation, which you have prepared in the sight of all people, a light for revelation to the Gentiles, and for glory to your people Israel."

JAMES: Wow. What was that part about the Gentiles?

SIMEON: Oh yes, I was very gentle.

JAMES: Not gentle. *Gentile!*

SIMEON: *What?*

JAMES: What did you mean about *Gentiles?*

SIMEON: The Messiah isn't just for the Jews, you know. He's going to be the light that will lead the Gentiles to God.

JAMES: Isn't that a kind of radical idea?

SIMEON: Goodness, no! Why, even the prophet Isaiah told us that the Messiah would be a light to the Gentiles. In fact, he said that the Messiah would bring salvation to the ends of the earth.

JAMES: So this baby is a shining light who's going to point people of all nations to God?

SIMEON: For a young feller, you catch on pretty quick.

JAMES: Well, uhh, thanks, I guess. This is James, reporting live from the temple at Jerusalem. Orpah, back to you.

ORPAH: Thank you, James. Quite a fascinating story. We'll pause now for station identification. But don't touch that dial! We'll be back with a story about some shepherds who may have spent a little too much time in the fields. *(Insert another activity here, such as singing a few Christmas carols.)*

(This scene opens in the shepherds' fields outside of Bethlehem.)

BAZ: Welcome back to Channel 14 News. In our People, Places, and Things segment, Nathan brings us a story about some shepherds who claim to have seen something rather unusual.

ORPAH: *Rather!*

NATHAN: Good evening. I'm standing in a field just outside Bethlehem on the exact spot where, one week ago, some shepherds claim to have seen a large group of angels singing praises to God. Here with me is Joseph, a boy whose father claims to have seen the angels.

BAZ: Umm. Excuse me, Nathan, you were supposed to be interviewing one of the shepherds.

NATHAN: Well, yes, but I can't find any of them. They're still running all over the countryside telling everyone about the Messiah.

ORPAH: Obviously whatever they saw addled their brains!

NATHAN: *(to Joseph)* Joseph, tell us about what your dad saw out in that field.

JOSEPH: Dad and the other shepherds were all out in the field watching the flocks when all of a sudden an angel showed up.

NATHAN: Just one? I heard there were hundreds of them! What's the big fuss about *one* angel?

JOSEPH: There was just one at first, but later there was a *ton* of 'em. They were all over the place!

NATHAN: So what did this angel have to say?

JOSEPH: He told them that a savior was born in Bethlehem, and that they would be able to find him if they looked in a hay manger at the local inn.

NATHAN: That's a strange place for a baby! What happened next?

JOSEPH: Then a chorus of angels showed up and started singing "Glory to God in the highest, and on earth peace to men on whom his favor rests!"

NATHAN: And what did your father and the other shepherds do?

JOSEPH: They went straight to Bethlehem to find the baby. He was lying in a manger just like the angel said!

NATHAN: And ever since then they've been running around the countryside telling everyone about what they saw?

JOSEPH: That's right.

NATHAN: You know, there's a man in Jerusalem who thinks this baby is the Messiah. What do you think?

JOSEPH: My dad says that this baby isn't going to fight against the Romans for us.

NATHAN: What? How can he be a savior if he won't free us from the Romans?

JOSEPH: I don't know, but my dad says he won't grow up to be a warrior.

NATHAN: Then what *will* he grow up to be?

JOSEPH: A shepherd.

NATHAN: A *what*?

JOSEPH: A shepherd. Just like my dad.

NATHAN: That's what your dad says?

JOSEPH: That's right!

NATHAN: Boy, this angel stuff is an awful lot of fuss to announce the birth of a shepherd, don't you think?

JOSEPH: Maybe he's a special kind of shepherd.

NATHAN: What do you mean, a *special* kind of shepherd?

JOSEPH: Well, in my history class we've been studying the prophet Isaiah, and do you know what he said?

NATHAN: What?

JOSEPH: He said all of us are like sheep that have gone astray, and each of us has turned to our own way.

NATHAN: So?

JOSEPH: Well, maybe this baby is going to grow up to be a People Shepherd to help rescue lost people.

NATHAN: I see. Well, uh, that is certainly an interesting idea—a shepherd who looks after people instead of sheep. But I would rather have someone free me from the Romans!

JOSEPH: But what good would it do a lost sheep to set it free? That wouldn't help it find its way home!

NATHAN: You have an answer for everything, don't you, boy?

JOSEPH: Not everything, sir. I'm just a lost sheep.

NATHAN: Yes, well, uhh, thank you for talking with me today. This is Nathan reporting to you live from a field in Bethlehem. Orpah, back to you.

ORPAH: Well, that was quite an interesting story.

BAZ: It certainly was, Orpah. *(MESSENGER suddenly runs on stage and starts talking to ORPAH.)* Our next major news story is about a plumber named

Ezra from the city of Nazareth who… *(ORPAH turns to BAZ and starts whispering frantically.)* Ladies and gentlemen we have an exciting story just in. Please stand by while we get details! *(insert activity here)*

(In this third scene Micah interviews a wise and wealthy visitor.)

ANNOUNCER: On in five, four, three, two, one! *(ORPAH and BAZ rush to their seats.)*

ORPAH: We apologize for that sudden delay in our program.

BAZ: We've decided to ditch our report on the plumber from Nazareth and bring you this news story on some distinguished visitors from the east instead.

ORPAH: It seems that some are very rich.

BAZ: And very wise.

ORPAH: Men from the east have paid a visit to one of our rural communities.

BAZ: At this point we don't know who they are.

ORPAH: Or what they want.

BAZ: But our roving reporter Micah is on the spot with this up-to-date report.

MICAH: Well, Baz, I'm here in Bethlehem.

ORPAH: Bethlehem?

BAZ: We just had a report from Bethlehem!

MICAH: Yes, well, it seems that you're going to get another one, so just pipe down and listen to me. *(ORPAH and BAZ look at each other and shrug.)* Some astronomers from the land of Persia journeyed to this town because a star led them here. We're not sure what they hope to find here, but one of the men has agreed to talk with me, so perhaps we can get some answers. Sir? *(MELCHIOR stares into the sky.)* Sir? Sir!

MELCHIOR: Eh?

MICAH: What are you doing?

MELCHIOR: Studying the stars.

MICAH: Why?

MELCHIOR: Because I'm an astronomer! That's what I get paid to do!

MICAH: Well, could you study the TV camera for a minute? *(points straight forward)* Otherwise, I'm not going to get paid! *(MELCHIOR looks forward.)* Now, what is your name?

MELCHIOR: Melchior.

MICAH: And what exactly why are you here?

MELCHIOR: Well, we've found the star, and now we're looking for the scepter.

MICAH: *What?*

MELCHIOR: It's all part of the prophecy.

MICAH: *What* prophesy?

MELCHIOR: The prophesy of Balaam. You should know all about that. It's in your Holy Scriptures.

MICAH: Yes, well, Balaam isn't one of our favorite prophets. He had to have a donkey tell him what to do.

MELCHIOR: That's better than most people I know. They wouldn't know what to do if a *camel* told them!

MICAH: So what does Balaam's prophecy say?

MELCHIOR: It says that a star will rise out of Jacob.

MICAH: That's the star you've been following?

MELCHIOR: Right. And then it says that a scepter will rise out of Israel.

MICAH: A scepter? You mean a king?

MELCHIOR: That's right. The prophecy tells us that a star will lead us to the king.

MICAH: And the star led you to Bethlehem?

MELCHIOR: Well, actually we went to Jerusalem first.

MICAH: Why?

MELCHIOR: Because we assumed that a king would be born in the capital of Israel.

MICAH: So what made you decide to come here?

MELCHIOR: Herod told us that the king was supposed to be born in Bethlehem. He asked us to find that baby, and then return to Jerusalem to tell him who the king was so he could go worship him.

MICAH: Did you find this king?

MELCHIOR: Oh, yes. We certainly did. His name is Jesus.

MICAH: Do you know what he is going to be king of?

MELCHIOR: Everything.

MICAH: Excuse me?

MELCHIOR: Everything! He's going to be king of everything.

MICAH: You mean all of Israel?

MELCHIOR: I mean *everything*!

MICAH: How can someone be king of everything? Isn't that a big job for one person?

MELCHIOR: Not for this person. He's the only one who can handle the job. Let's put it this way, have you ever been unsure of what's going to happen next? Afraid that things won't turn out the way they should?

MICAH: Sometimes. Why?

MELCHIOR: How does that make you feel?

MICAH: Worried. Scared. Nervous. Fearful.

MELCHIOR: Right. But when I knelt in front of this baby, what do you suppose happened to all of my fears?

MICAH: What?

MELCHIOR: They just melted away. Because I knew that this baby could handle anything, and there wasn't a problem anywhere that he couldn't take care of.

MICAH: That's crazy.

MELCHIOR: I know it sounds crazy, but it's true. Someday that baby will carry the weight of all the world's problems on his shoulders.

MICAH: I hope he grows up to have broad shoulders.

MELCHIOR: Perhaps you should visit the child and see for yourself.

MICAH: Perhaps I will. This is Micah reporting for Channel 14 News live from Bethlehem with the story of a baby who is going to be King of *(coughs slightly)* everything. Back to you, Orpah.

ORPAH: Thank you, Micah. This baby from Bethlehem seems to be in the news a lot tonight.

BAZ: When we come back, we'll have a report on how Herod responded to the visit of these astronomers from the east.

ORPAH: Don't touch that dial! *(Insert another activity here.)*

(Rachel interviews Herod at the palace in this scene.)

ORPAH: We're back.

BAZ: With an exclusive interview with King Herod. You know, Orpah, I'm curious to hear what he has to say about these visitors from the east.

ORPAH: Yes indeed, Baz. And I want to hear what he thinks of a King being born in Bethlehem.

BAZ: Let's hear from Rachel, our reporter inside the palace.

RACHEL: Hello, Baz.

BAZ: Uh, hello, Rachel. We're getting audio, but there is no picture.

RACHEL: Yes, well, our camera broke.

ORPAH: How did that happen?

RACHEL: Well, we set things up in the throne room and began asking the king about the wise men from the east.

BAZ: What did he have to say?

RACHEL: Nothing good.

ORPAH: What do you mean?

RACHEL: It seems that Herod didn't really want to worship the new King. He wanted to find the baby so he could kill him.

BAZ: How terrible! Someone should warn the wise men, so they don't go back to Herod and tell him.

RACHEL: Actually someone already did warn them. They didn't come back to Jerusalem.

ORPAH: Uh oh, Herod must be mad as a hornet!

RACHEL: Actually, if I was going to place him on an anger scale, I would say he's as mad as a pit-bull dancing *Swan Lake* in a ruffled tutu.

ORPAH: An appropriate description.

BAZ: But it doesn't explain what happened to the camera.

RACHEL: Well, next I asked Herod if he thought the baby was a king.

ORPAH: Yes?

RACHEL: And that's when he threw the Secretary of State at the video camera.

BAZ: *(looks at ORPAH) That* explains it! *(ORPAH nods)* So does that mean he doesn't think the baby is a king?

RACHEL: No. In fact, just as he was throwing me headfirst out the window, I heard him mutter, "How can he be king? He's just a carpenter's son!"

ORPAH: And what do you think?

RACHEL: Well, Orpah, I think it is interesting because most kings are born, taught, and grow up in a palace, so they never realize what it's like out here in the real world.

ORPAH: Yes.

RACHEL: Wouldn't it be great if we had a king who grew up the son of a poor rural carpenter? Now that's a man who would understand all of our problems!

BAZ: Hmm, an interesting idea, Rachel, but I don't think you'll get Herod to agree.

RACHEL: Definitely not! But some day it won't matter what Herod thinks!

ORPAH: And may we all live to see that day!

RACHEL: Amen to that!

ORPAH: Well, folks, that just about raps it up. Tonight we've witnessed some very unusual events.

BAZ: And we've heard a lot about one *very* unusual baby.

ORPAH: We've heard that he is the Messiah,

BAZ: And we've heard that he's a shepherd.

ORPAH: We've heard that he's a King,

BAZ: A king of *everything.*

ORPAH: But the official word from the palace is that this baby is nothing more than the son of a carpenter.

BAZ: The big question before you tonight is *who will you believe?*

ORPAH: Is he the Messiah? Or is he a Shepherd?

BAZ: Is he a king or just a carpenter's son?

ORPAH: Or is he somehow all of them at once?

BAZ: And will he someday carry the weight of all the world's problems on his shoulders?

ORPAH: As we leave you tonight, we leave you with these questions and many more. May you seek and find the answers in your own heart. This is Orpah for Channel 14 News.

BAZ: And I'm Maher-Shalal-Hash-Baz wishing you a safe and pleasant evening. Good night, and God bless.

END

CONTEMPORARY
SKETCHES

CONTEMPORARY SKETCHES

You can use these right-now, real-life scripts for everything from event announcements (that you can tailor to your own events) to dealing with emotional scars. These sketches help your teens examine everything from materialism and tithing to mistakes and forgiveness and temptation and purity. Perfect for meetings, talks, Bible studies, and even Sunday worship services. Use the Scripts by Topic index on page 7 to speed your search for the script that fits.

AMERICAN MASTER

Imagine that pushy phone salesperson who always calls during dinner. Then multiply that and picture her knocking at your door. She tells you how much you need what she has, that your life doesn't measure up, and you simply will not be happy until you accept and use the credit card she offers. She even points out things in the apartment that need to be replaced. Luckily, our heroine on page 95 knows where her values lie and kicks Ms. Pushy out the door.

This is a fun look at a serious influence in our lives—materialism. Cast someone who can work the role of the pushy salesperson. Timing is everything in this sketch. Plan enough rehearsal to get a good rhythm down. Use this to spark a discussion about the difference between wants and needs and what kind of life your students believe God calls Christians to lead. *Bryan Belknap*

WORKING PARTS
1 PETER 5:8–9, ROMANS 12:4–5

This sketch will make you remember every bad car you've ever owned! Not just one breakdown, but four,

make for an interesting date. Vince tries to keep a positive attitude through his obvious frustration. Brianne understands at first but soon moves from understanding to annoyed. The sketch on page 97 isn't the manual for a love connection, but it sure says a lot about relationships.

Little problems can create giant hassles. If all the parts of the car just do their jobs, the car moves forward. As each little part breaks, the overall effect gets bigger. One stumbling block is no big deal. Two, three, and four can change your whole outlook. This sketch helps students see what part of the body of Christ they play and how the little problems in life distract them from that purpose. Check out 1 Peter 5:8-9 to see what surprises Satan has in store around the corner. Use Romans 12:4-5 to remind your group of the parts of the body and how important each one is! Using both of these verses, your group should be deep into their discussion in no time! *Teresa McCasland*

LOVE ON THE BRAIN

This sketch is not for the faint of heart. The sketch on page 100 more than alludes to sex and dating. This look at a couple getting to know each other gives the audience the added bonus of knowing what's going on inside their heads! Their thoughts (indicated by a *TH* in the script) don't focus on the conversation at hand or how godly the other person is. In the end, nervousness gets the best of them and saves them from doing something they'd regret, and they create a friendship instead of anything else.

You'll need mature actors for this one! The sketch isn't necessarily risqué but the thoughts it provokes may be. Both characters have inner struggles with lust. The twist is that the girl has much more experience, and both are very aware of this. The more believable the scene is, the better your discussion will be at the end.

Prerecord the actors' thoughts before the rehearsals and performance. Use rehearsal time to get timing down with the prerecorded thoughts and to make it believable. If only real relationships worked this way! *John Cosper, Jr. and Laura Gray*

GOING UP?

Talk about missed opportunities! The guy in this sketch practically begs to be invited to Bible study. Unfortunately the Christians around him are so busy hanging out with each other they miss the chance to invite someone new to their group. The sketch on page 104 offers an example of exactly what *not* to do when it comes to witnessing. *Bryan Belknap*

SCREAMING ANNOUNCEMENTS

Give the kid with no volume control a perfect opportunity to use his talent! You get your announcements done and your students awake. Just prepare your announcements before the meeting.

Ask one of your extroverted kids to stand up at the appointed time and literally scream the announcements.

If you're up to it, try the ultimate: have two students (from different sides of the room) scream conversations concerning each announcement.

"Hey, Bobby!"

"What, Justin?"

"Did you know we're leaving at 4 p.m. on Saturday to go to the Newsboys concert?"

"Why, no, Justin, I didn't know that, but that's a good thing to know since I bought a ticket."

Kip Faught

THE FLOWER
BASED ON EPHESIANS 4:27

Only one person can receive our precious and fragile gift of purity. In the sketch on page 106, a dead flower symbolizes what once was. This sketch pushes the limits symbolically until only the flower's stem and petals remain to fall on the ground. The person who killed the flower closes the sketch by promising to care for the remaining stem.

Sad but true—many people struggle with the idea of remaining a virgin until marriage. People don't set out to have sex on the first date, but unless they guard against it, each step closer makes it more difficult. In this sketch about prevention rather than redemption, lies and broken promises seem to say that a damaged flower is worthless and may as well be destroyed. *Amy Norbie*

SILENT NIGHT

These three girls are tight. They shop together, laugh together, and even cry together. The shocker of the sketch on page 108 comes when you figure out that one of the three is no longer alive. A clever interplay of dialogue has two friends visiting the grave of the third. Confusion, questions, and a great deal of emotion flood the stage. As Luisa speaks, you soon realize that the other two can't hear her. Luisa pleads for them to look to Jesus. Obviously she no longer plays this guiding role.

This sketch takes careful blocking and timing. In the beginning the audience thinks that all three girls are present and talking to each other. As the conversation unfolds, it becomes increasingly obvious that the other two characters can't actually see or hear Luisa. You never know when your time to die may come. This sketch shows the effects of death not only on the one who died but also on the friends who are left behind. *Dave Tippett*

BAGGAGE
1 JOHN 1:9 AND PSALM 103:12

Life's past mistakes can be a pretty heavy load to carry around all by yourself. The sketch on page 111 shows two people waiting at a bus stop. One has learned to let go of past mistakes and accept forgiveness, but the other one is so loaded down she can hardly walk.

In this simple but powerful sketch, all but the last two lines are prerecorded. A couple of chairs or a bench and some baggage serve as the props and set. At the end of the sketch, the off-screen announcer reads 1 John 1:9 and Psalm 103:12. These verses can be used to guide the discussion afterward.

• What does being overwhelmed feel like?
• What causes you to be weighted down?
• Do you think anything can help you lighten the load?
• Who do you turn to for help?

- Do you believe God forgives sin?
- Why is it easier for God to forgive you than for you to forgive yourself?
- What would it feel like to be free of all of your past mistakes?
- How would this make you act differently today?

Larry Marshall

YOU DON'T HAVE TO PAY

Wouldn't it be cool if everything were just a *suggested* price? In the sketch on page 113, a theatre runs on the same principles as a church—with a suggested price. You pay whatever you think is fair and can afford. Needless to say, the theatre doesn't last long. In reality people pay for movies and candy without giving it a second thought, but the thought of tithing may not even cross their minds.

Money's always a tough subject, especially with teenagers who don't have much. Teaching tithing as a way to give back, to worship God, and to acknowledge that God gave it in the first place is a lesson we can never learn too early. You can use this sketch to talk about what tithing means, where the money goes, if you can tithe anything other than cash, and what scripture says about the concept of tithing. *Bryan Belknap*

CAN O' BLAME

Move over late-night infomercials—we've got a great new product! Now you can buy a way out of all the screwups you make. The sketch on page 115 offers the product and some examples of its possible uses. This backward look at responsibility shows how ridiculous people get when they try to pass the buck.

Choose actors who can create enthusiasm over any situation you give them, and you've got it made! This sketch can be performed live or videoed for more of an effect. Cover a spray can with construction paper to make a Can O' Blame. And just in case you're wondering, delivery doesn't get much more sarcastic than this! *Larry Marshall*

THE EXCHANGE SHOP

MATTHEW 6:25-26

This sketch takes genetic engineering to a whole new level. We all have some part of ourselves we'd love to change—hair color, big legs, no neck, whatever. So what would happen if we could? What if you could turn yourself in for a new model? The sketch on page 116 explores this option with some pretty startling results. When it comes down to it, both the bad and

the good make us who we are. And just as we are, we have worth.

This sketch has two characters: Martin the store clerk and Wayne the customer who wants to trade himself in. The sketch teaches that we are each one of a kind, and we're made in God's image. You can use Genesis 1:27 to drive this point home.
- What does being created in the image of God mean?
- Do you think some people are not created in God's image?
- How do you know?
- What do you believe God thinks of his creation?

Larry Marshall

GOD CALLING

Who can have a conversation with anyone, let alone God, while you're drinking and trying to make moves on a guy? In this sketch Abby wants someone to love her. But she can't see that God keeps calling and trying to get her attention to give her just what she wants.

This super-quick sketch gets across a big-time lesson! The only prop is a phone. Use the sketch on page 118 to start discussions about spending time with God, setting priorities, making choices, or realizing that you may already have the things you're looking for. *Charles Phillips*

DAILY DOSE

Sometimes we convince ourselves that a little dose, one song, one drink, one bad movie won't do that much damage. The sketch on page 119 shows that every time you do one little thing, it's like taking a daily dose of poison. It may not do much the first or second time, but eventually it's going to kill you—if not physically, then spiritually.

A bottle with the word *poison* written in large letters conveys the point of this sketch. One character requires a little coordination because one person speaks and another does the arm actions. In this sketch students see how the little choices they make can subtly poison their lives without them realizing the danger. *Dave Tippet*

BACKWARDS LIP SYNC CONTEST

Get your boy bands and girl groups warmed up! In this sketch you'll actually get to hear them! This is no traditional lip sync. Instead of turning up the sound and getting to act, this twist requires a video screen and live voices. It's a crazy version of a favorite youth activity. Movie clips or video clips roll with the sound down as your students fill in the dialogue and sound effects.

Select three to five teams (the number of students on each team depends on the number of actors in the movie scene.) Play a popular movie scene like the duel between Darth Vader and Luke Skywalker in *The Empire Strikes Back* for the entire group. Send the team members to another room with the video and do something else with the rest of the group.

Meanwhile, play the scene again for the team members, but this time, turn the sound all the way down. Give the teams time to discuss who will have what lines, what the lines are, et cetera. Play the scene with the sound off one more time, for the team members to quietly practice their lines.

When the team members return to the big group to perform in the Backwards Lip Sync contest, play the video for each team while they provide the voices and sound effects for the scene. Provide awards for best lip sync, most creative dialogue, et cetera.

This is a great late-night pick me up! *Rick Mumford*

UPGRADE

The sketch on page 122 offers a look at what can happen when we back up promises with the Holy Spirit, not just flesh. With some high-tech help from his computer, this guardian provides a change for his charge. With a little help from his guardian, this man, Jesse, gets an upgrade that changes his old way of making resolutions and keeps him from falling flat on his face.

The blocking for this sketch takes careful planning because Jesse moves backward and forward as the guardian reviews the tape of the Jesse's life. *Dave Tippett*

I'M LISTENING

Have you ever wanted to tape someone to a chair so you could have his or her full attention? Trying to talk while listening to the stereo, watching TV, and playing with a GameBoy just doesn't make for great communication. Unfortunately, that's what many people do when they're trying to talk with God. The sketch on page 124 shows what it's like to be so distracted that you can barely keep track of your own thoughts, let alone ever hear from God. *Bryan Belknap*

FLUNKING ENGLISH, FLUNKING LIFE
LUKE 9:23

More often than not, we never know the difference we make in someone else's life—especially someone's eternal life. Being a Christian means being obedient and sometimes doing things that just don't make sense in this world. The sketch on page 126—where a student chooses to fail English but honor God—illustrates his unexpected influence.

You can draw many lessons out of this sketch, including consequences of actions, witnessing, success by God's definition, and standing up for what you believe. Luke 9:23 wraps them all together. Following God, sharing beliefs, and living for Christ are all choices we make daily. And you don't have to wait until you're an adult to do any of them. *Curt Cloninger*

THE CHAT

Technology can be great—if it's used for good! The sketch on page 129 provides a heart-stopping reality check for parents, students, or the whole church! In this all-too-true-to-life situation about a girl in an Internet chat room, she thinks she's talking to a boy her age.

Two actors play a young girl and a grown man chatting on the Internet. The actors hold their scripts as they stand across the stage from one another. The sketch is pretty lighthearted until the end when everyone realizes what is going on. Be ready to field questions about the Internet, safety, and a host of opposing thoughts because the end of this sketch will leave everyone in a very sober mood. *Dave Tippett*

American Master

CAST

• Camille   • Stephanie

PROPS

• Couch   • Book   • Briefcase with papers inside

CAMILLE *sits on her couch in the living room reading a book. When someone knocks on the door, CAMILLE gets up and opens the door to find STEPHANIE standing at her door holding a briefcase.*

STEPHANIE: Camille Jones?

CAMILLE: Yes.

STEPHANIE: *(extends her hand)* I'm Stephanie Seymour with American Master credit cards. Mind if I come in?

CAMILLE: *(shakes her hand)* Sure.

(CAMILLE opens the door and allows STEPHANIE inside. STEPHANIE enters and looks around the room.)

STEPHANIE: Cozy little place you have here.

CAMILLE: Thank you. Won't you sit down?

STEPHANIE: Yes, thanks.

(STEPHANIE sits at one end of the sofa, and CAMILLE sits at the other. Stephanie opens her briefcase and pulls out some papers.)

CAMILLE: Is there something wrong with my credit card, Mrs. Seymour?

STEPHANIE: No, not at all! And please, call me Stephanie.

CAMILLE: Then how can I help you, Stephanie?

STEPHANIE: I'm here to help you!

CAMILLE: Really?

STEPHANIE: Yes. I don't think you're aware of the exciting life you have awaiting you.

CAMILLE: How's that?

STEPHANIE: With the help of your American Master card, of course.

CAMILLE: But I don't use it anymore.

STEPHANIE: That's why I'm here! Our records indicate that you stopped using your card approximately seven months ago. Is that correct?

CAMILLE: Sounds right.

STEPHANIE: Why did you stop using it? Did you get laid off?

CAMILLE: No. I just don't need anything else.

STEPHANIE: Pardon me?

CAMILLE: I've got everything I need, so there's no reason for me to use my card to buy more stuff.

STEPHANIE: Forgive me for being so bold, but I can think of lots of things you need.

CAMILLE: Like...

STEPHANIE: Come on. Look around you! *(stands and begins pointing)* You need a bigger TV, new furniture that matches, and a jukebox would look fab in that corner. This corner needs a ficus tree, or better yet, knock out a wall and make a greenhouse! Are you dating anyone?

CAMILLE: *(surprised)* No.

STEPHANIE: Get some new clothes then! Get a health club membership too. American Master can't buy you a man, but it can get you the tools you need to land one.

CAMILLE: *(irritated)* Thank you for your concern, but I'm perfectly content without all that junk.

STEPHANIE: Junk! It's the important things you need to live a happy, healthy life, and you can have it all right now by using your American Master card. Come on. I'll give you a ride to the mall.

(STEPHANIE grabs CAMILLE's arm and tries dragging her to the door. CAMILLE yanks her arm away.)

CAMILLE: No! I'm perfectly content with what I have, thank you. I know this might be hard to believe, but I'm happy without more stuff.

STEPHANIE: What about the American Dream? What about *Lifestyles of the Rich and Famous*? What about keeping up with the Joneses?

CAMILLE: I *am* a Jones.

STEPHANIE: Smiths then. What about the billions of dollars people spend on advertising a year? Are you going to let that go to waste?

(STEPHANIE takes CAMILLE's face in her hands like a caring mother lecturing her daughter.)

STEPHANIE: Do you want their children to starve?

(CAMILLE steps away.)

CAMILLE: No one is going to starve! *(calms down)* Listen, Mrs. Seymour…

STEPHANIE: Stephanie.

(STEPHANIE puts her hand on CAMILLE's shoulder. CAMILLE looks at the hand on her shoulder, slowly takes it, and lifts it off her shoulder.)

CAMILLE: I'm perfectly content with what I have. It may not be the nicest stuff in the world, but it works. Believe me, there's stuff out there I want, but definitely not anything I *need* or anything that would make me happy.

(STEPHANIE puts her hand flat on CAMILLE's forehead.)

CAMILLE: What are you doing?

STEPHANIE: Checking for fever. You're delirious.

CAMILLE: That's it! Get out!

STEPHANIE: I'm just trying to help you!

(CAMILLE grabs STEPHANIE's briefcase, shoves it into her arms, and pushes her toward the door.)

CAMILLE: I'll help you to the door.

STEPHANIE: That's another thing. This door is hideous! You should buy a new one right away.

CAMILLE: Goodnight, Mrs. Seymour.

STEPHANIE: But wait.

(CAMILLE shoves STEPHANIE out the door and closes it behind her. STEPHANIE pounds on the door.)

STEPHANIE: Your doormat's a little old here! Don't you want a new one?

(CAMILLE turns off the light, covers her ears, and exits.)

STEPHANIE: Did your light bulb burn out? Let's go buy some new ones! Hello! Camille? Are you there?

END

Working Parts

CAST

- Brianne
- Vince
- Tires, five people dressed in black
- Windshield wipers, one person dressed in a dark color
- Headlights, two people dressed in white
- Engine, one person dressed in gray

PROPS

- Two chairs
- Picnic basket
- Thunder sound

Arrange the car parts and the chairs center stage. The fifth tire is in the trunk. Meanwhile VINCE walks to one side of the stage and pretends to knock on a door. BRIANNE answers the door to greet him.

BRIANNE: Hi!

VINCE: Hi! Are you ready to go?

BRIANNE: Yeah, sure. Let me just grab the picnic basket.

(BRIANNE turns around and picks up a picnic basket. Together they walk to the car. He opens the door for her first, then he walks around and gets in the car. He then starts the engine. As he does the person playing the part of the engine along with the rest of the car parts begin to jiggle a little to give the impression of a car idling.)

VINCE: Here we go. *(pretends to back out of a drive way and shifts gears to drive)*

BRIANNE: It's a lovely day for a picnic!

VINCE: Something sure smells good! I hope you didn't go to too much trouble preparing it.

BRIANNE: Oh, it was no trouble at all. I hope you like fried chicken.

VINCE: I love fried chicken! As a matter of fact, it's my favorite!

(RIGHT REAR TIRE makes a loud pop noise and both actors pretend to swerve. VINCE stops the car. Both actors must move together to indicate the car stopping. He gets out to look at the tire).

VINCE: I can't believe this! We have a flat! Well, it'll take me only a few minutes to change tire.

BRIANNE: Okay, can I help?

VINCE: You can grab the keys and open the trunk for me if you want.

BRIANNE: All right. *(pretends to take the keys out of the ignition, opens her door, walks to the rear of the car, and opens the trunk)*

(VINCE pretends to take out a jack and jacks up the car. The rear tires rise just a little. He pulls the rear tire off and rolls it—the person should roll to the side—then kicks it.)

VINCE: Stupid tire! *(puts on the spare tire that he has rolled from the trunk. He finishes, and they get back in the car.)* Well, that didn't take too long, I guess. Sorry for the delay.

BRIANNE: Oh, that's all right. I'm glad you had a spare.

VINCE: Yeah, me too. Now, as I was saying, I love fried chicken, it's my favorite.

BRIANNE: I'm glad. I also made some potato salad, corn on the cob, and a fresh apple pie.

VINCE: Apple pie! My mouth is watering just thinking about it. I love apple pie!

(ENGINE *starts to cough, and other car parts begin to jerk until simultaneously everything stops, and the car dies).*

VINCE: Oh, what now?

(VINCE *gets out of the car and pretends to open the hood and starts poking on the engine. He asks* BRIANNE *to try to start the car as he pushes and pulls on different parts of the* ENGINE. *Each time* VINCE *pokes, the person playing the engine makes funny noises. Finally after several attempts, the car starts, and all the car parts begin to wiggle, signifying that the car is now running.* VINCE *gets back in the car).*

VINCE: Sorry about that, I just had the engine overhauled. I guess they didn't get all the bugs out yet.

BRIANNE: *(with a worried smile on her face)* That's okay. I'm sure it's just one of those things. You know, it is starting to look a little cloudy.

VINCE: Oh, don't worry, I listened to the weatherman this morning, and he said we'd have a warm sunny day, not a chance of rain.

(About *this time thunder sounds. They pretend that rain starts, rolling up the windows).*

VINCE: You've gotta be kidding! I can't believe this! Just this morning they said no rain! I'm going to start listening to another weatherman!

BRIANNE: I can't see where we're going. Can you turn on the windshield wipers?

VINCE: Oh yeah. (He *turns on the* WIPERS, *and they move very slowly, so slow that don't help clear the rain. The* HEADLIGHTS *flash on and off.)*

BRIANNE: What's wrong? Why aren't they going faster? Why are the headlights going off and on?

VINCE: I don't know.

BRIANNE: For goodness sakes, didn't you check this car out before you decided to take it out for a joy ride?

VINCE: I didn't check the wipers. It hasn't rained since I got the car. How was I supposed to know?

BRIANNE: Well, this isn't exactly the best time to see if they work—in the middle of a downpour. We could be killed!

VINCE: Don't get excited, I'll just pull over, that's all.

BRIANNE: I'll pull over, that's all! What's this, like the third time now?

VINCE: Hey, I'm sorry! It won't take but a second for me to fix them. *(under his breath)* I hope!

(BRIANNE *sighs as he gets out and tries to fix the wipers.)*

VINCE: Can you turn them off for a minute while I check them out, please!

(BRIANNE *leans over and turns them off.)*

(VINCE *jiggles things around moving the person's arms back and forth, tinkering with the headlights. The WIPERS take hold of VINCE's sleeve without him knowing it.*)

VINCE: Okay, I disconnected the lights. Try it now. (BRIANNE *turns the wipers on, and they go fast, jerking him back and forth across the car.*) Turn it off! Turn it off! Turn it off!

(BRIANNE *turns the wipers off, and VINCE jerks his sleeve out of the wipers' grip, looking a little irritated. He gets back into the car and smiles calmly.*)

VINCE: Well, I think we got that fixed.

(VINCE *turns on the WIPERS, which work properly now. They drive for a few minutes in silence, both feeling uncomfortable about what to say, acting like they're trying to think of something to say, smiling at each other, and acting fidgety.*)

VINCE: Hey, look! The rain is beginning to stop. That was fast, just a quick shower. (*turns off the wipers*) I guess we won't need these on any more.

BRIANNE: Guess not. I'm sorry if I seemed a little short with you earlier, I didn't mean anything.

VINCE: Hey, no sweat. I knew you were just kidding. I'm sorry about the car.

BRIANNE: No problem. It really is a nice car. (*car begins to slow down*) Why are we slowing down?

VINCE: I'm not sure. (*tries to shift gears, but the car parts slow their jiggling down until they come to a complete stop*) Oh no! What now? (*looks over at BRIANNE sheepishly as she rolls her eyes and puts her hands over her face*)

VINCE: The gas gauge says empty, but that's impossible, I filled it up just before I picked you up!

BRIANNE: You are kidding. You not going to use that, "We're out of gas" line on me are you?

VINCE: No, really! I filled it up just this morning before I came over to your house. Something else must be wrong. There's some kind of mistake!

BRIANNE: Vince, you got that right, and I made it! I should have never agreed to go out with you!

VINCE: It's probably nothing, just a loose wire or something.

BRIANNE: It's probably nothing, he says, a loose wire or something, he says. (*mockingly*)

(VINCE *gets out of the car, gets down on the ground, and looks under the car.*)

VINCE: Oh great! This is just great!

BRIANNE: What's wrong now?

VINCE: (*gets out from under the car, sort of chuckling*) The uh…the fuel line, it's, uh, well, it's got a hole in it.

BRIANNE: What?

VINCE: The fuel line has a hole in it. All of our gas drained out.

BRIANNE: You've got to be kidding! Please tell me you're kidding!

VINCE: I'm not kidding.

BRIANNE: Don't tell me—you'll have it fixed in just a minute! (*mockingly*)

END

Love on the Brain

CAST

- Jeremy, Christian teenager and committed virgin
- Jeremy's thoughts (heard, but not spoken on stage)
- Laura, Christian teenager, but barely a virgin
- Laura's thoughts (heard, but not spoken on stage)

PROPS

- Couch
- TV
- DVD player

The audience hears LAURA and JEREMY's thoughts throughout the scene. These may be pre-recorded or spoken off stage into microphones by other actors. JEREMY and LAURA walk into a living room with a couch, TV, and DVD player.

LAURA: So, this is the living room.

JEREMY: This is the living room.

LAURA: It's nice. I like the couch.

JEREMY: Thank you. I mean it's not my couch. It's my parents' couch. But I, uh, I sit on it a lot. You know?

LAURA: Oh.

TH-JEREMY: That's about the dumbest thing I've ever said. She probably thinks I'm an idiot now.

TH-LAURA: Gosh, he's so nervous tonight. Better compliment his dinner to calm him down.

LAURA: Thanks for dinner, Jeremy.

JEREMY: Oh. You're welcome. I'm glad you liked it.

TH-LAURA: Are you kidding? Spaghetti sauce with no meat? How many guys care enough to cook something without meat when their date is a vegetarian?

TH-JEREMY: Thank goodness she liked the spaghetti. After I burned those steaks, I didn't have anything else to cook.

LAURA: So what movie are we gonna watch?

JEREMY: My dad just got a DVD player. He's got *Forrest Gump*, *Sleepless in Seattle*, *Casablanca*, and *Highlander*.

TH-JEREMY: Please say *Highlander*! Please say *Highlander*!

LAURA: Anything but *Highlander*.

TH-JEREMY: Duh!

JEREMY: I'll get *Casablanca*.

(JEREMY exits. LAURA sits on the couch.)

TH-LAURA: *(to herself)* Man, did I get lucky! I've never met anyone so sweet. He's a gentleman. He's got a great…No, Laura, we're not gonna go there. Not with this guy.

(LAURA shakes her head and lays it in her hands. JEREMY walks in, sees her.)

TH-JEREMY: Laura looks so amazing. I can't believe this! She's actually here. On a date with me. In my house. *(pause)* Alone. No, no, no. She may be more experienced, but that doesn't mean I need to play catch up.

(LAURA looks up and sees JEREMY standing.)

LAURA: I can see the movie a lot better if you put it in the machine.

JEREMY: Oh. Oh, yeah. *(bends over to put CD in the DVD player with his back to LAURA)*

TH-LAURA: *(aside)* Hello, tush! That's gotta be at least a 9.5 on the cute scale.

(JEREMY steps back and sits beside LAURA.)

JEREMY: Comfy?

LAURA: Couldn't be more.

TH-JER and TH-LAURA: *(together)* Unless I was on top of you.

(JEREMY and LAURA look at each other, and then quickly look away.)

JEREMY: Can I get you anything?

TH-LAURA: Here it comes!

LAURA: What did you have in mind?

JEREMY: Coke? Iced tea? Lemonade?

TH-JEREMY: Did I just blow a signal?

LAURA: *(disappointed)* Oh, you mean a drink. Coke's fine.

TH-JEREMY: Yep, I blew it.

JEREMY: Be right back. *(exits)*

TH-LAURA: *(sings)* La, la la, la. I'm just sitting here, minding my own business, not lusting at all. Nope, nope, nope.

(JEREMY enters with a Coke.)

TH-JEREMY: Nope, nope, nope, no lust in my mind. Nope. Not at all.

JEREMY: Here you go.

LAURA: Thank you.

(LAURA takes the Coke, and JEREMY sits.)

TH-JEREMY: I wonder if I can get her to move closer. Maybe if she get's a whiff of my cologne…

(JEREMY leans over and brushes the scent toward LAURA who reacts unpleasantly.)

TH-LAURA: Boy went a shade heavy on the cologne.

LAURA: Tommy?

JEREMY: Who?

LAURA: Are you wearing Tommy?

JEREMY: Do you like Tommy?

LAURA: I prefer Hugo.

TH-JEREMY: Way to pick cologne, Jer.

TH-LAURA: Way to turn him off, Laura. Maybe he's waiting for me to make the first move. Of course if he was a gentleman, he'd know that's his job. Oh well. I'm a liberated woman.

(LAURA scoots closer to JEREMY, shoulder to shoulder. He smiles at her.)

LAURA: Am I too close?

TH-JEREMY: No way!

JEREMY: No, you're fine. Make yourself comfortable.

TH-LAURA: Take him!

LAURA: (eyes pop open) Okay!

(LAURA pounces on JEREMY. The two tumble off the couch onto the floor. LAURA stands up.)

TH-LAURA: That wasn't what I meant to do.

TH-JEREMY: That wasn't how I though it would go.

LAURA: (embarrassed) I'm so sorry.

JEREMY: (smiles) It's okay. It's okay. We'll sit on the floor. (pats the spot next to him)

(LAURA sits and shivers, nervously.)

TH-LAURA: I'm so nervous. I don't know what to do.

TH-JEREMY: She looks cold. Maybe I can share some body heat.

(JEREMY puts his arm around LAURA.)

TH-LAURA: Why is he making this so difficult?

TH-JEREMY: Why is it so difficult?

TH-LAURA: He's such a wonderful guy. I don't want to do the wrong thing.

TH-JEREMY: She's so incredible. I mean, we're still young and all, but I mean, if she were the one…

TH-LAURA: What's the harm in that? We'll do it all the rest of our lives.

TH-JEREMY: Why wait when we can get a head start?

TH-LAURA: Okay, I'm gonna do this.

TH-JEREMY: On the count of three, she gets lucky.

TH-LAURA: On the count of three, he gets lucky.

TH-JEREMY: One…

TH-LAURA: Two…

(JEREMY and LAURA lean in fast for a kiss and smack noses. Both reel back in pain.)

JEREMY: Oww, my nose!

(LAURA stands.)

LAURA: Look, Jeremy, I need to tell you something. (takes a deep breath) Ever since I met you, I thought you were someone special. I know you're not perfect but, compared to some of the guys I've been out with, you're an absolute saint.

JEREMY: That's good to hear. I've met some of the guys you've been out with.

LAURA: But honestly, I've been anything but a saint, and I've had a lot of experiences in the past. I want things to be different with you. It just feels like I can't help myself! I just want to…Never mind. But I want this to work. I like you, and I'd hate to lose you because I can't control myself. I guess this is all pretty hard for you to imagine.

JEREMY: Not at all. I know exactly how you feel.

LAURA: (surprised) You do?

JEREMY: Believe me, I've had the same thoughts you have, even if I haven't had the chance to act on them.

LAURA: How do you possibly avoid that?

JEREMY: I don't get many dates.

LAURA: That'll do it.

JEREMY: The point is, if I'd been in the same situations, I might have done the same things.

LAURA: (pause) I'm sorry I…

JEREMY: You don't have to apologize. It doesn't matter a bit if you've messed around.

LAURA: I was gonna apologize for smashing your nose.

JEREMY: Oh.

LAURA: But it's good to hear you say that. Especially since I can't change that about myself.

JEREMY: There's only been one perfect person in this world. All the rest of us can do is strive to be like him and hold each other accountable. (JEREMY hugs LAURA.)

LAURA: Is it really okay?

JEREMY: Yeah.

LAURA: Thanks. Hey, maybe we ought to set ground rules on ourselves. Like no touching in certain places, no parked cars…

JEREMY: No French kissing until we've gotten to know each other.

LAURA: Let's not take all the fun out of it.

JEREMY: It'll mean more if you take the time to get to know the person you're playing tonsil hockey with.

LAURA: (sighs) Yeah, I guess. (smiles)

TH-JEREMY: She's got the nicest smile. Man, am I lucky.

TH-LAURA: Look at those blue eyes. I wonder if he's thinking the same thing I'm thinking.

LAURA: Jeremy, what are you thinking about?

JEREMY: This could be the beginning of a beautiful friendship.

TH-LAURA: Yeah, he is.

(blackout)

END

Going Up?

CAST

- Jay
- Kristen
- Four elevator passengers
- Felipe
- Josephine
- Warren

Four people stand in an elevator, staring straight ahead. Jay enters the elevator and takes his place among the stone-faced passengers. Jay looks around and tries to make eye contact with any of the passengers.

JAY: Hi.

(No one acknowledges his presence.)

JAY: It's a great day, isn't it?

(Silence)

JAY: I just moved into town, and this is my first day on the job. I'm excited about being here. Are there any tricks I should know? You know, where not to eat, where the copy room is?

(Silence)

(JAY holds his finger out to the man standing next to him.)

JAY: Pull my finger.

(The man looks at him in disgust.)

JAY: I'm just kidding. It's a joke.

(JAY laughs a little, but no one else even acknowledges his existence. The elevator stops, and everyone gets off except JAY.)

JAY: Nice talking to you guys. Have a good day!

(JOSEPHINE gets on the elevator and stares straight ahead.)

JAY: Hi.

(JOSEPHINE glances at him nervously.)

JOSEPHINE: Hello.

JAY: I just moved here from Kansas. My name's Jay.

(JAY steps toward JOSEPHINE, his hand out to shake. JOSEPHINE shrinks away into the corner, terrified.)

JOSEPHINE: Please don't hurt me! I don't have any money.

JAY: No, ma'am. I just...

(The door opens, and JOSEPHINE runs out screaming.)

JOSEPHINE: Help!

JAY: ...want to make friends.

(KRISTEN, FELIPE, and WARREN walk into the elevator, watching the hysterical JOSEPHINE run away.)

KRISTEN: What's wrong with her?

JAY: She heard polyester was making a comeback.

(KRISTEN, FELIPE, and WARREN nod understanding and then turn to each other.)

FELIPE: So, what were you saying?

WARREN: We started this Bible study, and all kinds of people are coming.

KRISTEN: What a great way to meet people!

WARREN: We learn a ton about Jesus, too.

(JAY begins to lean in, moving closer, trying to listen in on the conversation. They stop talking and look at JAY, who stands up straight, embarrassed.)

FELIPE: Can I help you?

JAY: Oh, no. I was just, um, doing some exercises. Stretching is always good for the spine, you know.

FELIPE: I didn't know that.

JAY: That's what we learned in Kansas. I just moved here, and I'm trying to meet new people.

FELIPE: Oh. Good luck. **(turns to his friends)** Go ahead.

WARREN: We learned last night about how Jesus would reach out to anyone, especially those no one else would talk to, like prostitutes and lepers and tax collectors.

KRISTEN: You mean Jesus wants me to make friends with the IRS?

(JAY bursts out into an annoying laugh. The three turn and stare at JAY, who continues to laugh, slapping his knee in glee. Slowly, JAY realizes the three are staring at him. His laughter trails off, and the elevator is silent once again.)

JAY: IRS. That was a good one.

(The three ignore JAY again.)

WARREN: You're welcome to come with me. It's Thursday night at 7:30.

KRISTEN: That sounds fun.

FELIPE: Count me in.

(The elevator stops.)

JAY: This is my floor. I'll see you guys around, maybe on a Thursday night?

(KRISTEN, FELIPE, and WARREN mumble responses. JAY hurries out of the elevator, dejected.)

FELIPE: He was an odd one.

KRISTEN: Do you think he wanted to go to the Bible study?

(All three think about it.)

WARREN: I doubt it.

FELIPE: He would've said something if he wanted to go.

KRISTEN: You're right. See you Thursday.

(The three exit the elevator.)

END

The Flower

CAST
- Britt
- Jenna

PROPS
- Fresh flower

BRITT and JENNA enter stage right holding hands and staring at the sky and the incredible view at this lookout on the edge of the woods twenty miles outside of town.

JENNA: Britt?

BRITT: Yeah?

JENNA: How come you keep taking me out here?

BRITT: I like it out here. I like being with you out here.

JENNA: Not because it happens to be twenty miles out of town and gives us a chance to be all alone?

BRITT: I sure wouldn't have driven twenty miles if we just wanted to be alone. Look at this place. It's beautiful.

JENNA: *(pause)* So what do you want to do?

BRITT: I don't know, I thought maybe we could talk.

JENNA: Talk?

BRITT: Yeah.

JENNA: That's it? Again?

BRITT: Well, yeah. Jenna, I know a lot of guys would start acting like jerks in a situation like this, where no one else is even close to being around, but I just want you to know that I respect you.

JENNA: Britt?

BRITT: Yeah?

JENNA: I, I, um, I love you.

BRITT: Oh. Good. *(looks away with a stressful expression)*

JENNA: Oh, and Britt…

BRITT: Yeah?

JENNA: You know the flower people carry around in their back pocket until they give it away? Well, I was wondering if maybe, you know, I could have yours.

BRITT: My flower? The one I'm saving to give to my wife? No way!

JENNA: Are you sure you still have it? I think you are lying. I think you already gave it away.

BRITT: If I already gave it away, why would I be trying so hard to keep it from you? Hey! Speaking of that, where is your flower?

JENNA: I gave it away, all right? Look, most people have. I don't see what's so special about your flower that you gotta keep it under lock and key, anyway. You're gonna give it away sooner or later.

BRITT: Yeah. To my wife. Later.

JENNA: Oh, give me a break.

BRITT: Jenna, I thought we came out here to talk.

JENNA: Okay, fine. Let's talk.

BRITT: Okay.

(They fold their arms and stand silently.)

JENNA: Oh, come on, Britt! You know you don't want to sit out here and talk any more than I do. Okay, fine. You don't want to give your flower away. I can respect that. But I don't think it's gonna hurt anything to just bring it out into the sunshine for a few minutes.

BRITT: No!

JENNA: I promise I won't touch it. I'll try to not even look at it. Just give it a chance to breathe in a little of this fresh country air. Flowers thrive in this kind of environment.

BRITT: Then will you quit bugging me about it? All right. *Don't* touch it. (*carefully removes imaginary flower from his back pocket and shows it to JENNA.*)

JENNA: Britt, it's so beautiful! Look at all those colors! I've never seen anything like it.

BRITT: And you won't again. (*starts to put it away*)

JENNA: Oh, don't do that. It should be out soaking up this beautiful sunshine.

BRITT: Jenna, it gets plenty of sunshine. And water. And air. Fresh, country air.

JENNA: Well, okay. But can't I have just one little petal? I'll preserve it forever as a tribute to you. I'll stick it between the pages of my Bible.

BRITT: (*hopeful*) Your Bible?

JENNA: The dictionary, then. Whatever. Come on. I'll just take a small petal from underneath—one of the orange ones. You can't even see those. No one will ever be able to tell.

BRITT: Just a tiny one. Make sure you can't tell.

JENNA: Okay.

BRITT: Nope! Too big. Pick a different one. (*carefully goes underneath and pulls out a petal*)

BRITT: Oh, no! Look at all the other ones that fell off with it!

JENNA: Sorry.

BRITT: Now it's all lopsided. It looks terrible. What are you doing?

JENNA: I'm evening it out. (*pulls petals from other side and lets them fall to the ground*) There. Much better.

BRITT: It looks pretty sickly now.

JENNA: The petals are just arranged wrong. Here, let me… (*does some more arranging and plucking*)

BRITT: Oh, good going! It looks worse than ever.

JENNA: Yeah, it does. Looks like you pretty much have a glorified stem.

BRITT: But there are still a couple of petals. Hang on there, guys.

JENNA: Soon as this wind picks up, they'll be gone, too. Your flower is shot.

BRITT: Thanks a lot! Now what am I supposed to do?

JENNA: You might as well just give it to me.

BRITT: I told you I'm not giving you my flower.

JENNA: I sure wouldn't want to give that ugly weed to my wife. I've already got most of the petals. I'll keep them all together in a safe place.

BRITT: The petals are blowing around in the wind!

JENNA: Well, I might have dropped a few.

BRITT: All that care and safekeeping…

JENNA: I'll take good care of it, I promise.

(*BRITT reluctantly hands her the imaginary stem, which she promptly tosses over her shoulder as he turns and walks away from her, toward stage left. She exits stage right carelessly. He stops walking, sighs, and then exits stage left dejectedly.*)

END

Silent Night

CAST

- Joann, wearing a winter coat
- Kenda, wearing a winter coat
- Luisa

PROPS

- Nativity figurines of Mary, Joseph, and baby Jesus

At curtain, LUISA sits downstage center dressed in a nice dress, no coat. She looks off into audience with no expression. After several moments, KENDA and JOANN enter stage right dressed in winter coats. As they speak, they never directly address LUISA. KENDA and JOANN look around, then finally sit, facing stage left, pulling their coats around them.

KENDA: Hey, Luisa.

JOANN: Hey, Lu. We wanted to, uh, stop by and see ya on our way to church tonight. Christmas Eve and all.

LUISA: It's Christmas Eve? Already? *(long pause)*

KENDA: We were both shopping until, like, an hour ago. Joann bought this totally stupid Chia Pet for her brother at the 7-11.

JOANN: That's all they had left! He's lucky he didn't get a Slurpee with a bow around it! And what about you? What's that thing you got your Dad? A beef jerky gift pack?

KENDA: He likes that stuff!

JOANN: Uh, huh.

KENDA: He does!

JOANN: Bet he'll be all weepy eyed 'n' stuff.

LUISA: It's from the heart. They'll both like their gifts. *(pause)*

KENDA: Hey, Luisa, Joann finally got the guts up to ask Jeff Dixon out.

JOANN: He's cute.

KENDA: Yeah, in an under-the-rock kind of way.

JOANN: Oh, and what guy are *you* seeing? Which guy is giving *you* a Christmas present this year? Huh? Huh?

KENDA: *(thinks)* Santa.

JOANN: Ha!

KENDA: He's a guy.

JOANN: You're so lame.

LUISA: Jeff's cool. Nice choice, Joann.

(long silence)

KENDA: Yeah, it was fun, but it was a little expensive, too. My mom's gonna kill me when she sees her credit card.

JOANN: She sneaked her mom's Visa out of her purse, just in case we needed some extra cushion at the mall.

KENDA: I'm going to pay her back, of course.

JOANN: Yeah. What, at like a dollar a week for the next 200 years?

LUISA: You worry about having things, and not what really matters. *(long silence)*

KENDA: Hey, Luisa. They're doing that same Christmas play you were in at church again this year.

JOANN: You were *so* queer as that innkeeper's wife. Please!

KENDA: If I had been her, I woulda kicked the innkeeper's behind outta there, and let Mary and Joseph take *his* room.

JOANN: *(imitates innkeeper's wife)* Honey, if you don't let that nice couple from Bethlehem stay here tonight, just remember, I have the Judean Express Card, and I can do *a lot* of shopping with it, know what I mean? *(both laugh, then pause)*

JOANN: Hey, remember when the three of us helped out at that homeless shelter like two Christmases ago?

KENDA: Oh, yeah! Luisa, you kept getting that one gross looking guy coming over and asking for more food all the time? Remember?

LUISA: Oh, yes.

JOANN: I don't know *how* those people ate that food! It should have been donated to a museum. Hurl city. Grosses me out just thinking about it.

KENDA: I'm glad that place closed down, or else Pastor Rob would make us go there again.

LUISA: Those men needed us then. They still do. They're lost. They're hungry for more than food.

JOANN: Oh, someone else will help them. *(long pause)*

KENDA: Luisa, did you know you're the one that even got us to go to that church? It's pretty cool.

JOANN: The kids really accepted us. Especially after...

KENDA: Yeah. They thought a lot of you. You made an impact on a lot of them. Luisa, Luisa, Luisa. That's all they talked about. They really miss you.

LUISA: They're a good group. I miss them, too.

KENDA: But they are always talking about decisions we make in life, ya know? They talk about all this really heavy stuff in teen group. Like where you go when you die. What heaven's like. What the other place is like. I don't know. I think it's just too early to worry about that stuff...to decide now. You know?

JOANN: Yeah, they put the pressure on sometimes.

LUISA: Don't wait to decide. Please. Don't wait. *(long pause)*

JOANN: So, Luisa. Do you, uh, see your family at all? How's your mom? She was a mess last time I saw her, of course.

KENDA: Yeah. They all were. We all were.

LUISA: They've stayed away. Best therapy for them I suppose, especially this time of year.

JOANN: Funny, but I haven't seen them around the church much. Guess they want to put it all behind them.

LUISA: They need to be there. God misses them. *(long pause)*

KENDA: *(very quiet, moves downstage)* I, uh, I always wanted to tell you something, Luisa. But I never got a chance.

LUISA: Really?

JOANN: Kenda?

KENDA: I was, uh, really mad when you... I was mad at the other driver, but I was madder at you.

LUISA: I'm sorry.

KENDA: I know you didn't want to go, but I was left alone. Me and Joann both. You left us both.

JOANN: Kenda, don't dredge this all up.

KENDA: And I think about you, Luisa. All the time. Wondering. Wishing you were here. Talking to me. Listening.

JOANN: Come on, we better go.

KENDA: I think about where you are. Tell me. What's it like there? They tell us stories at church, but, well, I need to know.

JOANN: O.K., Kenda, it's time to go.

KENDA: Can you let me know? With a sign or something? Huh? Would that be too hard?

JOANN: Kenda, it's late. Let's go.

KENDA: How am I gonna know for sure? I need some proof. Proof. *(starts to weep)* That's all I need. That's all.

LUISA: You have proof. And you don't even see it. The baby. He's the proof. All he said. All he did. How he died and rose again. It's there in front of you.

JOANN: She can't hear you, Kenda. Come on. Come on.

KENDA: No. I can't. *(weeping, goes to knees)* Luisa. Please. Luisa. Talk to me. I miss you so much. So much.

JOANN: *(goes to her)* We all do. Kenda. We all do. *(stops and pulls out a package from her coat)*

KENDA: Wait. We forgot *(goes back)* Here, Lu. We wanted to bring something for Christmas *(puts several figurines on ground)* It's a nativity. You know, Mary, Joseph, and the baby. Hope you like it. *(long pause)* 'Bye.

LUISA: *(goes to figures and studies them for a few minutes)* Wait. Wait! Take it with you. Don't leave it here *(GIRLS don't hear her. LUISA picks up the manger.)* Don't leave these out here. In the cold. In the dark. In this cemetery. People need to see the baby. Know him. You need him. Take the baby home with you. Please. Please. Take him home. Take him home.

(after several moments)

KENDA: Rest in peace. At least you have some.

(KENDA and JOANN exit slowly, leaving LUISA holding the figures as the lights go out.)

END

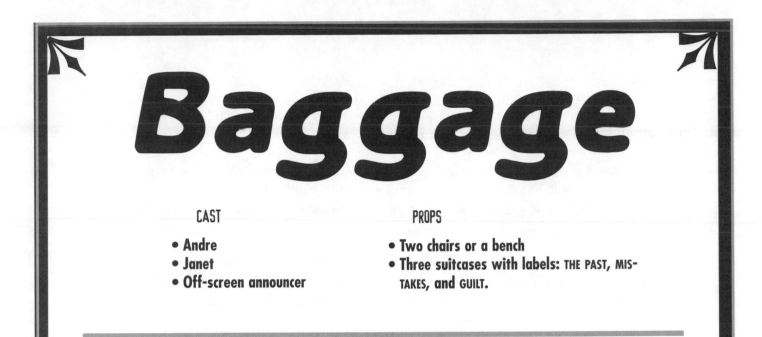

Baggage

CAST	PROPS
• Andre	• Two chairs or a bench
• Janet	• Three suitcases with labels: THE PAST, MIS-
• Off-screen announcer	TAKES, and GUILT.

ANDRE is sitting on a bus stop bench reading the paper. JANET enters with several suitcases. All of the voices are recorded or said by other actors offstage. The audience only hears the actors' thoughts until the last two lines of the skit when the characters on stage actually speak.

JANET: *(enters obviously struggling with bags)* Oh good! There's a seat. This stuff is heavy.

ANDRE: Yikes, she sure does have a lot of baggage!

JANET: Hope this guy doesn't mind if I sit here. I don't really care if he does mind; I don't think I can walk another step! *(drops suitcases and plops down, exhausted)*

ANDRE: She must be going on a pretty long trip with all of that stuff. Wait a minute, what am I saying? She's a girl. She's probably just going away for a night! Females have never been known for their concise packing ability.

JANET: It feels great just to sit down. My feet are so tired, and my arms are killing me from carrying these bags. I remember the good old days, when I didn't have that much to carry around. It sure was a lot easier back then. But, that was before.

ANDRE: Hmmm. *(investigating her baggage as she looks away)* From the looks of things, she's really hauling around a lot of stuff. I mean, lugging around the past everywhere you go can't be healthy. I wonder why a decent, normal, intelligent-looking person like her would continue to carry that around?

JANET: I mean, it's not that I want to keep holding on to the past, it's just that, well, I'm so ashamed of the things I did and the things that were done to me, it's just hard to forget. It's even harder to let go.

ANDRE: And mistakes, come on, give me a break! We all make mistakes. It's best to just learn the lesson that mistakes teach and move on. Doesn't she know that? Carrying your mistakes around with you can just lead a person into…

JANET: Depression. That's what I feel every time I look at this suitcase. I don't think anyone in the world has made as many stupid mistakes as I have. Stuff I don't want anyone to know about! I'm so ashamed of my mistakes; I'll probably carry this around with me the rest of my life.

ANDRE: I can't imagine how much guilt I would have if I held on to my past. I've had my share of stupid mistakes, and I've done some things that I wish I'd done a little differently, but I managed to move on with my life. Excess baggage can slow you down on a long trip. It's so much easier to travel light. Too bad she never learned that lesson.

JANET: I know I probably should just talk to somebody about my guilt. I'm just so ashamed of my life, I'm not sure I could talk about it. As hard as this is, it's easier just to keep carrying it all by myself. Well, there's the bus. I better get my act together.

ANDRE:*(speaking)* Uh, excuse me miss, but I couldn't help but notice you had a lot of baggage to carry. Would you like some help?

JANET: *(speaking)* Well, no, thanks. I'm gonna try it on my own.

ANDRE *exits left and JANET exits right.*

Projected onto a screen or read by off-screen announcer:

If we confess our sins, he is faithful and just and will forgive us our sins and purify us from all unrighteousness. (1 John 1:9)

As far as the east is from the west, so far has he removed our transgressions from us. (Psalm 103:12)

END

YOU DON'T HAVE TO PAY

CAST

- Jim
- Zack

PROPS

- Ticket window
- Movie ticket
- Concession stand
- Concession items: popcorn, Coke, and candy
- Chairs in a row to represent a church pew

JIM, *a fifteen-year-old boy, walks up to the box office of a movie theatre.* ZACK *stands behind the ticket window.*

JIM: I'd like a ticket to the next movie, please.

ZACK: Sure. *(hands JIM his ticket)* Here you go.

JIM: How much is it?

ZACK: We would appreciate it if you would pay $5.00, but you don't have to.

JIM: I don't have to?

ZACK: You can pay less if you want or more. You decide what you pay.

JIM: You're telling me that if I want to, I can just walk in and watch the movie without paying a dime.

ZACK: I guess you could. We'd rather you pay $5.00, but if you don't have that much, pay what you can.

JIM: I think today I'll just wander on in. Maybe I'll pay next time.

ZACK: If that's how you feel. Enjoy your movie!

JIM: I will; don't worry. *(walks away)* Since I have this extra money, I think I'll get some popcorn. *(walks up to the concession stand where ZACK stands ready and waiting)*

JIM: You work here too?

ZACK: I've always worked here.

JIM: But weren't you just back... *(looks back toward the box office, shakes his head, and turns back around)* Never mind. I'd like some popcorn, please.

ZACK: What size?

JIM: How much is the medium?

ZACK: We'd like you to pay $2.50, but you can pay however much you want.

JIM: You mean the concessions are just like the tickets?

ZACK: Yes. Every price in the theatre is a strong suggestion, but we don't force people who can't afford it to pay full price.

JIM: In that case, I would like a large popcorn, large Coke and some Milk Duds.

ZACK: Yes, sir. *(disappears behind the counter, getting the food)*

JIM: I can't believe this! I don't see how these guys can stay open.

(ZACK returns with the popcorn, Coke, and Milk Duds.)

ZACK: Here you go. I'll just ring this up.

JIM: Wait! I thought you said I could pay whatever I wanted to.

ZACK: Yes, that's right. I thought you might like to know our suggestion.

JIM: Don't bother. *(hands him a quarter)* Thanks for everything. *(walks into the movie, laughing to himself)*

JIM: This is great! I'm going to come to the movies every day now.

(blackout)

(JIM walks up to the ticket booth to find an OUT OF BUSINESS sign hanging there. JIM looks around inside the empty theatre.)

JIM: Hello! Is anybody here?

(ZACK appears and walks up to JIM.)

ZACK: I'm sorry; we're closed.

JIM: But you were open yesterday. What happened?

ZACK: Only a few people paid the prices we suggested, so we had to close. Sorry.

JIM: But you're the movie theatre! You can't close.

ZACK: Even the movie theatre has an electric bill. We couldn't pay the bills, so we closed. *(walks away, leaving JIM alone)*

(blackout)

(JIM, who is asleep, sits in a row of chairs with other students. ZACK sits next to him and shakes him awake.)

ZACK: Wake up, Jim. Wake up!

(JIM wakes up and looks around.)

ZACK: Church is almost over, man. You slept through the whole thing.

JIM: I had the weirdest dream. I went to this movie theatre, and you worked there.

ZACK: That's not weird. I do work at the movie theatre.

JIM: I know that. What was weird was I didn't have to pay anything if I didn't want to. It was like you made a donation, but you didn't have to. The theatre went out of business, though, because no one gave them any money.

ZACK: Of course they went out of business! Who ever heard of asking people to pay out of the goodness of their heart?

JIM: You're right. It was pretty dumb.

(The boys laugh. The offering plate comes by, and they pass it on, empty.)

END

Can O' Blame

CAST
- Winona
- Dimitri
- Announcer
- Eve (yes, the famous one)

PROPS
- Spray can labeled Can O' Blame
- Sappy music

ANNOUNCER: Ever have a day that goes something like this?

WINONA: Ah, man, I just got my English test back, and I got an F!

DIMITRI: I was at a party, had just a few beers, and wrecked my car! The cops nailed me for DUI! What am I gonna do now? *(sappy music could begin here)*

ANNOUNCER: Well, I'm glad you asked! You too can make all of your troubles disappear with a new product from X-Treme Productions. Just one whiff of Can O' Blame makes your troubles go down the drain!

WINONA: *(takes a spray)* Sure I got an F, but it wasn't *my* fault! It's very hectic at my house, and I just can't study! Yeah, that's where the blame should be—on my family, not me!

DIMITRI: *(takes a spray)* Well, it's not my fault that I had a few drinks. After all, everybody at that party was drinking, and I would have been out of place if I hadn't joined in. So, it's not *my* fault—it's theirs! They practically *made* me drink, then get in my car and drive!

ANNOUNCER: See how easy it is? Now you can do pretty much any stupid thing you want and just spray the blame onto someone else. Go ahead! Ruin your life and possibly the lives of those around you. With Can O' Blame, it's not your fault!

WINONA: Did you see Springer today? Some guy went ballistic on the Mayor McCheese statue at his local McDonalds. He emptied a gross of ketchup packets all over it! He was released from all charges because he claimed he had nightmares about the Fry Guys taking over the world. You see, it wasn't his fault! Thanks, Can O' Blame!

ANNOUNCER: Talk show hosts and crooked lawyers all agree: Can O' Blame really works!

DIMITRI: Just last week, some friends of mine were busted at school for drugs. Fortunately for them they knew about Can O' Blame. They told the police that because so many people were doing drugs, they didn't even think it was wrong! They blamed it on their ignorance! Can O' Blame to the rescue!

EVE: Hi. My name is Eve. Adam and I had no idea that our little spat with the apple incident would become the catalyst for this revolutionary new product. Pick up a can today, and keep on sinning! It's never your fault with Can O' Blame around the house!

ANNOUNCER: Order today, and we'll throw in a free bottle of It's Not My Fault—My Parents Screwed Me Up. Just one squirt after your morning shower, and it's good for the whole day! No more accepting blame—just blame it on your parents! Never admit you're wrong—put the blame on your situation! Remember, if you do something stupid, it doesn't have to be your fault! Order Can O' Blame today!

END

The Exchange Shop

CAST

- Wayne, customer
- Martin, store clerk

PROPS

- Lab coat
- Clipboard with papers
- Bell

The scene opens with MARTIN in lab coat with clipboard, looking over some papers. A bell rings, and WAYNE enters.

MARTIN: Good afternoon. Can I help you?

WAYNE: Yeah, is this the place where you, uh, trade stuff in?

MARTIN: You've come to the right place. What would you like to trade in today?

WAYNE: Me.

MARTIN: Excuse me? Did you say "me," meaning you?

WAYNE: Yes. I would like to trade myself in.

MARTIN: Okay. Let me get the paperwork. **(grabs a file folder from behind)** Let's see, trade a car, trade a video game, trade some jewelry, ah, here it is. How to trade yourself in. Boy, this is a lot more paperwork than most trades.

WAYNE: Whatever it takes.

MARTIN: Let's see, name?

WAYNE: Wayne Smith.

MARTIN: New name?

WAYNE: What you do mean, new name?

MARTIN: Well, if you're going to trade yourself in, you lose your old name. What would you like your new name to be?

WAYNE: Gee, I didn't think I had to lose my name. I need more time to think about that one.

MARTIN: Fine. How about brothers, sisters, or parents?

WAYNE: Well, I have a sister and brother, and a mom and dad.

MARTIN: Looks like all we have available right now is a mom, and she lives in Nome, Alaska. Do you like cold weather?

WAYNE: Wait just a minute! What about my family? Why do I need a new mom?

MARTIN: You came to trade yourself in, didn't you? If you want a new you, you have to get rid of the old you.

WAYNE: But my family? I mean, we have our moments, but I don't want to not have them around anymore!

MARTIN: Do you want a new you or not?

WAYNE: I wasn't prepared to make these kinds of decisions today. I need more time to think about this.

MARTIN: Fine. Let's talk about your new friends. Who do you want for friends?

WAYNE: Come on, you mean I need new friends? It's taken me so long to get the friends I already have. Why do I need new ones?

MARTIN: Look, you can't trade yourself in and keep your identity. You have to give that up, too.

WAYNE: Lose my identity? I thought I could just trade in the stuff I don't like. You know, like my inability to dunk a basketball. Or trade my face in for one of those Tom-Cruise-looking faces. Maybe get one of those Brad Pitt bodies. But that's all! Not lose my identity!

MARTIN: I'm sorry, but it just doesn't work that way.

WAYNE: Well, I actually like a few things about myself. I mean I've got a great sense of humor.

MARTIN: *(still writing, raising eyebrows)* Trust me on that one.

WAYNE: You're kidding, right? I've got to trade everything? I've got to start from scratch?

MARTIN: You've got it.

WAYNE: Well, I'm not prepared to make that kind of commitment.

MARTIN: You're the fifth person today who has been in here looking to trade it all in. Every time we get through one page of the application, they decide that trading themselves in would be a dumb idea.

WAYNE: Then why are you here? Why even make this service available?

MARTIN: Our job here at the Exchange Shop is to help people understand just how valuable they are. They never sacrifice themselves totally.

WAYNE: You mean people never trade themselves in?

MARTIN: Many try. They attempt to take on new identities, doing whatever it takes to fit in with the crowd. It never works, though. I mean, since you're so valuable, and there is no one else in the world just like you, why on earth would you want to be somebody else?

(blackout)

Projected onto a screen (or read from backstage): "There is far more to your life than the food you put in your stomach, more to your outer appearance than the clothes you hang on your body. Look at the birds, free and unfettered, not tied down to a job description, careless in the care of God. And you count far more to him than birds." (Matthew 6:25-26, The Message)

END

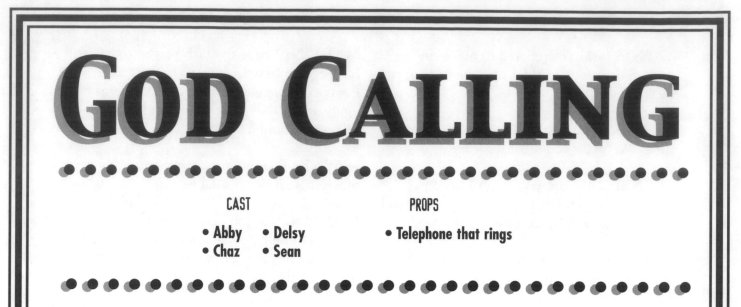

GOD CALLING

CAST
- Abby
- Chaz
- Delsy
- Sean

PROPS
- Telephone that rings

Three people (ABBY, DELSY, and CHAZ) sit at a party gossiping about people who aren't there. A telephone sits in the middle of them. They all talk at the same time so none of them can be heard. Each tries to talk louder than the others.

When the phone rings, no one seems to hear it except ABBY. She looks at the phone uncomfortably as though it's bothering her. She picks it up, annoyed.

ABBY: HELLO? What? I can't hear you. I'm sorry; you'll have to call back!

CHAZ leaves and comes back with some beer. They all start drinking. The phone rings again. ABBY hears it and finally picks it up.

ABBY: Hello? I'm sorry, what? Can you please say that again? I can't understand you. I'm not feeling quite right today. Hello?

DELSY and CHAZ come over and make her hang up the phone. Then they leave, and the place is a mess. ABBY tries to maneuver her way around the room, but it's not quite working. Enter SEAN, looking quite smooth. He looks ABBY up and down. He lifts a finger and beckons her to come here. The phone rings. She ignores it and goes to the boy.

SEAN: You are so beautiful. You are smart and funny.

Phone is still ringing. SEAN begins to get a little huggy. ABBY looks at the phone uncomfortably.

ABBY: Do you hear that?

SEAN: Hear what?

ABBY: I think I hear the phone ringing. *(It rings again.)* Yeah, I'm pretty sure that is what it is.

ABBY pushes him away, laughs at him, and goes to answer the phone. SEAN exits.

ABBY: Hello? What? I know we were gossiping, but I know we were partying. No, he is nothing like what I want in a guy, but he tells me what I want to hear. Yes, I heard you calling. What? You love me? What about the fact that I ignored you? I couldn't hear you. I felt far away. I'm so glad you called. It has been so lonely. Even with all the people, and the guy, I still felt alone. I love you.

END

DAILY DOSE

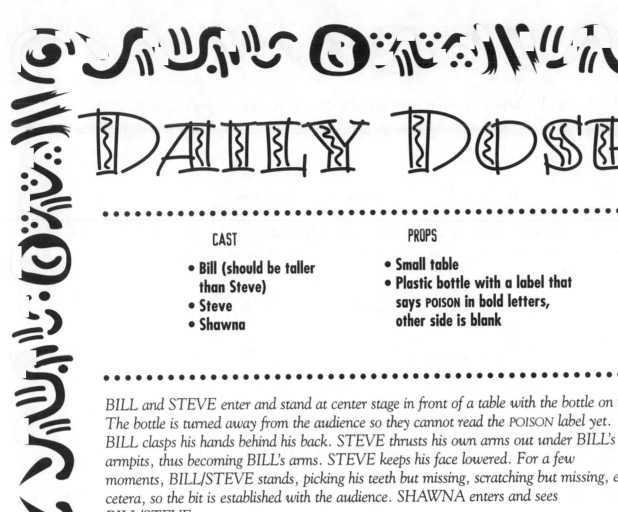

CAST

- Bill (should be taller than Steve)
- Steve
- Shawna

PROPS

- Small table
- Plastic bottle with a label that says POISON in bold letters, other side is blank

BILL and STEVE enter and stand at center stage in front of a table with the bottle on it. The bottle is turned away from the audience so they cannot read the POISON label yet. BILL clasps his hands behind his back. STEVE thrusts his own arms out under BILL's armpits, thus becoming BILL's arms. STEVE keeps his face lowered. For a few moments, BILL/STEVE stands, picking his teeth but missing, scratching but missing, et cetera, so the bit is established with the audience. SHAWNA enters and sees BILL/STEVE.

SHAWNA: Hey, Bill?

BILL/STEVE: *(BILL talks, STEVE gestures)* Hey, Shawna.

SHAWNA: *(looking at the setup)* Ah!

BILL/STEVE: Yes?

SHAWNA: Uh, what's going on?

BILL/STEVE: What do you mean? *(scratching himself)*

SHAWNA: Uh, don't you think this is, uh, strange?

BILL/STEVE: Well, sorry, but I have a rash, so I have to scratch.

SHAWNA: No, no. I mean, uh…*(looking behind STEVE)*

Permission to photocopy this page granted for use in buyer's own youth group.

119

Copyright Youth Specialties. www.YouthSpecialties.com

BILL/STEVE: *(looking behind himself)* What? Is there toilet paper on my shoe again?

SHAWNA: No! It's just…

BILL/STEVE: Do I have a booger? *(tries to swipe at his nose)*

SHAWNA: No! Uh, Bill, I hate to be the one telling you this, but, uh, there's some guy standing right behind you, and he's, uh, well, using his arms like they were yours.

BILL/STEVE: Huh? Oh, him. That's Steve. He's my new buddy.

SHAWNA: Steve?

BILL/STEVE: Yeah. Wave "Hi," Steve! *(STEVE waves.)*

SHAWNA: Uh, are you freaking out or something?

BILL/STEVE: Huh? No! It's like this. I was having a bad day, you know? Seemed like everything I did was wrong with my parents. I was listening to the wrong things. Watching the wrong shows.

SHAWNA: But how?

BILL/STEVE: But then, out of nowhere, Steve came along. He offered to, well, take over. You know, help me make decisions. Keep my parents happy. He wanted to help me, so I let him. What's the big deal?

SHAWNA: Uhhh.

BILL/STEVE: *(holds up bottle, but audience can't see label yet)* And Steve here is always feeding me great stuff. Stuff I never tasted before. And it's just little portions, so Mom and Dad won't think I'm getting too full. Steve says a little bit every day goes a long way. *(STEVE turns small bottle around so the POISON label shows and picks it up.)* Care for a sip?

SHAWNA: What? No!

BILL/STEVE: Suit yourself! *(STEVE puts drink up to BILL's mouth, and he takes a sip. It will probably spill.)* Ah! It's lemony. You sure you don't want to try some?

SHAWNA: Bill, that's, that's…

BILL/STEVE: Delicious! Steve gives me a little bit at a time because he says it's concentrated. He says my parents and I will never know how much I'm taking in if it's just these small doses. Makes sense to me. What's that, Steve? *(leans back and listens to STEVE)* Ah, okay. *(to SHAWNA)* Steve wants to know if you'd like him to come and help you, too.

SHAWNA: I don't think so.

BILL/STEVE: Oh well, you'll never know how good this can be! No more decisions. No more hassles from Mom and Dad. *(starts to slur his speech a bit)* Just enjoying what I'm given, a little bit at a time, and there's no harm, right? *(BILL's head starts to roll a bit. STEVE's hands try to keep BILL's head upright.)*

SHAWNA: Bill! Are you okay?

BILL/STEVE: Huh? Oh, no problem. Just feeling a little woozy. Just need a shot of this *(drinks more poison)* There. Better.

SHAWNA: Bill, don't you see what's going on?

BILL/STEVE: *(BILL gets woozy again)* Of course I do. Nothing is going on, that's what's going on. A little bit every day goes a long way. That's what Steve…Oh, I don't feel so good. *(BILL's head hangs down, and STEVE's hands hold his head up.)*

SHAWNA: Bill? Bill?

STEVE: *(This time STEVE's hand manipulates BILL's mouth, and STEVE is now talking for BILL.)* Oh, no problem. I can handle this. My buddy Steve here won't harm me. Right, Steve? Right.

SHAWNA: *(backs away in fright, then quickly exits)*

STEVE: *(STEVE is still talking for BILL.)* What's wrong with her? It's all perfectly harmless. As I say, a little bit every day. *(STEVE puts the bottle up to BILL's mouth and pretends to pour in the rest of the contents, shaking out the last drop.)*

END

UPGRADE

CAST

- **Guardian, man dressed in slacks, white shirt buttoned to the top**
- **Jesse, teen, dressed casually**

PROPS

- **Computer on small table, with chair**
- **TV remote control**
- **Fast forward tape sound effects**
- **Scarf**
- **Baseball cap**
- **Chair downstage center**
- **Coat**
- **Clip-on tie**

GUARDIAN *enters and sits at a desk with a computer monitor, hard drive, and keyboard at stage right.*

GUARDIAN: *(typing and talking)* Enter password. Guardian Angel 10521. Enter. *(waiting)* Yes, and welcome to the new year to you, too. No, I do not want to upgrade to Windows 3000. Okay, check mail. *(scrolling)* Uh-huh. Junk. Junk. Junk. Ju-Oops! An urgent message from the Lord. *(typing)* Locate the…Ah. *(typing and talking)*

Hey there Lord, it's me, Guardian Angel 10521. Pretty awesome New Year's, huh? A couple of the other guardian angels and I followed the midnight celebrations all across the world, and, boy, were our wings tired. Freddie's wings caught fire over Paris where they had a big fireworks display, and he was flying around fast trying to put it out. Some people on the ground thought he was a firework, and it was the funniest.

(pauses, looking at screen, then types) Oh, sorry, yes, uh, I got your message, sir. *(reads)* What? He did? Oh, man! *(typing)* Well, sir, uh, I thought I had backup with him that night, but apparently not. Sorry, sir. I'll get right on it. Huh? Download a special program? Fire away, sir! *(GUARDIAN holds screen and trembles as the program is downloaded*

into him. He stops and returns to keyboard.) Yes, I think that was a successful download. Thank you for the time and a big smiley face to you too, sir. *(gets up)*

I *knew* this was going to happen. I try and take one night off, just one, and my backup doesn't show. The Lord says my human, Jesse, is talking crazy again. Better rewind the celestial tape to his past New Year's Eve and see what happened.

(GUARDIAN holds up remote control and points it to stage right. JESSE, wearing a baseball cap, comes out walking backwards quickly, like a videotape being rewound. GUARDIAN makes rewind sounds. Then JESSE stops, moves quickly forward, and sits on a chair at downstage center. GUARDIAN pretends to stop using the remote and listens.)

JESSE: *(holding hand up, trying to get attention)* Oh! Oh! Pastor! Jesse here! Oh! Oh, thank you! I have this written down because it's so important. Well, as we close in on midnight, I just want to say that *this* coming year, the year _____ I
INSERT THE COMING YEAR
want to resolve to be a better person. A better son. A better worker. A better citizen. A better man. A

better gladiator in the fight against evil. A better coach. A better student. A better leader. A better follower. A better reader. A better fan. A better neighbor. A better, uh, uh, better overall guy! Thank you! *(GUARDIAN points remote at JESSE, and JESSE freezes)*

GUARDIAN: Oh, man, Jesse. Not again. Rewinding tape back to New Year's Eve _____. _{INSERT THE PREVIOUS YEAR} *(JESSE walks backward quickly, the forward quickly, putting on a scarf and losing the ball cap.)*

JESSE: Oh! Oh! Pastor! Jesse here! Oh! Oh, thank you! I have this written down because it's so important. Well, as well close in on midnight, I just want to say that *this* coming year, the year _____, I _{INSERT THE PREVIOUS YEAR} want to resolve to be a better person. A better son. A better worker. A better citizen. A better man. A better gladiator in the fight against evil. A better coach. A better student. A better leader. A better follower. A better reader. A better neighbor. A better, uh, uh, better overall guy! Thank you.

GUARDIAN: *(interrupts JESSE)* Hmmm. Go back one more year.

JESSE: *(same forward-then-back motion, losing scarf and putting on a coat)* Oh! Oh! Pastor! Jesse here! Oh! Oh, thank you! I have this written down because it's so important. Well, as we close in on midnight, I just want to say that this coming year _____, I want to resolve to be a better per-_{INSERT THE YEAR BEFORE LAST} son. A better son. A better…

GUARDIAN: That's enough. *(points the remote toward JESSE)* Fast-forward to today. *(JESSE moves around stage fast, then sits down, losing the coat, and adding clip-on tie in the meantime. He sits, looking intently forward. He keeps looking straight ahead as GUARDIAN talks to him. JESSE does not acknowledge his presence.)* Jesse, I know it's Sunday morning, and you're listening to the sermon, but let me speak to your spirit. Look. I'm your guardian angel pal, but I gotta tell you, these empty resolutions are getting old. I'm starting to catch some flak. I bet if we went back 10 years, we'd be hearing the same old resolutions. *(JESSE starts to listen without making eye contact.)*

I know we've talked about this before, but it's time to get serious. I got a download from the Lord this morning. It's a shareware program. You know, one of those things that millions of people can use. The one problem is that the receiver has to want it. Ask for it. *(pause, JESSE listening to preacher)* Yeah, like the pastor is saying. We do nothing in our own strength. Nothing we do is going to work. That's why your resolutions never work, Bud. *(JESSE listens some more)* But what he has for you makes all the difference. Just a simple download into your hard heart. *(JESSE looks uncertain, then listens some more and makes a decision, closes his eyes, and holds his head up.)* Atta boy. *(GUARDIAN puts his hand on JESSE's shoulders.)* Downloading strength and courage software to all files, overriding hard-heart hardware. *(GUARDIAN looks up for several moments, then slowly backs off and stands back. JESSE sits for a moment, then looks up and freezes.)*

GUARDIAN: *(points remote at JESSE again)* Fast-forward. *(JESSE moves forward fast, takes off tie, and sits in chair.)* Stop December 31, _____. _{INSERT THE CURRENT YEAR}

JESSE: *(holds up hand slowly)* Pastor. I, just, just want to thank God. Because this past year, _____, I didn't try to be a better, better, well, _{INSERT THE CURRENT YEAR} anything. But I was a better, better servant. A better follower. A better listener. A better Christian. Because it's no longer me trying. May I do the same in _____? *(JESSE freezes. GUARDIAN smiles _{INSERT THE NEXT YEAR} and returns to his computer. Types.)*

GUARDIAN: Upgrade complete. Logging out. *(both freeze, then exit)*

END

I'm Listening

CAST

- Janie
- Shannon

PROPS

- Book
- TV remote control
- Telephone
- GameBoy

• •

SHANNON sits on a couch in a living room reading a book. JANIE comes in and sits down beside her.

JANIE: Hey, Shannon. Can I talk to you?

SHANNON: Sure. *(puts down book)* What's up?

JANIE: Well, I've got a problem, and I'm not exactly sure what to do.

SHANNON: Okay.

JANIE: This girl in chemistry drives me completely psychotico, and I don't know why. Just a sec.

(JANIE jumps up off the couch and turns on the stereo. She sits back down. SHANNON thinks this is weird, but she doesn't say anything.)

JANIE: Where was I?

SHANNON: Chemistry.

JANIE: Oh, yeah. This girl, I don't know what it is, but everything she does makes me want to stick sea monkeys in her eyes and chia paste in her hair.

SHANNON: That's not right, Janie.

JANIE: Duh. That's why I'm asking your advice.

(JANIE picks up the remote, turns on the TV, and begins half watching it.)

SHANNON: What are you doing?

JANIE: I'm trying to avoid her.

SHANNON: I mean with the TV.

JANIE: I'm still listening.

SHANNON: Whatever. Okay. What's the thing that bugs you most?

JANIE: That's it. Everything about her bugs me! I'm trying to find one good quality to focus on.

(The phone rings, and JANIE answers it.)

JANIE: Hello? Hey, Hipster, whazzup? No, I'm just sitting here doing nothing.

(SHANNON rolls her eyes and starts reading her book again.)

JANIE: Sounds fab! Yeah, I'll be there in an hour or so. Fine. Later.

(JANIE hangs up. SHANNON puts down her book.)

JANIE: Okay, we've got a few minutes to talk before I have to get ready.

SHANNON: I don't want to be a hassle.

JANIE: No prob. Back to *her*. Everything she says is so unbelievably stupid. I want to submit her as a living brain donor. What are you reading?

SHANNON: Huh?

(JANIE picks up the book SHANNON was reading and reads the back cover.)

JANIE: Is it any good?

SHANNON: I just started. Look, Janie, let's talk about this girl later when there's not so much going on.

JANIE: No! *(lays down book)* I've got you right here. I'm afraid that I'm like this girl. You know, that whole log in the eye thing. So, am I like her?

SHANNON: You haven't told me anything about her other than she's buggin' you.

JANIE: What else do you need to know?

(JANIE pulls a GameBoy out of her pocket and begins playing it while SHANNON talks.)

SHANNON: Well, what does she say? How does she dress? Have you ever been around her outside of class? Who does she hang out with? What are you doing? *(raises her voice in irritation)*

(JANIE jumps a little, looking up from her game.)

JANIE: Don't do that! What are you freaking for?

SHANNON: You! You come to me for advice, and you keep doing other stuff.

JANIE: I can do two things at once, Shannon.

SHANNON: Just forget it. *(stands)* Let me know when you really want to talk.

(SHANNON exits.)

JANIE: Wait! I—geez! I just wanted to talk.

(JANIE puts down the GameBoy and picks up SHANNON's book and begins to read it.)

END

Flunking ENGLISH Flunking LIFE

CAST

- Paul
- Mr. Johnson, Paul's English teacher

PROPS

- Table or desk
- Two chairs
- Paper and pencil
- Newspaper

(MR. JOHNSON *sits at the desk, and* PAUL *approaches timidly.*)

PAUL: Excuse me, Mr. Johnson? Could I, uh, could I talk to you for a minute?

MR. JOHNSON: *(somewhat curtly)* Yeah. I was just finishing up some grading here. But, please have a seat. What can I help you with?

PAUL: It's about my English composition grade, sir. I've been doing really badly in this class, and I need to talk to you about my grades.

MR. JOHNSON: I'm all ears.

PAUL: *(uncomfortable pause)* Well, it's just that I've always done really well in all my other English classes. But in your class I've made a D or F on every paper I've written. I was just wondering if there's something I need to do, you know, to do better on my papers.

MR. JOHNSON: Ah, I see, Paul. You're asking me to give you some advice on writing. Is that it?

PAUL: Well, yes, sir, I guess that's it.

MR. JOHNSON: Well, to start with, I think you need to be more careful about your subject matter.

PAUL: Sir?

MR. JOHNSON: Your subject matter. The subjects you write about. I find your subject matter questionable.

PAUL: You mean, it's offensive?

MR. JOHNSON: *(pauses)* Offensive? Well, possibly to some. No, Paul, your subject matter is questionable because it's self-serving. It's gratuitous. And beyond that, you seem to be fixated on a subject that is not only inane but is also hopelessly outdated.

PAUL: Mr. Johnson, you've gotta forgive me here. I'm not trying to be a smart aleck, but I really don't know what you're talking about.

MR. JOHNSON: Look, Paul. You can stop with the innocent garbage. You know exactly what I'm talking about. Every paper you've written this semester has been about Jesus. I ask for a book review; you write one on the Gospel of Luke. Look, the Gospel of Luke is not a book; it's a propaganda piece.

PAUL: (interrupting) Mr. Johnson, I didn't...

MR. JOHNSON: (interrupting) Look, let me finish! I ask for a biography on somebody, and you give me a religious treatise on Jesus Christ. I ask for personal stories, you give me six pages on "How I Became a Follower of Jesus." You're fixated, son. Why don't you write about stuff the other kids are writing about? Why you hate your parents. Sex, drugs, rock and roll, Steven King. Why don't you write about those things?

PAUL: Well, at the beginning of the semester, you said this was a composition class, and we could write about anything we wanted. Jesus is what I want to write about. That's what's important to me.

MR. JOHNSON: (angrily) Well, it's not important to me. I don't happen to share your slant on life.

PAUL: (interrupting) Look, Mr. Johnson...

MR. JOHNSON: And I'm sick and tired of you Rich Wing Bible Bangers laying claim to my classroom. I didn't sign up to teach English so that a 17-year-old kid could spend a semester trying to convert me.

PAUL: (interrupting) Mr. Johnson, I'm writing a paper...

MR. JOHNSON: (interrupting) Now, in answer to your question. You're flunking English composition because I'm not comfortable with your subject matter. And if you

want to pass English composition, I suggest you change your subject matter. Is that understood?

PAUL: Yes, sir. (pause) Mr. Johnson?

MR. JOHNSON: Yeah.

PAUL: If I flunk your class, will I have you again next semester?

MR. JOHNSON: Not if I can help it.

PAUL: That's good, 'cause I'm afraid you're gonna have to flunk me, sir.

(Blackout)

Now the positions are switched with PAUL sitting at the desk and MR. JOHNSON approaching timidly.

MR. JOHNSON: Excuse me. Are you Paul Clark?

PAUL: (not even looking up) Yeah, I am. But I'm afraid I'm a little busy right now trying to get this column out.

MR. JOHNSON: Oh. I'm sorry. I can come back some other time.

PAUL: (still not looking up, still preoccupied) No. Please, come in. What can I do for you?

MR. JOHNSON: Well, actually, I, I just wanted to talk to you for a minute.

PAUL: (looking at his paperwork) That'd be fine. Please, have a seat. I'm sorry. I didn't catch your name.

MR. JOHNSON: Johnson. Alan Johnson. (uncomfortable pause) Twenty-five years ago I was your high school English composition teacher.

PAUL: Mr. Johnson? It *is* you! *(awkward pause)* Do you live here now?

MR. JOHNSON: Yes. I moved up here five years ago when I retired. I've been reading your column for five years now. But, I never knew you were the same Paul Clark I had in my class.

PAUL: Well, it's a small world, isn't it?

MR. JOHNSON: Yes, yes, it is.

PAUL: *(awkward pause)* Well, if you're one of my readers, I suppose you're here about one of my columns, eh?

MR. JOHNSON: Yes, you're a good writer, Paul. You have astute insights, politically and otherwise. Yes, I'm here about one of your columns. Last Tuesday's column, the piece you wrote on convictions…"Flunking Life" you titled it. I have it here. *(refers to newspaper)* You wrote: "I had a high school English teacher, Mr. Johnson, who flunked me for the year, essentially because of my belief in God. I'd like to thank him for that. He taught me a lesson that year. He taught me that true convictions don't come cheap and that sometimes flunking English is a whole lot better than flunking life."

PAUL: Ah. I suppose you're here because I mentioned your name. I'm sorry if I've offended you.

MR. JOHNSON: No, quite the contrary. I'm here to, to ask you a question. What exactly did you mean by that title, "Flunking Life"?

PAUL: Well, I suppose I meant basing your life on a wrong thing. Getting to the end of your life only to realize that you've been heading down the wrong path the whole time.

MR. JOHNSON: Yes. That sounds familiar. "Flunking Life"—I could write a book about that. Say, Paul? Do you think you may still have those papers that you wrote for my class?

PAUL: *(laughing)* My high school English papers? Yeah, I suppose I've got 'em somewhere. I think I've saved everything I've ever written. Somehow, even in high school, I knew I was gonna be a writer someday.

MR. JOHNSON: Would you mind maybe, if it's not too much trouble, digging those papers up for me. If it's not too much trouble.

PAUL: Or better yet, maybe we could have lunch and discuss what's in those papers.

MR. JOHNSON: Yes, I'd like that—to discuss what's in those papers—if it's not too much trouble.

PAUL: *(slowly)* I'd be honored, Mr. Johnson.

MR. JOHNSON: Please, call me Alan.

PAUL: I'd be honored, Alan.

END

THE CHAT

CAST

• Harold   • Melissa

HAROLD and MELISSA come out and stand stage left and right respectively. They hold black folders with their scripts inside. HAROLD, about 40 or 50, dresses casually with his baseball cap turned backwards. They stand for a moment, and then begin. During the sketch, HAROLD, taking baby steps, slides slowly sideways toward MELISSA until he's almost right next to her at the end. She does not move.

MELISSA: Hey everyone exclamation point, smiley face! Enter.

HAROLD: *(sounding like a teen boy)* Hey, Melgirl54. It's me, PrettyBoy. Enter.

MELISSA: PrettyBoy! How *are* you? Where have you been? I was worried about you. I haven't seen you in this chat room for like, ever. Enter.

HAROLD: Ah, my Ma busted me for not doing my homework. And she wouldn't let me get online. Enter.

MELISSA: Like, I thought maybe your band was finally gonna tour ya know, and that, maybe you'd be like near our town or somethin'. Enter.

HAROLD: Ah, man, the band's a joke. Our drummer dude was a jerk, and we split up. Who cares, you know? Enter.

MELISSA: I care, PrettyBoy! You know that! Enter.

HAROLD: Yeah. I know that, Mel. Hey, that's your real name, right? I mean all screen names are like that. They all like have parts of someone's real name. Enter.

MELISSA: Yeah. It's Melissa actually. I couldn't think of any better name. Pretty lame, huh? Enter.

HAROLD: No, no, it's great. Pretty. You know? Enter.

MELISSA: Thanks. So, okay, make with your real name. Enter.

HAROLD: Don't laugh. Enter.

MELISSA: Puh-leeease. Enter.

HAROLD: Dylan. Like in Bob. Whoever that is. Enter.

MELISSA: Cool name, dude. Enter.

HAROLD: You think so? Enter.

MELISSA: Yeah. Very cool. Look, I missed chatting with you. PrettyB…I mean Dylan. Try and stay in touch more, you know? Enter.

HAROLD: I will. It's just. Well, I've been down and stuff. My parents are on me, my grades stink, you know, stuff like that. And I'm kinda lonely. You know? Enter.

MELISSA: You don't have to be! I'm online, like all the time. Enter.

HAROLD: Naw, it's different when you can. Well, never mind. Enter.

MELISSA: What? Tell me! Enter.

HAROLD: Well, like talk on the phone. Or even in person. Enter.

MELISSA: *(quiet for a minute)* Oh. Enter.

HAROLD: It's not like I want your phone number or nothing. I'm not some creepo. I just, well, like to imagine what your voice sounds like. But…Enter.

MELISSA: I didn't think you were a creep. And it's not like I don't know you. We've been chatting online for like six months, right? Enter.

HAROLD: Right! Right! Enter.

MELISSA: My Mom's got this thing about giving out our number. She says people can tell what city you live in and stuff by getting your phone number. Whatever. Enter.

HAROLD: I don't care where you live. I do actually, but I just wanna talk. Hear your voice. What's the harm? Enter.

MELISSA: Yeah. What's the harm? Enter.

HAROLD: I really need to talk to you. Like real people do. You know? Enter.

MELISSA: Okay, look. You can't tell anyone about this. Let's go to a private chat room, and I'll give it to you. Enter.

HAROLD: Solid. *(waits a moment)* Hello? Mel? Enter.

MELISSA: Dylan? Cool. There you are. You have to swear that you won't give this out, and if my mom answers, hang up right away, Okay? Enter.

HAROLD: Don't worry. I'll keep it to myself. I promise. Enter.

MELISSA: Okay. It's 419-555-4563. Enter.

HAROLD: Wow. We've got the same area code! Enter.

MELISSA: You're kidding! I live in Oregon! Enter.

HAROLD: Yeah, Oregon. Sure. I'm just outside of there. Enter.

MELISSA: Walbridge? Toledo? Elmore? Enter.

HAROLD: Yeah, Walbridge. Enter.

MELISSA: This is *too* freaky! Wow! I could have heard your band anytime! Enter.

HAROLD: I can't believe we've been so close and yet, so like, far away. Enter.

MELISSA: Yeah. Oh, man, my mom's calling me. Are you gonna call? Enter.

HAROLD: Count on it. Enter.

MELISSA: Gotta go. Call me! Enter. Log out.

HAROLD: *(changes from his teen voice to deeper voice, turns his cap around)* Count on it.

(Both freeze and lights blackout.)

END

TV
TAKEOFFS

In a TV world of talk shows and sitcoms, sketches based on TV shows always kick off lively discussions. Familiar characters from television news and game shows offer new things to think about in these sketches. Some of these sketches are funny and some are very serious. They're great as openers at camps and conferences too.

THE BIG QUESTION

Dripping with sarcasm and the facade of a Hollywood game show, the sketch on page 134 will get you loathing most of the contestants almost as much as the host. The sketch does have one redeeming character. Only one guy is willing to say, "I don't know." After ridiculous trivia questions, he doesn't even pretend to have an answer. Ironically, that is the right answer! Salvation cannot be earned by knowing the right answer. It takes humility and a willingness to ask for help to get what you need from God. *Bryan Belknap*

PRIORITIES

So what activities do *you* think fill most people's time? According to our TV hosts on page 136 sleeping, eating, and watching TV pretty much fill our time! As you watch this segment from a top rated morning show, you can't help wondering if they're padding the numbers to keep their jobs. Notice church didn't even make it onto the list. If that's true, most of you reading this should be looking for a new job soon. *Stephen Smith*

WHO WANTS TO BE A CHRISTIAN?

You'll find Regis Philbin doing a bit of moonlighting in this sketch on page 137. Charlene Church, Gladys Goodworks, and Anna Apathy all fail on the very first question, but Ginny Genuine gets the answer just right.

This sketch takes a little more prep time than usual. It's better to have the lines memorized so the actors are free to overact instead of scrambling for their lines. Create a simple game show studio for a set and add show music. You'll also need slides, Microsoft PowerPoint, or butcher paper to display the answers to the contestants' questions. Allow yourself enough time to prepare.

Follow up with discussion questions after the sketch—
- Why do so many people live their Christian lives by playing church, doing good things, or acting as if it all doesn't even matter?
- Does a real Ginny Genuine exists? How do you know?
- Do all Christians have to be so perfect and goody-goody?

Grant Bowlus

The Big Question

CAST

- Pat Alex (host)
- Tonya, wearing a formal dress
- Cindy, dressed like a mom
- Jack, with glasses and alien-related T-shirt and book
- Miguel, dressed like a mechanic

PROPS

- Four podiums; three with the contestants' names on them
- Bullwhip
- Power drill
- Sound effects for a bullwhip cracking, a power drill revving, and a siren sounding

The game show contestants wear outfits to match their possessions. Any humorous torture devices or sound effects for Tonya add comedy. Pat Alex stands behind his podium, plastic smile firmly in place, when the lights come up.

PAT: Welcome to *The Big Question*, the game show everyone plays, whether they like it or not! I'm Pat Alex, your host, and here's our beautiful hostess, Tonya.

(TONYA walks out wearing a formal dress and waving like Miss America. She disappears backstage without saying a word.)

PAT: We'll see Tonya again later. Now, let's meet our contestants!

(CINDY, JACK, and MIGUEL jog out excitedly and take their places behind podiums with their names written on them.)

PAT: Welcome, Cindy.

CINDY: Hello, Pat.

PAT: Tell us a little bit about yourself.

CINDY: I'm Cindy Sanders from Oxnard, California. I'm a full-time mother with three kids and a wonderful husband who sells corrugated boxes.

PAT: *(patronizing)* That's fascinating. Really. *(turning to MIGUEL)* Miguel?

MIGUEL: Miguel Shatner, Pat, from Roswell, New

Mexico. I've been interviewing aliens for 17 years now and compiling the conversations into my new book, *Same Universe, Different Planet.*

PAT: Outer space aliens?

MIGUEL: Yes. I've met with over 20 different life...

PAT: *(interrupts)* That's out there. Really. Let's meet our final contestant.

JACK: Jack Jansen from Muleshoe, Texas. I can change a gasket in a Ford truck in 96 seconds flat.

PAT: How about a Volvo?

JACK: Can't touch foreigners.

PAT: Of course you can't. Well, then. Everybody ready?

ALL: Yeah!

PAT: Great! Cindy, you'll start. What would you use to remove a chocolate syrup stain?

CINDY: Lemon juice.

PAT: On carpet?

CINDY: Lemon juice and ice.

PAT: Excellent answer! Next question. What home remedy helps with a case of poison ivy?

CINDY: Baking soda mixed with calamine lotion and a dash of Diet Slice.

PAT: Very good, Cindy! Okay, your third question. What's the radius of the West African Piedmont beetle's artery?

CINDY: The what?

PAT: I'm sorry. We don't repeat questions.

CINDY: That's the most ridiculous question I've ever heard! How am I sup...

(A loud buzzer interrupts her.)

PAT: Oh, you've run out of time! The correct answer is .0217 micrometers. Tonya!

(TONYA appears holding a bullwhip. She leads CINDY away.)

CINDY: That wasn't fair! I'm a homemaker. I've waited on my family hand and foot for years. Who cares about a stupid bug anyway?

(TONYA disappears with CINDY backstage. We hear the crack of the bullwhip and CINDY's yell of pain. MIGUEL and JACK look at each other nervously.)

PAT: Okay, Miguel, your turn.

MIGUEL: I'm not so sure I...

PAT: *(interrupts)* Which was the last planet discovered in our solar system?

MIGUEL: That's easy. Pluto.

PAT: See? Nothing to worry about.

MIGUEL: I was a little worried after... *(makes whipping motion and sound)*

PAT: You're much more intelligent than she is, Miguel.

MIGUEL: I graduated summa cum laude from MIT.

PAT: Isn't your Mommy proud! Here's the next question. How many kernels of popcorn are popped each year in first-run movie theatres in the United States, including Puerto Rico?

MIGUEL: Popcorn? Who cares! Give me a real question.

PAT: Time's running out.

MIGUEL: Thirteen trillion.

PAT: The answer is 13 trillion, 5 billion and 72. Close, but no cigar, Miguel. Sorry!

(TONYA enters holding a power drill. She leads MIGUEL away by the arm.)

MIGUEL: Give me another chance. I know I can do it. My brain's insanely smart! Please!

(TONYA and MIGUEL disappear backstage. We hear the power drill revving up.)

PAT: Well, Jack, you're the last contestant. Are you up to the challenge?

JACK: No, not really.

PAT: What?

JACK: I'm not real smart. I didn't know the answer to any of them there questions. I shore could use some help answering 'cause I cain't do it myself.

(Sirens sound. JACK looks around, confused.)

PAT: Congratulations! You answered the big question correctly!

JAY: I did?

PAT: No one can answer the questions, Jack. Everyone needs help, and you were the only one to ask.

(TONYA walks out with a trophy and hands it to JACK, who is stunned. She exits.)

PAT: So, how does it feel to be a winner?

JACK: I don't know. I'm just a lucky loser.

PAT: We all are, Jack. Any last words?

JACK: *(motions backstage)* Does Tonya ever talk?

END

Priorities

CAST

• Hugh • Barbara

HUGH: Good morning. Welcome to the CBS morning magazine, *60 Seconds*. I'm Hugh Ups.

BARBARA: And I'm Barbara Falters. This morning we will be looking at America's priorities. What's important to you?

HUGH: Over a period of one year, CBS conducted a study of 1000 Americans. The people involved in this study were asked to meticulously record all of their activities during a one-week period.

BARBARA: The study found that people spend more time sleeping than doing anything else.

HUGH: Makes me sleepy just thinking about it.

BARBARA: The second most time-consuming activity for Americans was working. The average person spends 41.3 hours per week working.

HUGH: What other activities do Americans spend time doing?

BARBARA: Following sleeping and working came TV watching and eating.

HUGH: And family time?

BARBARA: Yes, family time. *(looking down the list)* I don't see family time on the list. I guess it didn't make the top twenty this year.

HUGH: What do Americans do after sleeping, working, watching TV, and eating?

BARBARA: Well, Americans spend an average of 10.2 hours per week involved in or watching sports. Movies were popular too, with the average American watching a video or going to a movie at least once a week.

HUGH: And church?

BARBARA: Sorry, Hugh. Church didn't make the list.

HUGH: What does that say about our society?

BARBARA: We're just too busy for church.

HUGH: Too busy sleeping, eating, and watching movies?

BARBARA: If given a choice, what would you do?

HUGH: I see your point.

BARBARA: In summary, Americans are sleepy, hungry, and addicted to TV.

HUGH: Yes! *(pumps arm)*

BARBARA: You're glad for that?

HUGH: You know, job security.

BARBARA: Until the next time, for all the staff and crew of *60 Seconds* this is Barbara Falters.

HUGH: And Hugh Ups, saying take time to smell the roses.

BARBARA: Have a nice day!

END

Who Wants to Be a Christian?

CAST

- Regis Philbin (emcee)
- Charlene Church
- Gladys Goodworks
- Anna Apathy
- Ginny Genuine

PROPS

- Studio setting
- Game show theme music
- Music stands
- Answers to questions displayed on slides, PowerPoint, or paper
- Confetti

The scene begins with applause as the show's theme plays. Regis is the host and is the lone person on stage. As the theme fades, Regis begins.

REGIS: Welcome to "Who Wants to Be a Christian?" What an exciting time we expect here in the next several moments. This is the show where people from all over the country try their wits at figuring out what it takes to become a fully devoted follower of Christ. Our contestants this evening were randomly selected before the show. Let's give a warm Gollywood welcome to our first contestant, Charlene Church! Come on in, Charlene! *(applause)* Charlene, we welcome you to our show. Tell us about yourself.

CHARLENE: Thank you, Regis. It's a dream come true to be here! I can't wait to play! I live in Jacksonville, Florida, and I'm a faithful member of the Competitive Community Church. I've been in that church all my life.

REGIS: That's just great, Charlene. Let's see if you learned anything in that church. Let's play "Who Wants to Be a Christian?" And now for your first question, Charlene. What must you do to enter the kingdom of heaven? Is it—

a. Be on all committees humanly possible.
b. Be in church for Easter and other important services.
c. Help out with local mission opportunities.
d. Admit your sins, believe, and commit your life to Christ.

Your thoughts? Take your time; this is eternal, Charlene.

CHARLENE: Regis, I feel confident on this one. The answer is "c," help out with local missions!

REGIS: Final answer?

CHARLENE: Yes, final answer!

REGIS: For heaven's sake, I'm sorry, Charlene! That was an admirable answer, but the correct answer is "d," admit, believe, and commit your life to Christ! Charlene, it's been a pleasure to have you on our show.

CHARLENE: But Regis, I want to use my lifeline.

REGIS: I'm sorry, Charlene. Jesus is your life-line. I'm terribly sorry for your outcome. Good luck to you! *(give time for CHARLENE to exit)* Our next contestant is Gladys Goodworks. *(applause as GLADYS takes her seat)* Gladys, welcome to our show! Tell us about yourself!

GLADYS: Well Regis, I'm from Salt Lake City and currently spend all my time doing good deeds for many people. I'm excited to be here to work for the prize!

REGIS: Good enough. Let's play "Who Wants to Be a Christian?" Gladys, your first question toward the prize is, "What must you do to enter the kingdom of God?" Is it—

a. Build homes for the less fortunate.
b. Have religious involvement in the community.
c. Admit your sins, believe, and commit your life to Christ.

Take your time. I'm here for you if you need me!

GLADYS: Regis, I actually think I know this one. I'll say "b," have religious involvement in the community. I think that's vital to the kingdom.

REGIS: Final answer, Gladys?

GLADYS: *(deep sigh)* Yes, final answer!

REGIS: Gladys, Gladys, Gladys. I'm terribly sorry. Good works are great, but the correct answer is "c," admit your sins, believe, and commit your life to Christ! It has been wonderful having you on our show.

GLADYS: *(with panic)* But Regis, I'd like to phone a friend.

REGIS: *(interrupting)* What a friend we have in Jesus. Gladys, you had your chance. I'm sorry. *(GLADYS leaves)* What a good worker. Our next contestant is Anna Apathy! Come on down! Anna, welcome to our show! Tell the folks about yourself!

ANNA: Regis, I don't know. I'm from Micanopy, Florida. Well, there isn't a whole lot going on down there. I guess I probably shouldn't even be here right now, but I guess I'll try to hang in there. I don't know.

REGIS: Wow, Anna that sounds exhilarating! We welcome you to our show, I think! Are you ready to play the game, Anna?

ANNA: *(deep, boring sigh)* Well, I guess.

REGIS: Anna, here is your first question! What must you do to enter the kingdom of God? Is it—

a. Wait for someone else to do it for you.
b. Sit back as life passes you by.
c. Do absolutely nothing.
d. Admit your sins, believe, and commit your life to Christ.

Anna, we need a winner, so take your time. We're talking eternity here!

ANNA: *(sarcastically as though this is annoying to her, sighs)* Well, if I'm forced to choose… *(thinking out loud)* God does love us all anyway. Regis, I'll guess "c," absolutely nothing! I don't like being bothered and obligated.

REGIS: Anna, is that your final answer?

ANNA: Yes, my final answer is "c."

REGIS: Wow, I can't believe this, Anna. I'm so sorry, but the only answer was "d," admit your sins, believe, and commit your life to Christ! This is devastating! You certainly have been an interesting addition to our show! Take care now.

ANNA: *(mumbling)* Oh, it doesn't really matter anyway! *(exits)*

REGIS: Well folks, that was hard to sit through. Let's welcome our final guest contestant this evening. Give it up for Ginny Genuine! Ginny, come on down! *(Applause. REGIS waits for her to be seated)* Ginny, welcome. Tell us who you are!

GINNY: Regis, it's more about *whose* I am than *who* I am! I'm Ginny Genuine from Jacksonville. Let me just say, I'm not perfect, just forgiven! It's a joy to be here with you!

REGIS: Ginny, let's play "Who Wants to Be a Christian?" Here's your monumental question! What must you do to enter the kingdom of God? Is it—

a. Absolutely nothing.
b. Do good for others.
c. Be involved in a local church.
d. Admit your sins, believe, and commit your life to Christ.

Ginny, please take your time. This has been a long night here in the studio.

GINNY: Regis, I have a genuine peace about the answer to this question. I know the answer is "d" because I have committed my own life to Christ. I have Christ in my heart, and he is the true living God! *He* is my final answer!

REGIS: That is unbelievable! We have never had a contestant so confident in their answer. Ginny, congratulations! You win the prize! *(confetti and applause)* Folks, from all of us here at ABC—that's A, Admit; B, Believe; C, Commit—thank you for tuning in. Join us next time for "Who Wants to Be A Christian?" or join us online at "There's room at the cross dot come!" *(applause)*

END

Life can be tough at times. These sketches offer insight into how to handle those rough times. Not all sketches with a serious message are themselves serious—some of these scripts wrap serious subjects in light-hearted banter and action. In any case, drama is a perfect medium for grabbing people's attention and priming them for a meeting, a talk, or a Bible study. If you have a particular topic in mind, check out the Scripts by Topic index on page 7.

TOO LATE?

Life moves pretty fast—for some teenagers, it moves a little too fast. The drug addict or abused or hateful kids aren't the only ones who need Jesus. Kids with good grades, involved in student government, seemingly perfectly normal but busy kids, need him too, but no one realizes it. They're often at the end of their ropes, looking for someone to offer them hope.

The sketch on page 145 tells Annie's story. On the outside she looks like she's got it all together, but on the inside she's dying. Her one Christian friend Chris isn't embarrassed about his faith; he just doesn't know quite how to share what it means to know Jesus. This sketch rotates between three scenes: a kitchen table with a TV, a school hallway with lockers and a trash can, and the black hole—a small space with two simple crates to sit on. The pace of the play moves faster and faster and Annie spins more and more out of control, until it all ends abruptly.

This is more than a standard sketch—its length alone requires multiple rehearsals. The technical additions provide important background noise and play off the dialogue, working together to create the complete scene.

Conclude the presentation with cast members sitting on the edge of the stage and telling the audience what they would say to Annie (as themselves, not their characters) if they had the opportunity. Then use this time to try to complete Chris' job for him.

The discussion time afterward can easily serve as an entire session with your group or as a youth-led service. This entertaining and all too realistic look at sharing faith makes the sketch too good to miss. *Robin Bolen and Cheryl Wooten*

THE VISIT

This sketch deals with something all youth ministers fear—the tragic death of one of their students. While Derrick's death affects everyone, no one's more affected than his best friend, Brad. The sketch on page 156 tracks Brad's reaction from the time he first hears about the death through the rest of that day. This sketch can be difficult to perform and watch. It raises tough questions, and we won't know the answers to some of them. As difficult as it might be, this sketch and its musical suggestions offer a way to cover an important issue before it becomes a reality in your group. *Jeff Dennis*

WITHOUT HER CONSENT

In the sketch on page 161, Samantha realizes that getting dumped by her date would have been better than being raped. She didn't mean for things to go so far, and when she said stop, he said it was too late. The sketch takes place a month afterward when a close friend helps Sam sort through what happened and tells her about God's redemption for her broken heart.

Rape is never an easy topic to cover. This sketch touches on just a few of the related issues. Fortunately for Sam, she has a good Christian friend to help her get through this. Use this sketch to educate your students about God's forgiveness and mercy, how he cleanses and heals the hurting, and to offer spiritual and practical tips for dealing with a sensitive subject.

John Cosper, Jr.

GUARDIAN ANGEL

Being at your wit's end isn't a unique feeling. However, your reaction to that feeling can change your life. Two girls give up on their families and strike out on their own with a grand total of $86. As they sit eating the tuna sandwiches they packed at home, a homeless man approaches them. The girls don't realize that they're all homeless now as they try to ignore the man. Persistence reigns, and by the end of the conversation, he convinces them that running away won't solve anything.

The sketch on page 163 brings a touching story to life. Not all runaway situations wrap up this neatly, so take time to talk about the outcome of this sketch.
• Is this situation realistic?
• What makes someone decide to run away?
• What are the alternatives to running away?
• What are some valid reasons for wanting out of your home?
• Do you know about resources to offer someone in this situation if you ever need to?

David E. Ruiz

THE ONLY WAY OUT

In this time of bombings, fires, and earthquakes, the sketch on page 169 could really happen. Three students get left behind in a building that has a gas leak and is ready to explode. Suddenly, two students hear a faint cry for help. They make a choice. One student leaves for safety, and the other searches to find the voice. Fear and panic settle in as the situation gets worse. Just when it looks like one student will save the other, their roles are reversed.

Death is real, and so are the choices we make while we are alive. In this sketch you'll come face to face with these life and death issues. The dialogue carries this performance without any sets or backdrops. An explosion occurs offstage with the lights down. In the blink of an eye, circumstances change!

Lara Willars

Too Late?

CAST

- Annie
- Andrea
- Mom
- Brenda
- Javier
- Sedric, wears an earring
- Kelley
- Dion
- Chris, wears a hat
- Isabella
- Dad
- Jeff
- Mrs. Sanchez
- TV news announcer (voice only)

PROPS

- Kitchen table
- Four chairs
- Timer with loud sound
- Cups
- Ice
- Papers on clipboard
- TV
- School hallway
- Lockers
- Trash can
- Fake gun
- Door with girls' bathroom sign
- Two crates to sit on
- Poster-sized report card with "A" grade
- Toy hammer

The first scene opens with ANNIE, her parents, and sister ANDREA at home. Friends stop by in small groups. ANNIE sits at the kitchen table with ANDREA, working on her speech for student council elections.

ANNIE: Now how does this sound? "As student body president I vow that we as students will have the right to take any test by e-mail."

ANDREA: Oh, is that a pig flying.

ANNIE: *(wads up paper and throws it at ANDREA, making an ugh-I'm-a-failure noise)*

ANDREA: Come on, Annie, you can do this. Let's just start with something smaller, like, maybe, nuclear disarmament.

ANNIE: Stop it, that's not funny. *(aggressively)*

ANDREA: Don't get so stressed out. It's just a speech.

ANNIE: That' s easy for you to say, Miss Graduated-valedictorian-and-got-a-full-scholarship-to-Princeton.

MOM: *(enters)* How's the speech going?

ANNIE: Not so great.

MOM: Maybe you just need to take a break, honey. Don't worry about it. You know you're going to carry on the tradition. Now, what kind of pizza should I order?

(BRENDA enters.)

ANNIE: Pepperoni, of course.

BRENDA: Ooh, pepperoni has the most fat grams.

ANDREA: Just like Brenda to make a dramatic entrance. Where's everyone else?

BRENDA: I think Javier is giving them a ride in his rebuilt Chevette.

(Horn sounds. Rest of friends enter. JAVIER runs in and hides behind ANNIE)

JAVIER: *(pushes ANNIE forward)* No, no, I can take 'em. You don't have to defend me.

SEDRIC: Man, Javier, you didn't tell me your car was part of the Hotwheels collection.

KELLEY: I'm never riding anywhere with you again. It's *right* turn on red, not left.

DION: I'm feeling kind of dizzy—I wonder if it's oxygen deprivation.

CHRIS: That's the closest I have ever come to a near death experience. I know I saw a bright light at the end of a tunnel when we pulled out in front of that truck.

ANNIE: My friends, happy to see me?

SEDRIC: *(sits in ANNIE's lap)* Oh, baby, you know we're glad to be here.

MOM: Okay, we've got chips and salsa, drinks, pizza's on the way; and we have a ton of brownies.

(DAD enters with huge tray with one brownie left in the middle. JAVIER snatches up the last brownie as DAD walks by and says, "Thanks.")

MOM: Maybe I spoke too soon.

ANDREA: Well I've got to upstairs and start reading *War and Peace*. Have fun, sis.

ISABELLA: Annie, let's go watch the movie.

ANNIE: What did you get?

KELLEY: I got *Up Close & Personal* but Javier brought *Ernest Goes to Camp*.

ANNIE: I know which one I'm watching.

DION: We'll see about that.

(ANNIE gathers her stuff off the table and finds a clock.)

ANNIE: Mom, what's this?

MOM: I got it for you. You'll need it to keep up with your life.

(JAVIER picks up the clock, holds it in front of ANNIE.)

JAVIER: *(speaks to the timer)* Aw, Annie's life—it doesn't look like you. *(Timer sounds and EVERYONE looks at clock like "What was that?")*

(As the second scene begins, ANNIE comes home from school. She's unpacking her books when MOM enters.)

MOM: Hi Honey. How was school? *(walks past Annie)*

ANNIE: Great! You'll never guess... *(follows Mom around kitchen table)*

MOM: Good, whew, am I worn out! Things were just crazy at the office today. Jenny called in sick, so I had to take on her load, too. Oh, it was a madhouse. Did you start dinner yet?

ANNIE: No, I just got home. I'm late because…

MOM: Argh. Sweetie, you know that helping out with the cooking takes just a little effort, but it's such a big help. That's okay. I'll go do it myself.

ANNIE: But Mom…

(MOM exits. DAD enters.)

DAD: I'm home.

ANNIE: Hey, Daddy. Guess what happened at school today.

DAD: How are you, Annie? *(hug)* Now what were you talking about?

(MOM enters to set the table.)

ANNIE: I...

DAD: Oh, hi, dear. How was work today?

MOM: Don't ask. It was insane. I'm just glad to be home. How about you?

DAD: Well, I had a patient throw up on me twice. That was exciting. Food poisoning. Oh, I'm supposed to get e-mail from Dr. Harper. Did you check the computer?

MOM: No, I just got home, and Annie hadn't started supper yet, so I've been busy with that. **(DAD exits.)** Annie, can you help me set the table?

ANNIE: Mom, do you want to hear about my day at school?

MOM: Sure, honey. I've been waiting for you to tell me about it.

ANNIE: You know the student body elections that I told you about? Well, we voted yesterday, and...

MOM: Oh, the water's boiling over! Hold on!

(MOM *runs back stage. DAD runs in.*)

DAD: I've got Harper on the phone long distance. He needs the case info. *(digs through briefcase)*

ANNIE: *(calmly)* Dad?

DAD: Yes?

ANNIE: The house is on fire.

DAD: Okay, Annie, just a minute.

(MOM *enters and fills cups with ice. ANDREA enters.*)

ANDREA: Hey, how's everyone doing?

MOM/DAD: Great, Andrea. How was your day?

(ANDREA *crosses to ANNIE.*)

ANDREA: Hey! Congratulations on your big day, my awesome victorious sister! I saw the sign when I rode by the high school on my way home.

MOM and DAD: *(still and quiet)* What?

ANDREA: Annie's just been elected student body president.

MOM and DAD: *(look at each other)* Oh. *(timer sounds)*

(*Scene three begins with ANNIE at her school locker.*)

DION: *(walks by)* Woohoo! Congratulations, Student Body President.

SEDRIC: Congratulations, Babe. Does this mean that I'm first lady of the student body? Ooh, I don't have my inaugural gown for the ball.

BRENDA: *(jokingly)* Hey Madame President, hope you're not too good to make it to volleyball practice today. It's at 3:30. Be there! *(exits)*

JAVIER: I can't believe I got beat by a girl. Our first meeting is today, and you're in charge. See you in the student council room at 3:30. *(exits)*

KELLEY: Hey, how are you?

ANNIE: *(shocked, not sad)* A little overwhelmed.

KELLEY: *(snaps picture of ANNIE and JEFF sneaks into the picture with his arm around ANNIE)* Good. Gotta make sure I get a picture of the new president. The first issue of the school paper comes out next week, so we need to get started. We're meeting at 3:30. Bring your first article, okay? *(exits)*

CHRIS: *(walks by)* Hey, Annie, how ya doing?

ANNIE: Never mind. Don't ask.

CHRIS: Tough day, huh? I'll call and check on you later, or hey, I could just pick you up for FCA at...

ANNIE: Let me guess, 3:30, right?

CHRIS: No, actually, it's 7:30. Hang in there. *(exits)*

SEDRIC: *(looks around to see if any more people are approaching, sees no one, and leaves)* Guess you're pretty busy. **(ANNIE *is left standing alone as the timer sounds.*)**

(*As scene four begins, ANNIE sits in the black hole looking at her clock. ANNIE is center stage, speaking her lines, and other characters speak from offstage—as if in ANNIE's thoughts.*)

MOM: You know that helping out with the cooking takes little effort, but it's such a big help.

ANNIE: Yeah, Mom, putting that pot of water on to boil is definitely going to clear up the hole in the ozone layer.

MOM: That's okay. I'll go do it myself.

ANNIE: Hmm. I'll go do my job as a mom.

DAD: Don't bother me now.

ANNIE: But the house was on fire *(plays innocent here as the timer sounds)*

(Scene five takes place around the kitchen table with a TV on the table, turned on all the time. ANNIE's PARENTS sit at the table eating and watching the news on TV. ANNIE enters.)

MOM: Hey, honey, I think your father and I need to discuss something with you. We met with your teachers and...

NEWS: Every day, the typical 14-year old watches three hours of TV and does one hour of homework. Every day, over 2,200 kids drop out of school.

MOM: *(said with same importance as above statistic)* You're making a "B" in AP Calculus.

DAD: *(points at TV)* Can you believe that?

MOM: *(punches DAD)* Honey.

DAD: Oh, I agree with your mother.

ANNIE: It's no big deal. We've only had one test.

MOM: You're trying to get into college. You need scholarships. You're trying to get into a good school aren't you? Do you want to live in Orangeburg and work at McDonald's the rest of your life? You know your dad and I can't afford to pay for school. You're going to have to help us out by getting good grades.

ANNIE: It's only a "B."

DAD: But a "B" is average and our daughter is above average. I know you can do better. *(looks at MOM and nods head as if to say, "I did good, didn't I?")*

NEWS: Every day 3,610 teenagers are assaulted, 630 are robbed, and 80 are raped.

MOM: Mrs. Sanchez said that you tested higher on the mathematics diagnostics skills test than anyone else in your grade. So what's the problem, Annie?

ANNIE: *(mutters under breath)* You are.

DAD: Try and do better. I think you're going to have to cut out some of these extra activities. We think your grades are suffering. You need to quit volleyball.

MOM: *(stands and leans over table)* Wait a minute. I think it's this guy Sedric. What kind of grades does he make anyway? He has an earring, and that can't be a good sign. What kind of guy wears an earring anyway? I don't think you should go out with him anymore.

DAD: *(suddenly stands and leans over table, ANNIE is caught seated in the middle)* Well, he may wear an earring, but I wear the pants in this family, and I say she quits volleyball.

MOM: You may wear the pants but I have the brains and I say it's that boy. I would have been a lot better off in high school if I hadn't gotten mixed up with you.

DAD: I could say the same about that.

ANDREA: *(enters)*

MOM and DAD: Hi, Andrea!

NEWS: Every day 500 adolescents begin using illegal drugs, and 1,000 begin drinking alcohol. Every day 1,000 unwed teenage girls become mothers.

DAD: *(walks to her and puts his arm around her shoulders)* Andrea's making all "A's" in her classes.

MOM: Yeah, why can't you be more like your sister? *(to ANNIE)* Let me get your dinner. *(to ANDREA as the timer sounds)*

ANNIE: I'm glad that's over.

(Scene six is at school. Kelley enters.)

ANNIE: *(enters feeling down)*

KELLEY: Hey, it's Annie! How ya doing, big girl?

ANNIE: Not so good.

KELLEY: Good! Good! *(not being mean, just not listening)*

JAVIER: *(enters on roller blades)* We're going to go rearrange the keys on Mrs. Sanchez's keyboard. Wanna come?

ANNIE: No, thanks.

(KELLEY exits.)

JAVIER: Annie, you don't look so good. Are you all right?

ANNIE: Just a fight with my parents,

JAVIER: *(skates around)* Oh, I know all about that. Remember that time I had purple hair? I thought my parents were going to get a divorce over that one. My mom cried for days, my dad slammed all the doors in the house, and my brothers and sisters weren't allowed to talk to me. My parents were so down on me they couldn't even look me in the eye. They made me use an entire bottle of shampoo in one night to get all the purple out. The shampoo bottle says "Lather, rinse, repeat," but I don't think it means 100 times! When I was done, my hair was brown but the bathtub looked like Barney's playground. Have you ever spent three hours in the bathroom? *(stops and slows for last line)* Oh, yeah, you're a girl.

ANNIE: Never mind. *(walks off)*

JAVIER: *(still moving, blocks ANNIE's path)* Hey, what do you girls do in there anyway? What could possibly take three hours? I mean, how bad can your face be that you have to cover it up every day with make-up? You know that commercial for the lipstick you can't kiss off? How do you know? Do you test the stuff? Do you get your money back if it comes off? I'd like to find out, but no one's ever tested it on me!

BRENDA: Hey, what's up?

JAVIER: *(suddenly stops, stands still)* I'm just listening to Annie, because she's bummed out.

BRENDA: Oh, what's the matter? Problems with Sedric? Boyfriends can be such a hassle.

ANNIE: No.

BRENDA: Well, if it's not your boyfriend, it's got to be fat grams. Don't worry about it. You don't look *that* much bigger. You can work it off in no time.

ANNIE: Actually it's…

BRENDA: Look, I know it's tough when your parents don't give you the back-to-school shopping spree, but last year's styles aren't that out yet. *(picks at ANNIE's clothes)* I'm sure most people don't even notice. Sorry I can't help you more, but I've got to go try on this new lipstick.

JAVIER: *(stands quickly)* Hey, is it the kind that won't kiss off?

BRENDA: Yeah. *(over her shoulder as she exits into girls' bathroom)*

JAVIER: All right! *(takes off after her, stumbles on roller blades, trips, falls into girls' bathroom)*

SEDRIC: What's this about kissing? *(SEDRIC moves to kiss her, and ANNIE pushes him away)* What's the matter with you?

ANNIE: I don't have any new lipstick.

SEDRIC: What?

ANNIE: Never mind.

SEDRIC: Come on, what's the matter?

ANNIE: You don't really want to know.

SEDRIC: Sure I do, I'm your boyfriend. Tell me all about your problems, baby. I'm here for you. Is it school?

ANNIE: Yeah, kind of.

SEDRIC: Is it grades?

ANNIE: Yeah.

SEDRIC: *(sarcastically)* Oh. Did my girlfriend make a "B"?

ANNIE: Yes.

SEDRIC: Look, don't worry about it.

ANNIE: I'm not.

SEDRIC: Oh, it's your parents.

ANNIE: Yeah, last night my loving parents told me how concerned they are about my future. Apparently, I can't get into college with one "B." Therefore I'm destined to spend my days flipping burgers, collecting garbage, and cleaning toilets. All because Annie made a "B" in AP Calculus. The real disgrace is the black mark this brings to the family name. Yes, here's Annie my daughter, the failure. She's only average.

SEDRIC: Oh, baby, you're anything but average. *(cuddles up to her)*

ANNIE: Well, you should have heard what they said about you.

SEDRIC: Huh?

ANNIE: Well basically, your earring means that you're the spawn of the devil and are destined to wreck my future.

SEDRIC: Let's start wrecking it right now. *(moves closer and laughs)*

CHRIS: *(enters, pushing between SEDRIC and ANNIE)* Hey, haven't you heard that abstinence is the only foolproof protection against pregnancy and disease?

ANNIE: Thank you. *(timer sounds and Annie walks off)*

CHRIS: Is she okay?

(In scene seven ANNIE sits at the black hole again, and the other characters' voices are heard from off stage.)

MOM: You're making a "B" in AP Calculus.

ANNIE: I'm a failure and an embarrassment to the family.

DAD: I say she quits volleyball.

ANNIE: That will sure help me take off the extra weight.

MOM: Why can't you be more like your sister?

ANNIE: Yeah, why can't I be perfect and adored by both of my parents?

JAVIER: How bad can your face be that you have to cover it up every day with makeup?

ANNIE: I'm ugly.

BRENDA: Don't worry about it. You don't look that much bigger.

ANNIE: Don't worry about it. Whales aren't that big.

SEDRIC: Oh, baby, you're anything but average.

ANNIE: I could be below average; I'm dating you, aren't I?

CHRIS: Is she okay?

ANNIE: I don't know.

CHRIS: *(enters)* Hey, watch out *(cuts around corner with fake gun in hand)* You ready for Mission Impossible Night at FCA? Where's your costume? *(timer sounds)*

(In scene eight ANNIE's PARENTS sit at the kitchen table, watching TV. Sound clips from Jeopardy *play in the background.)*

DAD: Where's Annie?

MOM: She's at the football game.

DAD: Have you noticed anything different about her lately? Do you think she's all right?

MOM: It's just one of those teenage girl things.

DAD: Yeah, I've never understood you women.

TV: ("Welcome to Jeopardy" and Jeopardy theme song play here.)

ANNIE: (enters after using breath spray right outside of parents' view. She leans over them from behind and speaks loudly.) Hey, what about a "welcome home, Annie"?

MOM and DAD: Welcome home, Annie.

MOM: What's got you so cheery?

DAD: Did you have a good time at the game?

ANNIE: I had a great time. I met this guy Jack and his friend Jim, (laughs) and their brother Bacardy.

MOM: Oh, good. I hope they're nice boys. They don't have their ears pierced, do they?

(Sound clip from Jeopardy of someone giving the wrong answer.)

DAD: Now, honey, don't start that again. Bacardy?

ANNIE: Bacardy, I met him at a party.

MOM: Now, Annie, you know I don't like those parties.

ANNIE: Mom, you'd be proud of me, somebody has to be the designated driver.

DAD: That's our Annie, always the responsible one.

ANNIE: Not responsible enough to make straight "A's." That's Andrea. Annie's only taking AP classes, student body president, and she used to play sports, but that's just not good enough for the world's greatest parents.

DAD: Annie, I won't have you talking to us like that while you live under our roof.

ANNIE: At least now you notice I'm under your roof.

MOM: That's it! Go to your room. (timer sounds)

(Clip from Jeopardy of host saying the show is over.)

(Scene nine is at school. ANNIE sits on a trash can. Her friends enter and stand behind her. CHRIS sits in the background and watches.)

BRENDA: It's Annie, the fallen angel.
DION: You just couldn't hold on to that halo, could you?

KELLEY: What's that say, going to FCA one night, and going partying the next? Isn't there something in the rulebook against partying?

DION: Chris, what do you think about all of this?

CHRIS: Well you know, to each his own.

SEDRIC: (enters and pushes friends away from ANNIE) Hey, leave my girlfriend alone. I know she was the life of the party, but no autographs please. (timer sounds)

(Scene 10 is in the black hole. All of these lines should be said in rapid succession.)

DAD: Bacardy?

ANNIE: Yes, my dad's an idiot; he missed the clue again.

DION: You just couldn't hold on to your halo, could you?

ANNIE: Annie messes up again.

DAD: Annie, I won't have you talking to us like that while you live under our roof.

ANNIE: Annie, we won't have you speaking what you really want to say.

CHRIS: Well you know, to each his own.

ANNIE: Get a backbone, Chris.

MOM: That's it! Go to your room.

(Pause here and go back to normal tempo.)

ANNIE: I hate you, too.

CHRIS: *(enters and stands behind ANNIE and slightly off to one side, twisting his hat in his hands)* Hey, Annie. How are you doing? Are you hanging in there?

ANNIE: I'm all right. I've just got a lot going on.

CHRIS: *(moves to front)* So, how's your life? *(points at timer)*

ANNIE: It's running.

CHRIS: *(sits)* Okay. So how are you doing?

ANNIE: I'm not sure.

CHRIS: I've been worried about you lately.

ANNIE: Me, too.

CHRIS: You want to talk about it?

ANNIE: Yeah, but I don't know how.

CHRIS: Just tell me what you're thinking.

ANNIE: I'm thinking that school's too much. I don't like my family a whole lot. And I don't think they like me either.

CHRIS: What do you mean? I thought everybody liked you.

ANNIE: I don't even like myself right now. *(after saying line, turns back to CHRIS)*

CHRIS: *(turns to face ANNIE's back, puts hand on her shoulder)* Someone likes you all the time, Annie.

ANNIE: What, are you gonna give me that God stuff?

CHRIS: No. *(gets up and walks off as timer sounds)*

ANNIE: To each his own.

(In scene 11 DAD and ANNIE are at home. Play clips from Touched by an Angel.)

ANNIE: *(enters)* Hey Dad, what are you watching?

DAD: *Touched by an Angel.* You want to watch?

ANNIE: *(sits down. Both sit in silence for a moment.)*

(Audience hears a clip from the show where the angel says, "God loves you.")

ANNIE: Do you believe that?

DAD: Well, there is a God, I think. And if there is a God, he probably loves us.

ANNIE: Well, if he loves us so much, why doesn't he help us out?

DAD: Well, I guess he does if you ask.

ANNIE: Then I'll be touched by an angel. *(Both laugh as the timer sounds.)*

(In scene 12 the FRIENDS are all in a hallway by school lockers. SEDRIC sits on a trash can. SEDRIC and JAVIER read and talk. Mrs. Sanchez enters and walks through the hallway.)

JAVIER: Hey, Mrs. Sanchez, if all this evolution stuff is true, how can boys and girls be so different? I mean, if we came from the same amoebas and everything?

MRS. SANCHEZ: *(unenthusiastically, by rote)* Well, as Darwin's research proves, all living things, despite their awesome diversity, originated from a single-celled amoeba formed in a warm pond. The life forms that grew from this amoeba then differentiated into a variety of life forms, proving that all life is a result of chance, of these precise elements combining on their own at just the right moment.

JAVIER: So you mean if I threw plankton in my swimming pool, and heated it to the right temperature, I could create a new pet. Cool!

KELLEY: This also explains why Javier looks so much like a monkey.

CHRIS: Mrs. Sanchez, what actual proof do scientists have to support evolution?

MRS. SANCHEZ: That's all right there in your book. If you'd read your homework, you would know.

CHRIS: Well, when I was reading my homework, I got confused about how this fish suddenly grew legs and walked out of the pond.

MRS. SANCHEZ: *(aggressively)* Well, Chris, how do you think life began?

CHRIS: Well, I think it had to be started by somebody bigger than us.

MRS. SANCHEZ: *(attacks)* You mean, like God? Well, which God?

CHRIS: I don't know. I just don't understand how all of the detail in nature could have happened by chance. You know, like eyelashes. How do those just happen?

JAVIER: Yeah, you know, I agree with Chris, like where did pit hair come from, and why do we have it?

SEDRIC: We all know *you* have it.

MRS. SANCHEZ: Chris, how can you possibly believe there is a God? Look at all the suffering in the world around us. If there is a God…*if*. He's either too weak to help us, or too cold-hearted to care. And speaking of proof, what proof is there for the existence of God? None, Chris. Now, Javier, fortunately, our next chapter is on hygiene. And…

ANNIE: *(to CHRIS)* Can I talk to you later? *(timer sounds)*

(In scene 13 ANNIE sits on a crate in the black hole again.)

MRS. SANCHEZ: This eliminates the need for God in our understanding of life.

ANNIE: How can anybody understand life?

MRS. SANCHEZ: Well, which God?

ANNIE: This is so confusing. I feel like I'm going to explode.

DAD: And if there is a God, he probably loves us.

ANNIE: Help me.

MRS. SANCHEZ: If there is a God…*if*. He's either too weak to help us or too cold-hearted to care.

ANNIE: Why am I even talking to you? I don't even know who you are, or if you even exist.

DAD: Well, I guess all you have to do is ask.

ANNIE: God loves me?

CHRIS: *(enters)* So Annie, how does this thing work anyway? *(points at timer)*

ANNIE: You really want to know?

CHRIS: Sure.

ANNIE: It's like my life. You know how the second hand keeps going and going.

CHRIS: You mean like the Energizer bunny? *(gives her a smile)*

ANNIE: No, like it's out of control. That's me.

CHRIS: Okay. *(stops)* So what did you want to talk about?

ANNIE: I want to know more about what you were talking about in class.

CHRIS: You mean, about creation.

ANNIE: No, about God.

CHRIS: *(nervously)* Well, what do you want to know?

ANNIE: No, you tell me. What do I need to know?

CHRIS: Uh, well, um, God loves you.

ANNIE: Well, thanks. Some angel on TV told me that. What's it all about?

CHRIS: It's about praying and going to church and stuff like that.

ANNIE: That's all? That's it?

CHRIS: No, it's just hard to explain. *(timer sounds)*

(In scene fourteen ANNIE's at her school locker.)

DION: Hi, Annie. *(walks up behind her)*

ANNIE: Oh, hey, Dion. What's going on? *(turns to face him, back to lockers)*

DION: You know people aren't allowed in this part of the building after 4:00. *(closes in on her, places one hand on lockers and leans in)*

ANNIE: Yeah. I just had to pick up my notebook for the test tomorrow. See ya. *(tries to turn and walk away)*

(DION places his other hand against lockers and pins ANNIE there.)

ANNIE: Dion, stop it. This isn't funny. *(timer sounds)*

(In scene 15 the family sits at the table, eating dinner. DAD and ANDREA are glued to the TV; watching a sitcom with lots of laugh tracks. ANNIE enters.)

MOM: Annie, you're late for dinner.

ANNIE: I, uh…

MOM: Well, sit down; you're food's getting cold. *(ANNIE sits down. During a silent pause, audience hears sitcom, punch line, and canned laughter. DAD and ANDREA crack up.)*

ANNIE: Mom, what do you do when… A strange thing happened today. This guy…well, he followed me after school. We were alone, and…

MOM: Annie, What are you trying to say? What happened?

ANNIE: Not *that*, but…

MOM: Whew. You scared me.

ANNIE: Well, he did back me up.

MOM: Oh, he was probably just flirting.

ANNIE: No. Listen to me. We were in the hall alone.

He wouldn't let me leave. He backed me up.

MOM: Annie, stop it. This isn't funny. *(ANNIE stares at MOM. Audience hears laugh track. DAD and ANDREA crack up at the TV. Timer sounds.)*

(In scene 16 CHRIS sits at the black hole, waiting for ANNIE.)

ANNIE: *(enters)* Explain it. What does this all mean? I've got to know.

CHRIS: Well, it's kind of like an invisible friend. He's always there for you, even though nobody else can see him.

ANNIE: What? Things just aren't making sense right now. *(timer sounds)*

(If possible, change lighting here to indicate these scenes aren't necessarily realistic by the way ANNIE interprets them. Scene 17 happens at school.)

BRENDA: *(whacks volleyballs at ANNIE with overhead spikes after each line)* Now that you're off the team, I'm the most valuable player. *(whack)* Why did you quit the team anyway, couldn't hack it? *(whack)* How's student council going, Miss President? You know you only won because nobody in their right mind would vote for Javier. *(whack)* How are you and Sedric? You better hang on to him, because he's the only thing good you've got going for you. *(whack)* You know he's shopping around, and with the way you look…*(whack, timer sounds)*

(In scene 18 ANDREA comes in waving poster-sized report card with "A" on it, skipping around ANNIE and her PARENTS who are already seated at kitchen table eating.)

ANDREA: I got an "A"! I got an "A"!

MOM: Now what did you get?

(ANNIE tries to take bite of food, and it falls off her fork.)

DAD: You can't do anything right, not even eat.

ANNIE: What's going on? *(to herself, as if she knows she's seeing this unrealistically)*

ANDREA: I'm the perfect one.

DAD: Remember, she's only average.

MOM: You mean the Loser. **(Whole family does "L" sign on their foreheads and timer goes off.)**

(In scene 19 CHRIS sits in the black hole.)

ANNIE: *(runs in)* This invisible friend, how do you know he's there?

CHRIS: You can feel him talking to you. It's like this feeling in your heart. Because you know that he's talking to you, but you can't, like, hear a real voice. But you know it's real, for some reason. He's like your best friend, you know he'll never leave you, but it's not like you can really see him there in the first place.

ANNIE: You can hear him, but you can't see him. So what's this feeling?

CHRIS: I can't describe it. You'll know it when it happens.

ANNIE: How do you make it happen?

CHRIS: Uhh...**(timer sounds)**

(In scene 20 all of the school characters walk through and spin ANNIE around when they touch her.)

ANNIE: Help me.

KELLEY: I've got to get the newspaper ready by the deadline. By the way, you just got voted most likely to become a bad memory.

ANNIE: Help me.

JAVIER: I've got to go preside over the student council meeting. **(whacks ANNIE with toy hammer)** That should be your job.

ANNIE: Help me.

BRENDA: I can't help you, chubby. I've got a game.

ANNIE: Help me.

SEDRIC: I don't date people who need help. See ya.

(timer sounds)

(In scene 21 ANNIE is at home watching clips from Charter Rivers commercials. She takes her timer up to DAD (from Charter Commercial, "know someone who's depressed...").

ANNIE: Fix this.

DAD: What's wrong with it?

ANNIE: It's broken. It's running too fast.

DAD: I can't. Honey, it's beyond repair.

MOM: *(enters)* Don't worry about that, we'll just buy a new one. **(timer sounds with a broken clock sound)**

(Clip from Charter Commercial, "If you don't get help at Charter, please get help somewhere.")

(In scene 22 ANNIE and CHRIS meet at the black hole.)

ANNIE: *(enters)* You've got to tell me how this happens. I don't have time to waste.

CHRIS: You've got to believe.

ANNIE: Believe in what?

CHRIS: Well, you know.

ANNIE: Hurry!

CHRIS: There's got to be somebody else who can help you more with this.

ANNIE: No! You tell me.

CHRIS: Look Annie, I've never tried to explain this to somebody else before.

ANNIE: Just do it. I'm counting on you.

CHRIS: Annie, I don't know how.

ANNIE: *(looks at the timer)* It's stopped.

(blackout)

END

The Visit

CAST

- Ashley
- Brad
- Miss Johnson
- Principal (voice)
- Seth
- Derrick
- Mom

- Slip of paper
- Recording of the song "Life Goes On" by PFR
- Bible
- Wastebasket

PROPS

- Recording of the song "The Love I Know" by PFR
- Chairs in rows, for funeral scene
- Recording of the song "I'll Lead You Home" by Michael W. Smith
- Cross

Scene opens on a typical school at the beginning of the day as several students walk into a classroom, talking as they go.

ASHLEY: (running to catch up) Hey, Brad, wait up! How's it goin'?

BRAD: Good. What's up?

ASHLEY: Nuthin'. Hey, have you seen Derrick today?

BRAD: Yeah, he stopped by my house this morning to give me a ride, but I wasn't ready, so I told him I'd catch up with him at school. I haven't seen him yet, though.

ASHLEY: When you see him, tell him I need to talk to him before youth group tonight, okay?

BRAD: When I see him, I'll let him know.

ASHLEY: Hey, I heard the both of you were accepted into Bible college!

BRAD: Yeah.

ASHLEY: Congratulations! Imagine the two of you terrorizing such a nice campus. I hope they're ready for you guys!

BRAD: Cute, real cute. *(They walk into the classroom and sit in their seats.)*

MISS JOHNSON: All right gang, settle down! Has anyone seen Derrick this morning?

BRAD: I saw him earlier this morning, Miss Johnson. He's probably just running a little late.

MISS JOHNSON: Okay. Well, until Mr. Thatcher joins us, let's clear off our desks. It's test time!

(The class moans. MISS JOHNSON passes out the test, and the students begin. MISS JOHNSON notices a student standing in the doorway, crying, and holding a slip of paper. MISS JOHNSON goes over and reads the note. She hugs the student and slowly walks back to the front of the room.)

MISS JOHNSON: (in a muffled, choked-up voice) Class, stop your tests. Put your pencils down. *(waits)* I have some news, and I don't know how to say it.

ASHLEY: Miss Johnson, are you okay? What happened?

MISS JOHNSON: *(tries to regain composure)* This morning, on his way to school, Derrick Thatcher lost control of his car and slid off the road. *(looking at BRAD)* He was killed instantly. I'm sorry.

(BRAD looks in disbelief, then runs frantically from the room. ASHLEY follows.)

ASHLEY: *(calling)* Brad! Wait! Brad!

PRINCIPAL: *(over the loudspeaker)* Students, please stop what you're doing now and listen. You've heard about the loss of Derrick Thatcher this morning. Your parents are currently being notified. We will have counselors in the auditorium for anyone who needs to speak with someone. Tonight our thoughts and prayers are with the Thatcher family.

(In scene two BRAD enters an uncrowded hallway in the school with ASHLEY pursuing him.)

ASHLEY: Brad, wait! Please stop!

BRAD: It's not true! It can't be! I just saw him this morning. They're wrong! It's somebody else, not Derrick!

ASHLEY: *(tries to calm BRAD)* Brad! Brad! *(crying)* It's okay. *(holding him)*

(SETH enters, walking quickly)

SETH: Brad, Ash, you guys okay?

ASHLEY: We're doing all right.

SETH: I'm sorry. I came from the church as soon as I heard.

BRAD: Yeah, well, you heard wrong. It's not him.

SETH: Brad, it was him. There was nothing they could do.

ASHLEY: It's okay, Brad. *(holds him tighter)*

BRAD: *(pushes her away)* No! No, it's not *(hesitates)* It should've been me!

SETH: Brad...

BRAD: *(sobs)* I was supposed to be with him! He was all alone. He died alone.

SETH: Brad, Derrick wasn't alone. He knew that since he gave his life to the Lord, he would never be alone. You know that's true.

BRAD: *(belligerently)* If God was there, why did he let my best friend die? Why didn't he save him?

SETH: He did, and now he lives with God for all eternity. No more pain, no more suffering.

BRAD: *(angrily)* So, I imagine that's supposed to make me feel better?

ASHLEY: Brad, just listen.

SETH: No, Brad, just help you understand a little bit more.

BRAD: *(calmly)* No, I understand. I understand just fine. *(bitterly)* I understand that my best friend is dead, and he shouldn't be! And God did nothing about it! He just let him die. *(BRAD runs off sobbing)*

ASHLEY: *(gets ready to run after him)* Brad!

SETH: *(catches ASHLEY by the arm)* Let him go, Ash. He needs some time to sort things out. We need to pray for him and be here for him, when he's ready.

(Both walk off.)

(In scene three, Derrick's funeral, the song "Life Goes On" by PFR plays in the background. No one talks. Derrick's parents sit in the front row. Other guests sit in the first two rows. Pallbearers enter carrying Derrick's coffin. ASHLEY places Derrick's senior picture on top of the coffin. Once everyone is seated, and the service begins—pastor mouths words, but doesn't speak—the congregation sings a song. As they sing, BRAD enters from the back slowly, and places a flower in front of the picture. He looks at SETH, and they acknowledge each other. BRAD then places his Bible in front of the picture. He goes to Derrick's mother and hugs her. BRAD then exits to the back slowly, looking straight ahead, without expression. Then the scene freezes.)

(Scene four opens the next day with SETH at BRAD's house with BRAD's Bible in hand. He knocks on the door, and Brad's MOM answers.)

SETH: Hi. Is Brad here?

MOM: *(shows fear and concern)* Come on in, Seth. He's in his room. He's been in there since the funeral. He hasn't eaten. I heard him up walking around all night long. I'm scared.

SETH: If it's all right with you, I'd like to try to talk to him.

MOM: *(She nods and shows SETH to BRAD's room; then she leaves.)*

SETH: *(knocks)* Brad? It's Seth. Do you mind if I come in? *(no sound, SETH slowly opens the door to find BRAD standing in the middle of the room holding a jersey)* Hey, how are you doing? Still hanging in there? *(BRAD ignores him)* Well, I just stopped by to drop this off. You accidentally left it yesterday. I thought you might want it back. *(no response from BRAD)* You know, everyone is pretty worried about you; your parents, Ashley, the rest of the youth group, *(pause)* and me. Are you sure you don't want to talk about it? *(pause)* Okay. *(starts to walk off, then turns around)* Listen, we're having youth group tonight at church to talk about it. I'd really like to see

you there. I know everyone else would too. If you can make it, it's at 6:30. *(pause)* Well, I guess I'll see you later then. *(begins to leave)*

BRAD: *(abruptly)* Have you ever lost your best friend before, Seth?

SETH: *(surprised)* No, no, I haven't.

BRAD: Then you have no idea what I'm going through.

SETH: Let me see if I can figure it out. You feel sad and angry at the world—at me, Derrick, and even God. You feel like you're all alone.

BRAD: I am alone! No one knows what I'm feeling! See this jersey? I bought him this for his 16th birthday. This is all I have left! This is all I have left, because God took the rest away from me!

SETH: Brad, that's not true. You will always have the memories you shared together.

BRAD: Memories. Memories of plans we made together. Plans that will never come true because God is punishing me! Well, if God can turn his back on me, then I can turn my back on him! And everyone else for that matter!

SETH: God has not turned his back on you. He loves you with everything he is.

BRAD: Is the only reason you came here is to harass me? Well, I don't need it. I want you to go.

SETH: But Brad...

BRAD: I said go!

(SETH sets the Bible down and leaves the room. When he leaves, he begins to pray.)

SETH: Father, in the name of Jesus, please lay your hand of blessing on Brad tonight. He needs your touch more now than ever.

(*Scene five takes place in BRAD's room. It is night, and he is alone—or so he thinks.*)

BRAD: (*sits in a chair, still holding the jersey in his hand.*) Yeah, I remember the time we got up at, like, 8 a.m. Saturday morning and played one-on-one all day long. We were so tired, we crashed on the living room floor before we even ate dinner. Man, I miss you so much it hurts. There are so many things I wanted to do with you. We were going to go to college together. You were going to be the best man at my wedding someday. Our families were going to take vacations together, and now it's gone. It's all gone. I have nothing left. (*DERRICK quietly enters the room unseen. He moves to the table where Brad's Bible rests, and he gently pushes it to the ground. BRAD walks over and picks it up.*) And all this time, I thought you actually cared about me. Now I realize that you were never really here at all.

(*He puts the Bible in the wastebasket. Derrick picks it up and sets it on his chair, open, before he can sit down. BRAD notices it as he sits down and grabs it like he's ready to throw it, but then stops, sits down, and begins to read the verse aloud.*) And Jesus said to her, "I am the resurrection and the life. He who believes in me will live, even though he dies, and whoever lives and believes in me will never die. Do you believe this?" I don't know what to believe anymore! Why did you take my friend? Why him? (*DERRICK goes over quietly and touches BRAD on the shoulder. BRAD spins around and stares in disbelief.*)

DERRICK: Brad.

BRAD: (*falls over himself in disbelief*) Derrick?

DERRICK: Brad, it's okay.

BRAD: I knew it wasn't true! Where have you been?

DERRICK: (*hesitantly*) Brad, I don't have much time.

BRAD: What do you mean? Time for what? I don't understand. (*BRAD sits, realizing the truth.*)

DERRICK: A lot of people are worried about you.

BRAD: How do you know that?

DERRICK: Let's just say, (**glancing upward**) I have it on good authority.

BRAD: Now what? No, let me guess, you're an angel sent here by God to set me straight, right? Well, I've stopped believing in fairy tales.

DERRICK: Brad, I'm not here to set you straight. That's something only you can do. I'm here to help you find what you've lost.

BRAD: And what would that be?

DERRICK: Your faith.

BRAD: I have none left. I put my faith in God, and he took it away!

DERRICK: Brad, God loves you with all that he is. He never forsakes us, and he'll never leave our side. You should know that better than anyone. Five years ago, you introduced me to a new life— a life through Jesus Christ. Through him and his love, I grew into a person committed to serving God the Father. You helped me to realize what faith truly was, a belief that with him all things are possible. I was living proof of that. Now you tell me that faith no longer has any meaning for you. Those words are not from God the Father, but straight from the Father of Lies. He's using your grief as a way to gain a foothold in your life. Think about it. You know what I'm saying is true.

BRAD: But God took you away from your family, from me.

DERRICK: No, Brad. He simply brought me home. Remember, we do not belong to this world, and God has prepared a place for us to live with him and dwell forever. Earthly death is not the end, only a new beginning.

BRAD: But it still hurts. It's like losing a part of myself.

DERRICK: Lamentations 3:32 says, "Though he brings grief, he will show compassion, so great is his unfailing love." God's never going to give you anything you can't handle through him. He still loves you, and he always will.

BRAD: How could he? I've spent the last few days hating him for what I thought he did to me. How can I go back? He has no reason to forgive me.

DERRICK: Because his love has no boundaries, no conditions. It never fails or keeps records of wrongs. You just need to reach out and take it.

BRAD: How? How do I come back to the one I've hurt so much?

DERRICK: You already know how. He's waiting for you. If you knock, he will open the door.

(BRAD kneels at the side of his bed and sobs)

DERRICK: Just ask from your heart. Remember, he will never leave us, even if we leave him. He'll just wait for our return.

(DERRICK rests his hand on BRAD's shoulder and bows his head in prayer as "The Love I Know" plays softly. As the song ends, BRAD falls asleep beside the bed. DERRICK walks away as BRAD'S MOM enters the room. They pass each other, unnoticed.)

MOM: Brad? Honey, are you okay?

BRAD: Mom, *(hugs her)* I'm sorry for everything.

MOM: Honey, are you all right?

BRAD: *(wipes the tears from his eyes)* I am now. I'm sorry for scaring you. I guess I just got a little sidetracked.

MOM: Are you sure you're okay?

BRAD: *(picks up his Bible)* Yeah, really, Mom. I just needed to sort things out. Hey, Mom, what time is it?

MOM: It's 6:30. Why?

BRAD: *(runs out the door)* I've gotta go. I need to take care of something. *(BRAD begins to run from the room, and then stops at the doorway)* Mom? I love you. *(BRAD leaves the room)*

MOM: I love you too.

(In scene six BRAD enters from rear of the church sanctuary and walks quietly toward the front of the church, eyes fixed on the cross at the front of the room. Play "I'll Lead You Home" by Michael W. Smith in the background. BRAD kneels in front of the cross and prays silently as music plays.

After a few seconds, ASHLEY enters quietly from the rear and stands silently in the aisle. BRAD stands wiping the tears from his eyes. She runs to him and hugs him. SETH and the other youth group members enter from the rear after watching from the doorway, quiet but noticed by the audience. They approach the pair on the stage. SETH stands face to face with BRAD. They comfort each other.

After BRAD hugs SETH, he moves away from the group, unnoticed. He stares at the back of the sanctuary where DERRICK stands watching. They exchange glances and a brief wave good-bye. DERRICK turns and slowly walks out the back of the sanctuary, smiling. BRAD rejoins the group. The group gathers around each other, hugging and comforting each other. Then they form a circle and pray.

END

Without Her Consent

CAST

- Samantha
- Danielle
- Corey

PROPS

- Banner that says PROM NIGHT: A WONDERFUL TONIGHT

● ●

A banner sits on the stage floor. COREY and DANIELLE walk onstage toward the banner.

DANIELLE: Can I see it yet?

COREY: In a minute. I want to make sure it's dry.

DANIELLE: Come on, Corey. You can't keep me in suspense forever.

COREY: It's ready.

DANIELLE: Let me see!

(They pick up the banner.)

DANIELLE: Corey, it's awesome!

COREY: Thank you.

(They set the banner down.)

DANIELLE: I'm so excited! This is going to be the best night of our lives!

COREY: I don't know about the *best* night.

DANIELLE: Oh, come on. You'll have a great time and you know it.

COREY: Yeah, well, my idea of a best night would involve something a little more comfortable than a tuxedo.

DANIELLE: I know—flannel and blue jeans.

COREY: Shouldn't you be getting ready? I thought it was the law that all girls take eight hours to get ready on prom night.

(SAMANTHA walks in timidly.)

DANIELLE: My manicure and pedicure are at two. I've got plenty of time. *(turns, sees SAMANTHA)* Samantha, you're just in time! *(gestures to the room around her)* What do you think?

SAM: *(with no emotion)* Looks great, Danielle.

DANIELLE: Let's not be enthusiastic about it.

SAM: Sorry. Guess I'm not in the mood.

COREY: Are you okay?

SAM: Fine.

DANIELLE: No you're not. I know you too well to believe that.

(DANIELLE gives COREY a hinting glance.)

COREY: I, I'm going to go help Missy with the centerpieces.

DANIELLE: Bye.

(COREY exits.)

DANIELLE: (to Samantha) What's wrong?

SAM: I need to sit down.

(They sit on the floor.)

DANIELLE: Is it about Kevin? *(pause)* He didn't dump you for tonight, did he?

SAM: I dumped him.

DANIELLE: *(surprised)* When did this happen?

SAM: Last night.

DANIELLE: I don't understand. I thought you were all excited about going.

SAM: I don't even care any more.

DANIELLE: What happened?

SAM: Danielle, you swear this doesn't go anywhere but between us?

DANIELLE: Of course.

SAM: I'm so scared right now. I have to tell some one, but I don't want you to think less of me.

DANIELLE: Samantha, you're my best friend. What ever you did, I'm not going to think less of you.

SAM: I didn't do anything. It was more about what I didn't do—what I couldn't stop. *(pause)* You know how I feel about guys and love and, and sex. We were always taught that true love waits, and I believed that with all my heart. I told Kevin how I felt right from the start, so it wasn't like he didn't know. *(another awkward pause)* Things started to get physical with us. It started slowly at first. Just touching on the outside and all. *(stops, trying not to cry)* I didn't do anything to stop it from going further. It seemed so innocent, you know? There wasn't anything specifically forbidding it in the Bible. I thought I could keep it from going further. Then it just sort of happened.

DANIELLE: What happened?

SAM: It was a month ago at his house. We were on the couch kissing, and he started to touch me. It was like we always did, you know? Nothing new. But that night he was so different. He was more aggressive. Then all of a sudden he started to take my clothes off. I tried to pull away but... *(crying)* He was too strong for me to do anything.

DANIELLE: *(pause)* He raped you?

SAM: It hurt so bad. I begged him to stop, but he told me to stop fighting and enjoy it. I was bleeding all over the couch, and he didn't even care! When he finally finished, he kissed me. He told me he knew that I loved him now that I'd let him do it. I wanted to throw up, I felt so sick. He kept telling me everything was okay. All I could do was cry.

(DANIELLE nods.)

DANIELLE: *(letting it sink in)* My gosh. Why didn't you tell someone when it happened?

SAM: Because he told me…he said it was my fault it happened.

DANIELLE: What?

SAM: I was just as involved in the touching and the making out we did. He told me I could have stopped him at any time if I really didn't want it to happen.

DANIELLE: Samantha, it wasn't your fault. He had no right to do this to you. What he did is a crime, and you need to tell someone what happened.

SAM: What good will that do? Everybody loves Kevin. Even my parents. Who's gonna believe a guy like him would rape his own girlfriend? *(pause)* I loved him so much! I trusted him! *(lays her head on DANIELLE's shoulder)* He stole my virginity. And there's nothing I can do to get it back. Why would God allow him to do that to me? How could he let anyone be hurt like that?

DANIELLE: *(hugs SAMANTHA)* I don't know why, Sam. But I know he still loves you, and to him, you're still as pure as the day you were born.

SAM: I want to believe that, Danielle, with all my heart. I just don't know how I can.

(DANIELLE hugs SAM again. Blackout.)

END

Guardian Angel

CAST

- **Tammy**
- **Jessica**
- **Homeless man, William**

PROPS

- **Backpacks**
- **Sandwiches**
- **Money**
- **Crates**
- **Trash cans**
- **Cardboard**
- **Dog (optional)**

It's early evening when girls two enter. Each has a small suitcase and a backpack. They wear warm clothes and look discouraged.

TAMMY: You know, Jessica, nothing I do ever pleases my parents. They want me to get straight A's. I bring home a B+, and they get on my case.

JESSICA: Well at least your parents know you're there. My parents are so busy with their careers, I could be sick and dying and they still wouldn't notice me.

TAMMY: Sometimes I wish I had your problem.

JESSICA: No, you don't, Tammy, I'm telling you—you don't want to know how it feels to have parents who don't care about you.

TAMMY: Well, maybe you're right. But just the same, my parents don't give me room to grow and be myself. I always have to meet some quota or something.

JESSICA: Tammy, I don't think running away is going to solve anything. I've heard so many stories about teenage runaways. They're kind of scary.

TAMMY: That's because they trusted the wrong people and made bad decisions. Besides, anything is better than staying at home.

JESSICA: So, where are we going?

TAMMY: I don't know. I need time to think. Thanks for coming with me. You're a true friend.

JESSICA: Don't take this the wrong way, but I don't think a true friend would have come with you. I should have thought of a way to make you stay.

TAMMY: Nothing was going to make me stay.

JESSICA: Look, Tammy, why don't we just go back? If we leave now we could get back in time for our favorite TV program.

TAMMY: I'm not going back. Listen, I don't know why you're making such a big deal out of it—you're not wanted at home.

JESSICA: At least it's a place to stay. A place with a roof over my head…

TAMMY: Yeah, but no love.

JESSICA: That's not true. My parents love me. They just don't know how to show it.

TAMMY: That's not love to me.

JESSICA: Well, it's better than being alone in a big city. I just feel funny about the whole thing.

TAMMY: Look, you just said how bad it is at home. I bet you've wanted to run away all along, but you just didn't want to do it alone—you needed an extra push. Well, I'm that extra push. We can do it together.

JESSICA: But what if something happens to us?

TAMMY: Nothing's going to happen to us. This is our chance to be free. We don't have to answer to anyone. Not our parents, our teachers, our brothers and sisters—nobody!)

(They sit down on a curb and think for a moment.)

TAMMY: Did you bring anything to eat?

JESSICA: I only brought a couple of tuna sandwiches. *(frowns for a moment)*

TAMMY: What's the matter?

JESSICA: I just remembered my mom was going to make spaghetti for dinner tonight.

(both are deep in thought again)

TAMMY: Yeah, your mom does make great spaghetti. Who cares…Look, I brought a couple of TV dinners. Now all we have to do is find a microwave to put them in.

JESSICA: They just bought a new TV too.

TAMMY: I hope you're not getting cold feet. We've come this far; now let's just go all the way.

JESSICA: *(sighs)* Okay.

TAMMY: Now, how much money did you bring?

JESSICA: Well, after gathering all my allowances and cashing in the aluminum cans, I have thirty-nine dollars. How much do you have?

TAMMY: Forty-seven dollars… Put it together and that gives us…*(hands her money to Jessica)*

JESSICA: Eighty-six dollars. *(puts the money back in her backpack)*

TAMMY: Well, that's a good start.

164

JESSICA: I wonder if my parents will miss me.

TAMMY: Well, I don't know about you, but I'm hungry. How about we eat those tuna sandwiches now?

JESSICA: *(reluctantly)* All right...

(JESSICA opens her backpack and takes out the tuna sandwiches. She hands one to TAMMY, and they begin to eat. While they're eating, they're thinking. Suddenly they hear someone yawning from the background. They're startled and on their guard.)

JESSICA: Did you hear that?

TAMMY: I hope that was you yawning.

JESSICA: No, it wasn't me. No way. It came from back there.

(The HOMELESS MAN suddenly gets up from behind the appropriate props—crates, trash cans, card board, etcetera, possibly with a dog. His clothes are tattered and torn.)

MAN: *(looks at the girls)* Now, I thought I smelled some fish. Smells just like Chicken of the Sea too. *(fixes himself and carefully approaches the two girls, who at this point don't quite know what to do)* Would you by any chance have an extra tuna sandwich? I just woke up and suddenly feel hungry.

(The girls look at each other cautiously. Then they shrug their shoulders in agreement.)

JESSICA: I just happen to have an extra.

(They each encourage the other to give the sandwich to the HOMELESS MAN. Both hesitate, then they do it together.)

MAN: Are you girls a couple of Siamese twins or something? I'm not going to hurt you. I'm just hungry. *(eats the sandwich aggressively while the girls look at each other in disbelief)* Now what are you two girls doing here at this time of night? *(looks around and sees the suitcases and backpacks)* You wouldn't by any chance be running away, would you?

TAMMY: Yes, we are. Now if you don't mind, we must be on our way.

MAN: You know you shouldn't be running away like this—you could run into some really strange people. *(laughs)* Hey, I may be a bum, but I do have a sense of humor.

TAMMY: Thanks for your concern, but we've got to get out of here. *(Girls start to pick up their belongings.)*

MAN: Wait a second. Why don't you just stay for a minute or so? People don't talk to me. It's been a long time since I had a decent conversation with another person.

(The girls look at each other, shrug their shoulders in agreement, and set their stuff down.)

TAMMY: All right, but just for a minute. And please keep your distance, okay? No offense, but...

MAN: I know, I know. I smell bad, right? And I look bad, too. I'm sorry, but they canceled my subscription to GQ magazine.

(The girls laugh unintentionally.)

MAN: So, what is life like out there in the real world?

TAMMY: It's bad, okay? In fact, you, me, and my friend here may have something in common.

MAN: What do you mean?

JESSICA: You don't have a home, and we're not wanted in ours.

MAN: Wow, that's pretty sad. I may be better off than you, if you think about it. What's the problem?

TAMMY: Look, I'm sorry, Sir, but the minute's up, okay? We've got to go.

(They get ready to leave then stop. JESSICA slowly gives the rest of the sandwiches to the HOMELESS MAN. The HOMELESS MAN begins to eat another sandwich. He sits on the curb and continues to eat. The two girls start to walk away again. Then they stop, thinking. They look at each other and nod their heads in agreement. They go back to the HOMELESS MAN and sit next to him, one on each side. He notices them but continues to eat as the girls watch closely.)

MAN: What's wrong? Haven't you ever seen a bum eat before?

(The two girls smiles vaguely.)

JESSICA: Look, you don't have to eat fast. We have more food if you want it.

TAMMY: *(resisting the smell)* Can I ask you something?

MAN: Sure.

TAMMY: When was the last time you took a bath?

(The HOMELESS MAN thinks for a moment.)

MAN: 1993…

(The girls' faces show their shock.)

MAN: I'm just kidding. But I don't get to bathe that often. So when I do, I take a good long bath.

JESSICA: Don't you have a home?

MAN: I had one, but it was taken away because I couldn't afford the payment anymore.

TAMMY: Well, don't you have any relatives or something?

MAN: I have a mother up in San Francisco… We sort of lost communication, though…

(They all stop to think.)

MAN: My mother was a great lady. She used to say that life was like a box of chocolates—it's just going to melt away. She said you can tell a lot about people just by the shoes they wear.

(The two girls look at his shoes and are sad.)

MAN: Enough about me, though. Tell me, what could make two sweet little girls like you run away from home?

TAMMY: Things just are not working out between my parents and me.

JESSICA: Same here.

(The HOMELESS MAN laughs.)

JESSICA: What's so funny?

TAMMY: Why are you laughing?

MAN: I'm sorry. Sorry I laughed, but I don't think that's a valid reason to hit the road.

TAMMY: It's more than that.

JESSICA: Did you ever have problems with your parents when you were young?

MAN: Oh, sure we had problems, but I never wanted to run away. Life would have been much too hard.

JESSICA: Well how did you solve things? *(thinks hard while she listens)*

MAN: We just worked things out.

TAMMY: It's not always as easy as it sounds.

MAN: I know it's not. We've got this thing we can't get rid of called "flesh" and that always gets in the way.

TAMMY: Well, my parents are the pick of the litter. Nothing will ever please them.

JESSICA: Well, how did you resolve things?

MAN: We just did. I don't know any magical solution. It's not written down like a recipe. You just resolve things. It may take days, months, and sometimes even years, but you get through it togeth-

er. That's what family is all about. People are always going to be related to one another, and no matter how bad you may think it is, it'll get better. I guarantee it.

(They all think for a moment.)

JESSICA: When was the last time you saw your mother?

MAN: Oh gosh, it must be at least 22 years.

TAMMY: But you know where she lives, don't you?

MAN: Yes.

JESSICA: Then why don't you just go visit her?

MAN: I can't afford to with my budget. I'm only making 32 dollars a week, and that's a good can week. I use all that money to get me through the next week. *(laughs)* I guess you can say I live paycheck to paycheck. I'll need at least 86 dollars to get there by plane.

JESSICA: Eighty-six dollars?

(The HOMELESS MAN nods humbly. The two girls look at each other, think, and nod their heads in agreement. JESSICA takes their money out of her backpack.)

JESSICA: Listen…um…gosh, you never even told us your name. We didn't tell you ours either. My name is Jessica.

TAMMY: And my name is Tammy.

MAN: It's nice to meet the two of you. My name is William.

JESSICA: We would love to see you make it back to San Francisco to see your mom. And we just happen to have eighty-six dollars with us…

TAMMY: And we want you to have it.

(JESSICA hands the money to WILLIAM, who is touched as he humbly accepts the money.)

MAN: I don't know what to say.

TAMMY: You said enough already. Thank you for everything, but we have to go now. *(They gather their things and get ready to leave.)* Hurry, Jessica! If we hurry, we can get home in time to see our favorite TV program.

(They say good-bye to WILLIAM and leave. WILLIAM is left alone.)

MAN: Wow! *(firmly grabs the money and prays silently for a few seconds. Then he gets up and sings softly.)* Oh how I love Jesus. Oh how I love Jesus. Oh how I love Jesus. Because he first loved me. *(walks off stage.)*

END

The Only Way Out

CAST

• Chuck • Sergio • Glory

PROP

• Cardboard box decorated to look like a locker

CHUCK: *(to SERGIO)* Did you hear that? It sounded like someone crying for help!

SERGIO: No, I didn't hear anything. Come on!

CHUCK: *(looks around)* I heard it again! Someone needs help! *(turns to go up center stage)*

SERGIO: Where are you going? The gas might explode any minute! You'll be killed!

CHUCK: I don't care! I have to find her! *(goes up center stage)*

SERGIO: Be careful! *(exits)*

CHUCK: *(stops up center stage)* Come on, yell again. *(loudly)* Where are you?

GLORY: Help! Someone, please! I'm in the locker rooms!

CHUCK: Hang on! I'm coming!

(CHUCK approaches GLORY down stage right. She's in pain and tries to get her leg out from underneath locker.)

GLORY: *(as he reaches her)* Oh, thank goodness! I thought everyone was gone!

CHUCK: *(surveying the area around her)* What happened here? *(kneels beside her leg)* Are you all right?

GLORY: I think so. When the earthquake happened, these lockers fell on my leg, but now I can't get them off.

CHUCK: Well, the earthquake also caused a crack in the gas line, so we have to get out right now! Can you feel your foot?

GLORY: Yes, it hurts a lot, but I can't move it.

CHUCK: All right. Just hold still, I'll try to move these lockers. *(tries to move invisible lockers)* They won't budge. I think they're wedged.

GLORY: *(frantic)* What do you mean, they're wedged? You can lift it off. Try again!

CHUCK: *(tries again but fails)* It's no use. I'm sorry.

GLORY: You're sorry! You're sorry! Oh, I'm sure you're sorry, because I'm going to die!

CHUCK: You won't die. Maybe someone else in the building can help us.

GLORY: Maybe. Let's call for help. *(They yell for help, but then GLORY stops.)* No one is coming. They've all left!

CHUCK: No, they haven't. We just have to have a little faith.

GLORY: Oh, sure, I have faith. I have faith that the gas line will explode, and I'm going to die!

CHUCK: You will not die! Someone might still be left who can help us. Wait here. I'll be right back. *(starts to leave)*

GLORY: No! Don't leave me!

(CHUCK stops.)

GLORY: If you go, I'm sure I'll die.

(CHUCK turns around.)

GLORY: Stay here and keep trying. Someone will hear us eventually, and I know you can move these lockers. Please stay.

CHUCK: All right. I will. How's your foot doing? *(begins to move the lockers)*

GLORY: I don't know, I can't feel it anymore, but I'm sure it's still there.

CHUCK: *(tries to sound cheerful)* Well, that's good! *(As he continues, she calls for help. Then he tries to pull her foot out.)*

GLORY: Ow! Stop! I can feel that! It hurts!

CHUCK: *(stops and sits down beside her, obviously tired)*

GLORY: This is ridiculous. We shouldn't both die! Go on, and save yourself.

CHUCK: No.

GLORY: What? But that's crazy! If you stay, you'll die!

CHUCK: I have to keep trying.

GLORY: But you have to go!

CHUCK: I will not leave you!

GLORY: *(pause)* I don't understand. Why did you come?

CHUCK: Why? Because when I heard you crying for help. I couldn't leave knowing someone was still inside that I could have saved.

GLORY: But weren't you afraid you would die?

CHUCK: The thought crossed my mind, but it didn't matter.

GLORY: *(laughs)* Well, if that had been me, I wouldn't have risked my life for a total stranger. So why did you?

CHUCK: Because a long time ago, a man named Jesus Christ gave his life for me and saved me from a terrible death, so how could I do any less?

GLORY: Oh, I've heard of Jesus before, but I didn't think I needed him.

CHUCK: Everybody needs Jesus. Don't you think you need him right now?

GLORY: *(desperately)* We need somebody to save us!

CHUCK: Exactly! You need somebody to save you from a terrible death. The sin in your life is like this locker. It weighs you down and causes you pain, and because of it, you eventually die. And you may die, but you don't have to go to hell. You see, God is perfect, and we're sinners, and he can't let sinners into heaven. So he sent Jesus, his son, to die for all the bad things we've done. If we put our faith in him, he'll forgive us, and we'll be in Heaven with him when we die.

GLORY: Jesus would save me and forgive me?

CHUCK: And love you.

GLORY: *(nervously)* I want to be with Jesus when I die, but how do I ask him?

CHUCK: Just talk to him. He's listening.

GLORY: God, if you can hear me, I just want to thank you for what you did for me. I want you to come into my heart and forgive me of all the stuff I've done. I can't wait to be in heaven with you, Jesus, when I die.

CHUCK: Amen.

GLORY: *(looks back at him)* Thank you. *(pause)* Now go. Please don't stay here. You helped save my life today. Now save your own. I'm not afraid to die any more.

CHUCK: *(looks around fretting, then turns back)* No. I can't. Besides, Jesus once said, "I'll never leave you, nor forsake you." And I shouldn't either.

(The lights go out and an explosion is heard. When the lights come back on, the two huddle together on the stage.)

CHUCK: *(looks up slowly)* What happened? Where are we?

GLORY: *(moves her foot, then grabbing it)* My foot! It doesn't hurt any more! What happened to the lockers? *(looks around)*

CHUCK: *(stands up and points downstage left)* Hey, look! Isn't that light beautiful?

GLORY: It is, and listen. *(she pauses and stands)* It almost sounds like angels singing to us. *(turns to him and smiles rapturously)* Where are we?

CHUCK: I'm not sure, but I have an idea. *(starts to walk downstage left and then turns around)* So come on! *(offers his hand)* I think someone's been waiting for us.

(They exit hand in hand.)

END

Does your youth group's dramatic talent reside in only one or two students? Or do you want to raise interest in starting a drama ministry? In both cases, a monolog is your ticket! These one-person scripts require few or no costumes or props—yet they can be as powerful as a three-act play. Topics range from silly to serious, so check the Scripts by Topic index on page 7 to find one that covers your group's interests best.

WAITING FOR THE COMMERCIAL

Prepare your group for an intimate and serious look at how an abortion affects the guy in a relationship. This young man gives a heartfelt plea about the choice he helped make to abort his baby. The monologue on page 176 speaks of regret and a surreal wish to turn the whole situation into a TV story with a neatly wrapped up ending instead of the pain of reality. *Curt Cloninger*

THE VALLEY GIRL HISTORY OF THE WORLD FROM CREATION TO, LIKE, THE BIRTH OF CHRIST

Oh my gosh! Like, she's back! Straight from the valley and with a seminary degree behind her, Buffy presents her dissertation on all of creation! Believe it or not, page 178 goes all the way from Adam and Eve right up to the birth of Christ. History will never be the same after this totally rad version gets told. And, like, the best part's that it takes no props, no set, and only one actor! Of course there's that whole memorizing-a-whole-bunch-of-lines thing but, fer sure you have someone who can do it! *Gary Cantwell*

GENERATION X

A Nike commercial couldn't say it better than this. A whole generation out there is searching for something with substance—something with meaning inside and out. The monologue on page 181 runs the gamut of emotions from angry to frightened to pleading—all packed with passion. Not wanting to be a Christian isn't the problem. Wanting to be something genuine and have examples who aren't hypocritical is. Choose a strong speaker to portray this character and offer this unique perspective. *Lara Willers*

Waiting for the Commercial

(A young man speaks directly to the audience. He speaks from his heart, not overly dramatically, just with a great deal of resignation.)

It all seems so easy on TV, you know? People meet in a bar, on the street, or in some kind of funny romantic sort of setting. They fall in love or out of love. They're lonely, or they just have the hots for each other. They go somewhere. They, you know, fool around. And then there's a two-minute break for a commercial. Somebody comes on the tube trying to sell you an Audi or a piece of the rock or a Michelob Light. Who says you can't have it all? And then there they are again, and everything's fine. Or, if everything's not fine you just wait until next week. Everything gets worked out before the next episode, you know? It all seems so easy.

People don't get pregnant too much on TV. In fact, when it comes to sex, nobody hardly ever pays. Nobody ever gets hurt. If they do, the pain fits nicely into a 30-minute time slot. Then they just break away to a commercial. You know? You know what's weird? It's weird when somebody up in New York messes up in the control room, and they run the same commercial twice. Twice, right in a row. It sort of embarrasses you. Like, it hits you, the second time through, "Oh yeah, this is a commercial." You're whistling the tune, right? But the second time through, you're thinking, "This ain't necessarily so, but I bought it the first time, hook, line and sinker." It's embarrassing.

"Who says you can't have it all?" I say it. I say it. I'm not on TV. I mean, I've been waiting for the commercial, but it just doesn't seem to come. You know, somebody with a cheerful voice breaks into my crappy situation with a nice little jingle, pushing some fast food fix, and then the show's over till next week, when we discover that amazingly, everything's worked out fine. Well, I waited till next week, and everything didn't work out fine, you know? She just kept on being pregnant. Four weeks, five weeks, six weeks pregnant. Everything is very unfine. It's like the second time through the commercial, and it hit me: You can't really have it all. That's a lie.

So you do something about it. Look, I don't really believe in abortion, but I did drive her to the clinic. It's amazing what a little pressure will do to your beliefs, huh? I guess it makes you do things you don't really want to do. I just never thought it would end up like this. I thought it would be like the movies or television. You know: You meet a gal. You hit it off. You date awhile. You go out to dinner. You go to the movies and watch some folks on the screen who hit it off, and they go home and hop in the sack. It seems like the natural thing to do. I guess they just don't forget to take their pill, or something on TV. Or maybe their clinics are off camera. I don't know. I don't know. I don't know what to think. For whatever it's worth, I guess I thought I loved her. That seemed like a good enough ticket for admission into bed. It always is on TV, anyway.

But I don't think I loved her. Oh, I guess I loved her enough to drive her to the clinic, but not enough to be a daddy. And probably not enough to see her anymore. I just didn't think sex was gonna be this complicated. Maybe if I get calloused, things will get simpler. I don't know. Something's got to change. I can't go on like this.

Look, I know you're thinking I'm a jerk. Right. Tell me something I don't already know. "The beer commercial is about to come on, and who says you can't have it all? Next week is a whole new episode." I'll swallow that, hook, line, and sinker. That's what I'm really ready to hear.

END

The Valley Girl History of the World from Creation to, Like, the Birth of Christ

Okay, so here's like, you know, how the world began, ya know, billions of years ago. No, I mean like millions. Wait—was it thousands? Who cares? Anyway, in the beginning some people think the earth was made with, like, this Big Bang. I'm like, "Yeah, right. Whatever!" The Bible says, like, God just said it, and it happened. So I guess it was more like the Big Mouth.

Can you imagine making something happen just by talking? I'm like "That is *so* cool! I could do, like, *so much* every day!" I wonder if that would work on housework and stuff. I'm all like, "Let my room be clean! Let the dishes be put away!" Reality check! Anyway, God made the world. It took, ya know, like, maybe a week, and then God was all, "This is so tight. I'm takin' a day off."

So, then there was that whole deal with, like, Adam and Eve and the apple and that slimy thing and God is all, "Thou sinneth! Thou art banished from the garden!" And Eve must have been all, "What*ever*! I'm going shopping for some clothes. I don't have a thing to wear." Well, I don't know, but that's what I would've been like.

So, then Adam and Eve, they had a bunch of rug rats and their rug rats had rug rats, and well, you know. Anyway, it got to where there was a whole bunch of people on the earth, and they were, like, all screwed up, except for this one guy, Noah. He thought God was, like, totally tight, even if he did make Noah build this humongous boat in the middle of nowhere. But everybody else was all, "Duh, God who?" And God's like, "I don't *think* so". And then it rained and rained big time and yada yada yada, and everybody, like, dies except for Noah, his family, and all the fuzzy little animals. But I've always wondered—was Noah even thinking when he let spiders and snakes and stuff on the boat? That was so lame!

Anyway, then Noah's family, like, did the complete rug rat thing again, and yada yada yada, then Abraham was born. He was, like, this complete dude who lived near Kuwait. But I think it was, like, before that Saddam guy was around and had that nasty golf tournament, you know, the Golf War. Anyway, so God was all thinking Abraham was, like, to die for. So God told Abe to move to Israel, but it, like, wasn't Israel yet. It was just all dirt and grass and mountains and stuff. And God told Abe that all this land was his forever and ever and made him promise to do that whole rug rat thing all over again. So yada yada yada, Isaac, Jacob, Joseph.

So this is, like, 2000 B.C. and that's about when they built Stonehenge in England. You know, that, like, big pile of rocks that everybody gets all hyper about. I mean, what's the big deal? My little brother could so completely do that.

Anyway, that's so totally beside the point. Where was I? Oh yeah. Joseph...

So Joseph's brothers really, like, think Joseph's a total dork and, like, sell him to be a slave in Egypt. I wonder if you can still do that today? Anyway, eventually everybody in the whole world runs out of food, and Joseph has it all. He became, like, the Ronald McDonald of Egypt. So his whole family figures he's not such a total dork after all, and they move in with him. And of course they do the whole rug rat thing again and yada yada yada. Now there's a million or two Jews in Egypt.

And did you know the pyramids had been built, like, a thousand years before they even got there? And what was *that* all about, those pyramids? *What* is the point? I mean did they have a life, or what?

Anyway, Joseph's family, the Jews, somehow they all wound up being slaves in Egypt until this guy Moses comes along and goes, "I don't *think* so!" to Pharaoh Fawcett who was, like, the major dude in Egypt–I think he was bald. Anyway, Pharaoh got on the bad side of Moses, who was, like, this big movie star, special effects guy, so it turned out bad for the Egyptian dude, like completely.

So the Jews left Egypt and went through the Red Sea staying, like, totally dry. I *so* don't know how they did that! I think God had something to do with it. What's his deal? I mean, first he floods them, then he keeps them dry. Whatever! But then they all go, "Duh, God who?" and hang out in the desert for, like 40 years. Can you imagine what that would do to your complexion?

So eventually they wind up back in Israel, the land that God promised to Abraham, except, like, there's other people there now, so this guy Joshua, who's like the Schwarzkopf of the Jews, kicks some serious *be-*hind and goes, "Leave or we'll kill you, and your little dog Toto, too." And I guess God is, like, on their side because the Jews win *big time*. And they all go, "Yeah God!" and get back to that whole rug rat thing again. So now we're at about 1400 B.C.

So I'm gonna skip about 400 years here. 'Cause, like, nothing happened. I mean King Tut died in Egypt and wrote that cool song. And Samson was, like, the Clint Eastwood of Israel. He's like, "Go ahead, make my day." And he had this awesome hair. And then, like that whole Trojan horse thing happens. And some Chinese guy invents multiplication and geometry. I'm like, "Thank you very much, major dork. Get a life!"

But then in about 1000 B.C. this big dude Goliath goes, "You Jews are a bunch of wimps!" And this little Jewish sheep guy goes, "Are not!" And Goliath goes, "Are too!" And David, he's the sheep guy, he goes, "Are not!" and pulls out his slingshot and, like, *Bam!*, gets the big ugly dude right between the eyes. And David goes "My God's bigger than your god! Nanny-nanny boo boo!" And before you know it, the little sheep guy is King of Israel, which is, like, all the land God promised to that dead guy Abe and all his rug rats forever and ever.

So David was, like, this *way* cool king. Except for this one deal with a lady who took a bath on the roof. What was she *thinking*? I mean do you really think people aren't gonna look? Anyway, David was like a colossal dork and, like, had her husband killed. Was he even thinking?

Anyway God forgives them, and they have some rug rats, and one of them named Solomon becomes King when David croaks. Solomon was this completely smart dude and built this, like, totally awesome church, but they called it a temple back then. And Solomon had, like, hundreds of wives. Can you imagine what his MasterCard bill was like? Anyway, when he died, his sons messed everything up, and Israel divided in half. So now we've got, like, Israel in the North and Judah in the South. One of them is bad and the other is worse, I don't remember which is which.

Meanwhile in the rest of the world, the Chinese figure out astronomy, which is *so* better than geometry. And

Homer writes the Odyssey, which is, I guess, what he did before the Simpsons. And they start ice skating in Europe, which is awesome because you get to wear these cool outfits. Except for Tonya Harding, who's like the mother of all dorks. Oh, that reminds me, the first Olympics were held in Greece in 776 B.C. And did you know that in the Olympics back then they didn't wear any outfits at *all*, if you know what I mean. How *weird*! I guess that's why they hang the medals around your neck instead of pinning them to your shirt.

So anyway, back to the Jews, who were divided between, like, Israel and Judah. Eventually they were both all, "Duh, God who?" and God's all, "I don't *think* so!" and they both got kicked out of the land God promised to Abe and his rug rats forever and ever. And when they were getting booted out, this guy Isaiah, who was, like, a prophet told the Jews that God was gonna be mad at them for awhile but that things would eventually chill and that God would send them a new major leader dude called the Messiah who would, like, really solve all their problems forever. The Jews are all, "I can handle that." But the hard part was that they had to wait and wait and wait.

Anyway, while they were waiting, there was this cool guy Daniel who was like a Jewish lion tamer, or something, in Babylon. I guess they called it that because the people would just babble on and on about stuff. Don't you hate when people do that? Then this fat old Buddha guy becomes a major dude in India. Aesop becomes, like, the Mr. Rogers of ancient Greece. And Confucius makes fortune cookies in China. I'm not sure, but I think he makes up stuff to put on little pieces of paper in the cookies to make them sell better, because, you know, I don't think they taste that good anyway.

So, back to the Jews. A bunch of them come back to Jerusalem in about 450 B.C. They're, like, building a new temple and a big wall. They hang out waiting and waiting for this Messiah guy. I mean, what is his problem? They've been waiting for, like 300 years—no joke.

While they're waiting, Greece, like, decides it's really hot stuff. You know, those guys, Socrates, Aristotle, Plato (I so love that clay stuff he invented, especially how you can, like, make really cool animals. I can make a totally radical snake.) And then there was this one Greek soldier dude, Alexander, who thought he was so cool he called himself Alexander the Great. I would have been all, "Excuse me? Can you move over? I can't see because your big head is so in the way!"

Anyway the Greeks get a little cocky and before you know it this Roman guy named Julius Caesar takes over and gets appointed, like, Emperor for Life, God of Everything, and Maker of All Salads. I mean, can you believe it? He's all, "Bow down and worship me, you mortal peons!" Get real! Anyway, some of his buds are all, "I don't *think* so" and go like, "Mr. Caesar, meet Mr. Knife. *Umph*! " But Rome was still ruling the world like a *big* dog, and they're, like, the biggest world power *ever*. I mean practically the whole world was ruled by Rome, and they're all speaking the same language and paying taxes big time. These Roman guys with their little short skirts ran even Israel, which God promised to that Jewish guy Abe and his rug rats forever and ever.

Of course, the Jews are totally ticked at the Romans for making their life miserable, and they're wondering about God, because that Messiah dude hasn't showed. And it's been, like, over 700 years since Isaiah said he was gonna come! So the Jews are totally hoping the Messiah will come and be all, "I don't *think* so" to the Romans. Then the Jews will be, like, completely the *big* dogs for a while.

So Marc Antony and Cleopatra do their little thing—isn't that romantic? Except they lose, commit suicide, and Rome conquers Egypt. And then the Romans make Herod the Great. What is it with this "the great" thing, like, King of Judea, which is what they started calling Israel.

And then a Jewish girl named Mary gets engaged to Joseph, and they have a baby boy in a barn on Christmas Eve. Wouldn't you hate having a birthday on Christmas? That would be *so* not fun! I mean, a rip-off, *bigtime*! I *know* you're only getting half as many presents. Anyway, like, that's the birth of Christ and that's it.

END

Generation X

(seriously)

I am Generation X.
I am alone.
There is no one else around me.

(voice rising)

I am Generation X.
There is no one I can trust.
There is no one who is real.

(louder, annoyed)

I am Generation X!
I feel no love.
These momentary highs of happiness leave me
    empty inside.

(calm)

My family, my friends, my life; everything to me,
    are all just meaningless parts of life.
Is there really a God?
Is he the King of the Universe or just a figure
    carved in stone?

(mocking)

Or maybe I am God.
Maybe I control the world with my fingertips.

Or maybe I have no boundaries.
Maybe I am free to set my own standards, make my
    own rules, live my own life.

(almost frightened)

What is my future?
What will become of me?
Does this crazy life I live truly have a meaning?

And does this God know, or does he really just not
    care?

(fretful, agitated)

I don't know where to go.
I don't know where to turn.
And I don't know who to turn to.
Everyone keeps telling me where to go, and what
    to do, and what to believe.

(painful)

But I'm so tired, so tired!
I want to escape this pain with everything I've got!

(mocking)

This world is *so full of hypocrites!*
They know nothing.
They too, toss and turn in their beds at night,
    wondering how to make sense of all this.
I have no reason to live by the standards they
    make!

(angry)

I am Generation X!
I refuse to live life this way!
They tell me where to go. They tell me what to
    believe!
And yet, all I want is for them to tell me where
    they go. What they do. What they believe.

(pleading)

Please, is this so hard?
I have not lived, I do not know!
Please, someone, show me. Show me.

END

READER'S THEATER

The actors read their lines instead of memorizing, but don't get the idea that these are lightweight in content. These sketches cover a wide range of subjects from the Old and New Testament to hot topics like racism and discrimination that can overwhelm today's students. Some are powerful and to the point and some, like the modern-day Cinderella, are just for fun!

THEY'RE NOT LIKE US

ACTS 10:34-35

We'd all like to forget that racism and discrimination still have a strong foothold in our society. The sketch on page 187 hits this issue head on with a creative and captivating example of what happens if we don't try to stop prejudice. The hate builds up one piece at a time.

In the background a dialogue runs about everyday stereotypes and prejudices used against people. The words are harsh but still suitable for all audiences. While a tape plays this dialogue, the characters build with each new vignette. By the end they have built a box they can't escape from.

Use this sketch with caution. Be sure to give enough explanation at the end so you don't leave any room for misinterpretation. The sketch combines powerful imagery with words that are familiar to too many people. The sketch intends to belittle as many peoples and groups as possible. If you want you can tailor it to fit more appropriately for your particular area.

Acts 10:34-35 tells us that God does not show favoritism. Read in context, these verses follow on the heels of Peter learning not to be prejudiced against the Gentiles. Scripture gives us no greater mandate against such behavior. This sketch should leave people thinking about even the smallest comments they make. *Jeff Bursch*

WHERE IS GOD?

Information bombards us constantly in this day of video and multimedia everything. This stage is no exception. The intense reader's theatre on page 192 throws around all of the hot topics that can overwhelm students. When Jesus' words interrupt the rush of information, the sketch takes a distinct turn. He is loyal. He is constant. He won't hurt you or leave you. Most of all, he cries with you, he hurts for you, he suffered and died for you. That message closes this disturbing but ultimately hopeful piece.

You can precede or follow this presentation with musical selections or hymns and opportunities for prayer and reflection. Some suggestions are "Where Is God?" by Church of Rhythm to open and "He Won't Let You Go" by The Kry to close. Do not read the parenthetical scripture references aloud.

Cast members wear signs to let the audience know which life situation they represent. *Steve Hoekstra*

REMOTELY ENTERTAINING

This fast-paced surf through channels will keep you laughing. As our couch potato flips from station to station, the dialogue creates a hilarious running commentary with totally unrelated conversations tying together. The sketch on page 196 is your instruction book for operating the remote. You'll only need to get off the couch to gather costumes to help tell the characters apart.

Line the cast up across the stage, preferably behind a curtain while the emcee reads the introduction. If no curtain is available, the characters should come on stage and freeze after the introduction. Characters don't interact with each other at any time during the production. They simply say their own lines until they are cut off by the imaginary remote control. Each time they're cut off, they freeze until the next time they speak. *Bonnie Zimmer*

FOR GOD SO LOVED

JOHN 3:16

Sometimes messages we've heard hundreds of times hit us the hardest. The sketch on page 198 offers a powerful and to-the-point readers' theatre rendition of John 3:16.

Every line comes straight from scripture, and they combine to present the message of God's love and desire to be with us.

Schedule a rehearsal with enough time to run through lines and work on the timing. Your students can hold the scripts, but they should be familiar with the lines. For Christians, most of this is a passionate reminder of what God promises. For non-Christians, it's an invitation to a personal relationship with God. Whether you use this sketch as part of a lesson or as the entire lesson, go back through the script and discuss what each scripture means to the people in your group. Readers should not read the Scripture references during the performance. *Maranda Kneep*

They're Not Like Us

CAST
- Carol
- Sara
- Hank
- Joey
- Gary

PROPS
- PVC pipe and connecting joints to build a five-foot by five-foot box

---

This drama illustrates the effect of racism and prejudice. Two things happen simultaneously as this skit unfolds. First, a recorded tape plays with the voices of all the participants reading the script. On the tape they discuss different groups, races, and stereotypes. As they talk about each group, they reveal their prejudice. The dialogue continues conversationally on the tape, going through every stereotype one can think of. It's one long conversation of bigotry and prejudice. Following each section someone says, "They're not like us."

While the tape plays the people whose voices are on the tape enter and begin to silently construct something. Using PVC pipe and connecting joints they begin to put something together. The audience is both listening to the tape of stereotypes and watching the actors make something on stage. What the actors are making remains unclear until the very end when they put everything together. By the end of the tape, the actors have constructed a cage out of the piping with themselves inside. The completion of the cage and the end of the tape come at the same time with the actors joining the taped voices in saying, "They're not like us. They're not like us. They're not like us."

This sketch illustrates that prejudice not only places others in a box, but it puts us in a box by limiting our conception of the world. Practice reading before you record the tape and have good recording equipment. The cage should be about five feet by five feet with five actors working to construct it. This script is divided into five parts but could be adapted to fit your situation.

CAROL: Did you see that new girl at school today?

JOEY: Oh, yeah, what a prep!

SARA: Does that girl live at the Gap or what? And

easy on hair spray, girl.

CAROL: Preppies and snobs—I can't stand 'em. *(mockingly)* "We live in the suburbs. My daddy just bought me a cell phone."

JOEY: "We're going to the mall in my new car to buy clothes with my daddy's credit card."

SARA: There are so many snobs in this school.

GARY: They're not like us.

JOEY: Hey, check out Dave over there.

HANK: What a grunger. Dude, Nirvana rules!

JOEY: *(sarcastically)* Nice clothes!

HANK: When's the last time you think he took a bath?

SARA: He's probably going to ride his skateboard to go see his other druggie friends.

GARY: Yeah, those guys never saw a brain cell they couldn't destroy.

SARA: Or a gas fume they didn't inhale?

GARY: You can tell just by the way they dress that they're potheads.

JOEY: Man, they're not like us.

HANK: You know what I hate?

GARY: What?

HANK: Fat people.

GARY: Like John in chemistry. Oh, yeah, he makes me sick.

HANK: Fat people are so lazy.

CAROL: They're disgusting.

JOEY: I can't even look at them.

CAROL: Yeah, but sometimes I'll just stare at one of them for a long time. Just to make 'em mad.

SARA: How can they even stand to live with themselves?

GARY: They're not like us.

GARY: Did you see that new Jap girl at lunch?

CAROL: She's Korean.

HANK: No, she's Chinese.

SARA: No, I think she's Vietnamese.

GARY: Ah, what's the difference, they're all the same.

CAROL: No kidding, with their cameras and squinty eyes.

HANK: I don't even like to be around them.

SARA: Yeah, there's just something about 'em that's creepy.

GARY: Hey, let's face it—they're not like us.

HANK: They're almost as bad as Mexicans.

JOEY: Lazy, drunk, beaners.

HANK: They come up here and take away our jobs.

JOEY: You know, our country wouldn't be broke if the Mexicans weren't here.

SARA: They should just put up a wall at the border and shoot people who try to cross it.

GARY: There's so many of them, it's not like it would matter.

HANK: They're just not like us, you know?

JOEY: You know who the most annoying people are, though?

GARY: Who?

JOEY: White people.

HANK: No kidding. White people have it so easy. They get everything given to them. And if they see something they want that isn't theirs, they just take it.

CAROL: And they're all prejudiced. They see a white pillowcase, and the next thing you know they've got it over their head and they're burning a cross.

SARA: I hate white people.

JOEY: They're not like us.

SARA: Hey, look at that! Isn't that Kristin?

GARY: She's a preacher's kid.

HANK: *(sarcastically)* She knows how to have a good time.

JOEY: Religious people make me sick.

SARA: I saw her talking to Eric the other day. Eric, that guy is such a geek.

GARY: I didn't think he talked to anyone but his computer.

HANK: You need an encyclopedia to understand him.

JOEY: Get a life! He spends his Friday nights at the library with all the other geeks. It's like Nerds are Us.

SARA: Man, they're not like us.

GARY: I can't believe how many black people got into this school.

CAROL: Yeah, why can't they just go back to Africa where they came from?

GARY: They're just a bunch of ignorant gangsters. Saggin' their pants, listening to Rap.

CAROL: Doin' drugs and gang bangin'.

GARY: The world doesn't need people like that.

HANK: You know, they're all on welfare.

SARA: Really?

HANK: Oh yeah, all of them. They don't work. They just sit around and collect their government checks. They're all just getting rich off the government.

GARY: Man, those people are not like us.

CAROL: There are just too many foreigners in our country.

HANK: I know what you mean. Have you seen that guy that works at the gas station down the street?

CAROL: Yeah, what's his problem?

HANK: I think he's some kind of Arab or something. Every time I get gas there I think he might blow my car up or something.

GARY: Why's that?

HANK: You know those Arabs are all crazy, don't you? They got this weird religion where you have to kill people to go to heaven or something.

JOEY: They shouldn't let them into our country at all.

CAROL: They're definitely not like us.

JOEY: Isn't the janitor at school an Arab?

CAROL: No, he's an Indian.

JOEY: You mean like cowboys and Indians?

CAROL: No, he's from India.

JOEY: That's the same thing, right?

CAROL: I don't think so, but I don't like him either.

JOEY: He's strange.

SARA: He talks funny.

HANK: He smells. He smells like he ate a whole spice rack.

CAROL: He's not like us.

SARA: I saw this Indian guy once who was just like drunk and passed out and I said, "Why, don't you go back to the reservation."

GARY: Go back to your teepee.

HANK: Go back to your casino.

SARA: I'm tired of them crying about how we took their land.

GARY: Yeah, just deal with it, okay.

SARA: They're not like us.

GARY: You know who I saw yesterday at the mall?

CAROL: Who?

GARY: Craig.

CAROL: Really? That guy is stuck in the '60s.

GARY: What a flower child.

  189

CAROL: (mockingly) "Peace, man."

HANK: "Make love, not war."

SARA: "Groovy!"

GARY: Those guys have no clue.

CAROL: No class.

HANK: No style.

SARA: Join the new millennium and get a life.

GARY: They're not like us.

CAROL: Hey, tell me this, where did all the rednecks in our school come from?

JOEY: I know. Like Jason over there.

CAROL: Look at him. Flannel shirt, cowboy boots, big belt buckle.

JOEY: Those guys are so stupid.

HANK: And prejudiced.

GARY: All they think about is killing things and getting drunk.

JOEY: Someone should round up all the white trash and rednecks in our school and ship them off somewhere else.

HANK: Send 'em down south where the rest of their kind live.

JOEY: Yeah, they don't belong here.

CAROL: They're not like us.

JOEY: You know who else they should round up? All the old people in the world.

SARA: No kidding. With their blue hair and big cars.

JOEY: They've got no purpose in society.

SARA: They're useless.

CAROL: Washed up.

HANK: Good for nothing.

JOEY: They're not like us.

SARA: Did you hear that joke about the Polack?

GARY: No, how did it go?

SARA: I don't remember exactly, but they're so stupid!

GARY: Yeah, not like us.

GARY: You know what I heard about Cindy?

HANK: What?

GARY: She's easy.

HANK: Well, duh. Look at the way she dresses.

JOEY: What a slut.

SARA: She's just a pregnancy waiting to happen.

HANK: You know just by looking at her that she has no morals.

GARY: She's not like us.

CAROL: How about John?

HANK: Man, what a fairy.

CAROL: Big time.

GARY: Queers like him make me sick.

SARA: They don't belong.

HANK: They're different.

CAROL: They're not like us.

JOEY: How about Jews?

HANK: What about 'em?

JOEY: Well, do you hate 'em?

HANK: Oh, yeah! They're just a bunch of money-loving rats.

GARY: Somebody should just round 'em all up and shoot 'em.

CAROL: Why hasn't anyone ever thought of that?

HANK: I think Hitler tried that.

JOEY: Yeah, but he was a German.

HANK: I hate the Germans.

JOEY: They're not like us.

HANK: This world is so screwed up.

GARY: If we could just get rid of all the…

GARY: Preps…

CAROL: Gangsters…

JOEY: Grungers…

SARA: Snobs…

GARY: Druggies…

HANK: Potheads…

CAROL: Flower children…

JOEY: Geeks…

SARA: Losers…

GARY: Nerds…

HANK: Rednecks…

CAROL: Hicks…

JOEY: Tramps…

SARA: Posers…

GARY: Fairies…

HANK: Mama's boys…

CAROL: Blacks…

JOEY: Jews…

SARA: Japanese…

GARY: Chinese…

HANK: Whites…

CAROL: Mexicans…

JOEY: Indians…

SARA: Arabs…

GARY: Polacks…

HANK: Canucks…

CAROL: Germans…

JOEY: Fat people…

SARA: And old people…

GARY: This world would be a better place.

HANK: After all…

ALL: They're not like us! They're not like us! They're not like us!

END

Where Is God?

CAST

- Brooke (breakup)
- Dennis (divorce)
- Rhonda (date rape)
- Dirk (death of relative)
- Polly (peer pressure)
- Perry (peer pressure)
- Della (death of peer)
- David (biblical references)
- Jon (biblical references)
- Ben (biblical references)
- Abdul (abuse)
- Angie (abuse)
- Stewart (depression/ suicide)

PROPS

- A sign for each cast member

This sketch opens with all of the cast members sitting (on chairs and on the floor) and standing in a group on stage. They can move as they talk, changing positions, using hand motions when they speak, switching from standing to sitting as the sketch progresses. The people playing David, Jon, and Ben can stand apart the rest of the group, if you want.

BROOKE: Then he told me we should stop seeing each other.

DENNIS: My dad told me that he and Mom are getting a divorce.

ANGIE: Why did he touch me there?

DIRK: That was when my grandfather passed away.

POLLY: Everyone else was doing it.

PERRY: My parents have no clue about half of the stuff I've done.

RHONDA: I said no, but he kept going.

DENNIS, STEWART: Didn't anyone care about how I felt?

BROOKE, DENNIS, RHONDA: Was it my fault?

DIRK, ANGIE, STEWART: Why couldn't I make the pain stop?

POLLY, PERRY: My parents are going to kill me when they find out.

BROOKE, DENNIS, ABDUL: Deep down I knew it was my fault.

RHONDA, ANGIE: I was probably asking for it, right?

DELLA: We fought the last time we were together.

BROOKE: I must've done something wrong, somewhere. Bad karma.

POLLY, ABDUL, STEWART: No one knows how I feel inside.

BROOKE, DENNIS, RHONDA, DIRK, ABDUL, ANGIE: What did I do to deserve this?

BROOKE: Just friends, he said. Can you believe that? After all we'd been through?

DELLA: My Mom called me and told me he had died.

RHONDA: He just grabbed me and threw me down. There was nothing I could do.

BROOKE, STEWART: Was there something I could have said?

BROOKE, DELLA: Before I knew it, she was gone.

DELLA: An accident, they said.

BROOKE, DIRK, DELLA: Why did God take her away?

DENNIS, POLLY, ABDUL, ANGIE: I've been good. I went to church.

STEWART: He was only 15.

RHONDA: I closed my eyes and wished with all my might that I was somewhere else.

ANGIE: Somewhere safe.

ABDUL: She didn't know any better.

DIRK, DELLA: I never got a chance to say good-bye.

POLLY, PERRY, STEWART: I go to youth group regularly.

BROOKE, DENNIS, DELLA, DAVID: Why?

BROOKE, RHONDA, PERRY, ABDUL, ANGIE, STEWART: Why me?

BROOKE, DENNIS, DELLA: Why now?

RHONDA, POLLY, DELLA, ANGIE, STEWART: I felt so helpless, so out of control.

PERRY: The room was full of strangers.

RHONDA, ABDUL, ANGIE: I couldn't tell anyone.

DENNIS, RHONDA, POLLY, STEWART: I'd never felt so alone before.

DAVID: "What is man that you are mindful of him, the son of man that you care for him?" (Psalm 8:4)

JON: "Are not five sparrows sold for two pennies? Yet not one of them is forgotten by God. Indeed, the very hairs of your head are all numbered. Don't be afraid; you are worth more than many sparrows." (Luke 12:6-7)

BEN: "O Lord, you have searched me and you know me. You know when I sit and when I rise; you perceive my thoughts from afar. You discern my going out and my lying down; you are familiar with all my ways. Before a word is on my tongue you know it completely, O Lord. You hem me in—behind and before; you have laid your hand upon me. Such knowledge is too wonderful for me, too lofty for me to attain." (Psalm 139:1-6)

DAVID: "Where can I go from your Spirit? Where can I flee from your presence? If I go up to the heavens, you are there; if I make my bed in the depths, you are there. If I rise on the wings of the dawn, if I settle on the far side of the sea, even there your hand will guide me, your right hand will hold me fast. If I say, 'Surely the darkness will hide me and the light become night around me,' even the darkness will not be dark to you; the night will shine like the day, for darkness is as light to you." (Psalm 139:7-12)

BEN: "For you created my inmost being; you knit me together in my mother's womb. I praise you because I am fearfully and wonderfully made; your works are wonderful, I know that full well. My frame was not hidden from you when I was made in the secret place. When I was woven together in the depths of the earth, your eyes saw my unformed body. All the days ordained for me were written in your book before one of them came to be." (Psalm 139:13-16)

DAVID: "How precious to me are your thoughts, O God! How vast is the sum of them! Were I to count them, they would outnumber the grains of sand. When I awake, I am still with you." (Psalm 139:17-18)

POLLY, DELLA: What if I had only been there for her?

BROOKE, DENNIS, RHONDA, PAUL: Could I have done anything to make a difference?

ABDUL, ANGIE, STEWART: I prayed and prayed, but there was no answer.

BROOKE: How could God do something like this?

DENNIS, PAUL, DELLA, ANGIE: Could I have stopped them?

RHONDA, ABDUL: How could God just sit by and let something like this happen?

BEN: "When Mary reached the place where Jesus was and saw him, she fell at his feet and said, 'Lord, if you had been here, my brother would not have died.'" (John 11:32)

DAVID: "But some of them said, 'Could not he who opened the eyes of the blind man have kept this man from dying?'" (John 11:37)

ALL: Jesus was there too.

JON: "At the sixth hour darkness came over the whole land until the ninth hour. And at the ninth hour Jesus cried out in a loud voice, 'Eloi, Eloi, lama sabachthani?'—which means, 'My God, my God, why have you forsaken me?'" (Mark 15:33-34)

ALL: Jesus felt abandoned too.

BEN: Did you know that Eloi is a term for a familiar? So this could be translated as "Daddy, where are you?"

ALL: God knows. God listens. God feels.

DAVID: "At that moment the curtain of the temple was torn in two from top to bottom. The earth shook and the rocks split." (Matthew 27:51)

DENNIS, ANGIE: God isn't here. If he were here he would do something!

DIRK, POLLY, STEWART: Just give me some proof that you're here for me, Lord!

DAVID: "Now Thomas said to them, 'Unless I see the nail marks in his hands and put my finger where the nails were, and put my hand into his side, I will not believe it.'" (John 20:24-25)

JON: "Then Jesus told him, 'Because you have seen me, you have believed; blessed are those who have not seen and yet have believed.'" (John 20:29)

RHONDA, DELLA: I never thought it would happen to me.

BROOKE, DENNIS, ANGIE: Everything seemed to be going along just fine.

RHONDA, ABDUL: Why did this happen to me? What did I do?

JON: "Do not let your hearts be troubled. Trust in God; trust also in me." (John 14:1)

BROOKE, DELLA: I knew something was wrong by the look on his [her] face.

JON: "You will grieve, but your grief will turn to joy. A woman giving birth to a child has pain because her time has come; but when her baby is born she forgets the anguish because of her joy that a child is born into the world. So with you: Now is your time of grief, but I will see you again and you will rejoice, and no one will take away your joy." (John 16:20-22)

ALL: Jesus struggled too.

BEN: "He withdrew about a stone's throw beyond them, knelt down and prayed,"

JON: "'Father, if you are willing, take this cup from me; yet not my will, but yours be done.'" (Luke 22:41-42)

DAVID: "Going a little farther, he fell to the ground and prayed that if possible the hour might pass from him." (Mark 14:35)

JON: "'Abba, Father,' he said, 'everything is possible for you. Take this cup from me. Yet not what I will, but what you will.'" (Mark 14:36)

BEN: And through it all he remained faithful.

DAVID: "The rest said, 'Now leave him alone. Let's see if Elijah comes to save him.' And when Jesus had cried out again in a loud voice, he gave up his spirit." (Matthew 27:49-50)

DENNIS, RHONDA, POLLY: It was all over. My life, as I knew it, was changed forever.

ABDUL: My father disowned me again. He kicked me out of the house.

ANGIE: Maybe if I made him mad, he'd hit me instead of Mom.

ALL: Jesus felt pain too.

DAVID: "When Jesus saw her weeping, and the Jews who had come along with her also weeping, he was deeply moved in spirit and troubled." (John 11:33)

BEN: "Jesus wept." (John 11:35)

PAUL: It seems so overwhelming, so out of control.

JON: "Come to me, all you who are weary and burdened, and I will give you rest. Take my yoke upon you and learn from me, for I am gentle and humble in heart, and you will find rest for your souls. For my yoke is easy and my burden is light." (Matthew 11:28-30)

ALL: Jesus cares for us.

JON: "Peace I leave with you; my peace I give you. I do not give to you as the world gives. Do not let your heart be troubled and do not be afraid." (John 14:27)

ALL: Jesus feels for us.

JON: "You did not choose me, but I chose you and appointed you to go and bear fruit—fruit that will last." (John 15:16)

ALL: Jesus will hold us up.

JON: "Righteous Father, though the world does not know you, I know you, and they know that you have sent me. I have made you known to them, and will continue to make you known in order that the love you have for me may be in them and that I myself may be in them." (John 17:25-26)

ALL: He will strengthen us and nurture and protect us.

JON: "And surely I am with you always, to the very end of the age." (Matthew 28:20)

END

REMOTELY
Entertaining

CAST

- Emcee—no costume necessary
- Cowboy—in western garb, holding a rope, and resting his foot on a stump or a hay bale
- Ballet instructor—in bright bodysuit, ballet slippers and tutu
- Grandmother—wearing a shawl and long skirt, old-fashioned glasses, seated in a rocking chair holding a children's storybook
- French teacher—wearing a brightly colored suit (or suit and tie if male), seated on a high stool behind a lectern, or standing in front of a portable chalkboard
- Dentist—in traditional white smock, seated on a stool, rig up a dentist's chair and cover with a white sheet. Some dentist's tools would be helpful, and he should have a toothbrush
- Patient—nonspeaking part

PROPS

- Costumes (see above)

EMCEE: Ladies and gentlemen, we now take you to the living room of Mr. Carl Couch Potato. He is about to spend his afternoon watching TV. As Mr. Couch Potato lives in the country, he has only five channels to choose from:

On Channel 6, the health channel, the network features a program called A Day in the Life of a Dentist.

Channel 7 offers a self-improvement show called Ballet Lessons with Brenda.

Channel 9 has Granny Gab-a-Lot reading children's stories to her young viewers.

Channel 13 offers long-distance French classes with Madame Foufou.

And Channel 15 shows a documentary filmed in Alberta called There's a Cowboy in my Cornfield.

Now Carl Couch Potato could watch any one of these fine programs, but like many people, he prefers to use his remote control to flip from channel to channel. Let's watch the results.

TEACHER: Now, students, in today's televised French class, I'm going to be talking about how to improve your pronunciation. To begin, we will read a short passage from your textbook. Please turn to page 41 and…

DENTIST: …spit out the little bits of old filling. Fortunately, with the rubber dam we now have, that isn't a problem anymore. Now, I need you to open your mouth a little wider and just try to relax as I…

GRANDMOTHER: …tell you the story of The Ugly Duckling. Once upon a time there was a mother duck and three baby…

BALLET INSTRUCTOR: …ballerinas. To be a true ballerina, you must spend years practicing your jumps, your pirouettes and your…

COWBOY: …calf ropin'. Now this rope is a pretty good un, but if you happen to come across a calf that is heavier than your ordinary run of the mill calf, you might have to…

TEACHER: …speak French with a better accent. The only way to do this is to practice rolling your rrr's. For example, the word for garage is the same spelling in both languages, but when you say it in French you say…

GRANDMOTHER: Quack! Quack! The mother duck led her ducklings down to the pond. The ugly duckling didn't like to swim, so he asked his mother to…

DENTIST: …do an extraction. Personally, I don't really like extractions. I'd prefer to fill this tooth because I think we can make it last until…

BALLET INSTRUCTOR: …the second act of the performance when Juliet appears on the balcony and calls out to Romeo…

COWBOY: …git along, little doggie. You see, you hafta talk to animals like you talk to people. They may not know exactly what you're saying, but they can tell by the tone of your voice when you say, "Here Bossie," you actually mean…

TEACHER: … "Your homework's not done again! It's important to keep sending in those assignments, because if you don't I'll have to phone your principals and tell them that you…

GRANDMOTHER: …need to fluff out your feathers to dry off properly, said the mother duck. So the little duckling flapped his tiny wings, and wiggled his…

DENTIST: …dental floss at least once a day. And don't forget the importance of fluoride. If you drink fluoridated water, you will be able to…

BALLET INSTRUCTOR: …maintain your balance during the love scene when Romeo and Juliet become engaged. A graceful deep plié would certainly…

COWBOY: …frighten them cattle all to blazes. Those ornery critters would take off like a bat outta…

TEACHER: …*Hello*, as you know, means *bonjour*, but *salut* is better for less formal occasions. Now, on tomorrow's show, we will interview Mr. Jonathan Bright, the bilingual superintendent of the local school division that sponsors our show. You'll be interested to know that Mr. Bright is the…

GRANDMOTHER: …ugliest creature on the pond had turned into an incredibly beautiful…

COWBOY: …pile of manure. And there I was, facin' all those angry steers, equipped with nuthin' but my trusty…

BALLET INSTRUCTOR: …pink tutu. For the death scene, though I think Juliet should be wearing a long gown so she will look more like…

COWBOY: …that heifer. But after that experience, I'd decided I'd always carry my…

DENTIST: …toothbrush. You'll never regret it if you…

TEACHER: …keep on studying, students, and soon you'll be speaking French…

COWBOY: …while you're cleanin' out the feedlot…

DENTIST: …with a sparkling white smile…

GRANDMOTHER: …happily ever after!

END

For God So Loved

CAST

- Narrator
- Readers 2 through 10

NARRATOR: John 3:16—"For God so loved the world that he gave his one and only Son, that whoever believes in him should not perish but have eternal life."

NARRATOR: For God…

READER 2: There is no one holy like the Lord: for there is no one besides you; there is no rock like our God. (1 Samuel 2:2)

NARRATOR: So loved…

READER 3: The Lord hath appeared to us in the past, saying: "I have loved you with an everlasting love; I have drawn you with loving-kindness. (Jeremiah 31:3)

NARRATOR: That he gave…

READER 4: Thanks be to God for his indescribable gift! (2 Corinthians 9:15)

NARRATOR: His only begotten son…

READER 5: God made him who had no sin to be sin for us, so that in him we might become the righteousness of God. (2 Corinthians 5:21)

NARRATOR: That whosoever…

READER 6: The Lord is not slow in keeping his promise, as some understand slowness. He is patient with you, not wanting anyone to perish, but everyone to come to repentance (2 Peter 3:9)

NARRATOR: Believeth in him…

READER 7: That if you confess with your mouth "Jesus is Lord," and believe in your heart that God raised him from the dead, you will be saved. For it is with your heart that you believe and are justified, and it is with your mouth that you confess and are saved. (Romans 10:9-10)

NARRATOR: Should not perish…

READER 8: If anyone's name was not found written in the book of life, he was thrown into the lake of fire. (Revelation 20:15)

NARRATOR: But have everlasting life…

READER 9: Jesus said to her, "I am the resurrection and the life. He who believes in me will live, even though he dies; and whoever lives and believes in me will never die. Do you believe this?" (John 11:25-26)

READER 10: Who shall separate us from the love of Christ? Shall trouble or hardship or persecution or famine or nakedness or danger or sword? For I am convinced that neither death nor life, neither angels nor demons, neither the present nor the future, nor any powers, neither height nor depth, nor anything else in all creation, will be able to separate us from the love of God that is in Christ Jesus our Lord. (Romans 8:35, 38-39)

END

SO WHAT CREATIVE SCRIPTS HAVE YOU WRITTEN LATELY?

Are your kids still talking that drama or skit you invented for last month's meeting or event? Youth Specialties pays $50 (and in some cases, more) for unpublished, field-tested ideas that have worked for you.

You've probably been in youth work long enough to realize that sanitary, theoretical, tidy ideas aren't what in-the-trenches youth workers are looking for. They want—you want—imagination and take-'em-by-surprise novelty. Ideas that have been tested and tempered and improved in the very real, very adolescent world you work in.

So here's what to do:

- Sit down at your computer, get your killer script out of your head and onto your hard drive, then e-mail it to Ideas@YouthSpecialties.com. Or print it and fax it to 619-440-0582 (Attn: Ideas).

- If you need to include diagrams, photos, art, or samples that help explain your dramatic idea, stick it all in an envelope and mail it to our street address: Ideas, www.YouthSpecialties.com

- Be sure to include your name, addresses, e-mail address, and phone numbers.

- Let us have a few months to give your game idea a thumbs up or down*, and a little longer for your 50 bucks.

*Hey, no offense intended if your idea isn't accepted. It's just that our fussy Ideas Library editor has these really meticulous standards. If the skit isn't creative, original, and just plain fun in an utterly wild or delightful way, she'll reject it (reluctantly, though, because she has a tender heart). Sorry. But we figure you deserve only the best skit ideas.

RESOURCES FROM YOUTH SPECIALTIES

YOUTH MINISTRY PROGRAMMING

Camps, Retreats, Missions, & Service Ideas (Ideas Library)
Creative Bible Lessons from the Old Testament
Creative Bible Lessons in 1 & 2 Corinthians
Creative Bible Lessons in Galatians and Philippians
Creative Bible Lessons in John: Encounters with Jesus
Creative Bible Lessons in Romans: Faith on Fire!
Creative Bible Lessons on the Life of Christ
Creative Bible Lessons in Psalms
Creative Junior High Programs from A to Z, Vol. 1 (A-M)
Creative Junior High Programs from A to Z, Vol. 2 (N-Z)
Creative Meetings, Bible Lessons, & Worship Ideas (Ideas Library)
Crowd Breakers & Mixers (Ideas Library)
Downloading the Bible Leader's Guide
Drama, Skits, & Sketches (Ideas Library)
Drama, Skits, & Sketches 2 (Ideas Library)
Drama, Skits, & Sketches 3 (Ideas Library)
Dramatic Pauses
Everyday Object Lessons
Games (Ideas Library)
Games 2 (Ideas Library)
Games 3 (Ideas Library)
Good Sex: A Whole-Person Approach to Teenage Sexuality & God
Great Fundraising Ideas for Youth Groups
More Great Fundraising Ideas for Youth Groups
Great Retreats for Youth Groups
Great Talk Outlines for Youth Ministry
Holiday Ideas (Ideas Library)
Hot Illustrations for Youth Talks
More Hot Illustrations for Youth Talks
Still More Hot Illustrations for Youth Talks
Hot Illustrations for Youth Talks 4
Hot Illustrations CD-ROM
Ideas Library on CD-ROM
Incredible Questionnaires for Youth Ministry
Junior High Game Nights
More Junior High Game Nights
Kickstarters: 101 Ingenious Intros to Just about Any Bible Lesson
Live the Life! Student Evangelism Training Kit
Memory Makers
The Next Level Leader's Guide
Play It! Over 150 Great Games for Youth Groups
Roaring Lambs
Screen Play
So What Am I Gonna Do With My Life?
Special Events (Ideas Library)
Spontaneous Melodramas
Spontaneous Melodramas 2
Student Leadership Training Manual
Student Underground: An Event Curriculum on the Persecuted Church
Super Sketches for Youth Ministry
Talking the Walk
Teaching the Bible Creatively
Videos That Teach
What Would Jesus Do? Youth Leader's Kit

Wild Truth Bible Lessons
Wild Truth Bible Lessons 2
Wild Truth Bible Lessons—Pictures of God
Wild Truth Bible Lessons—Pictures of God 2
Worship Services for Youth Groups

PROFESSIONAL RESOURCES

Administration, Publicity, & Fundraising (Ideas Library)
Dynamic Communicators Workshop
Great Talk Outlines for Youth Ministry
Help! I'm a Junior High Youth Worker!
Help! I'm a Small-Group Leader!
Help! I'm a Sunday School Teacher!
Help! I'm an Urban Youth Worker!
Help! I'm a Volunteer Youth Worker!
How to Expand Your Youth Ministry
How to Speak to Youth...and Keep Them Awake at the Same Time
Junior High Ministry (Updated & Expanded)
The Ministry of Nurture: A Youth Worker's Guide to Discipling Teenagers
Postmodern Youth Ministry
Purpose-Driven™ Youth Ministry
Purpose-Driven™ Youth Ministry Training Kit
So That's Why I Keep Doing This! 52 Devotional Stories for Youth Workers
A Youth Ministry Crash Course
Youth Ministry Management Tools
The Youth Worker's Handbook to Family Ministry

ACADEMIC RESOURCES

Four Views of Youth Ministry & the Church
Starting Right: Thinking Theologically About Youth Ministry
Youth Ministry That Transforms

DISCUSSION STARTERS

Discussion & Lesson Starters (Ideas Library)
Discussion & Lesson Starters 2 (Ideas Library)
EdgeTV
Get 'Em Talking
Keep 'Em Talking!
Good Sex: A Whole-Person Approach to Teenage Sexuality & God
High School TalkSheets—Updated!
More High School TalkSheets—Updated!
High School TalkSheets from Psalms and Proverbs—Updated!
Junior High-Middle School TalkSheets—Updated!
More Junior High-Middle School TalkSheets—Updated!
Junior High-Middle School TalkSheets from Psalms and Proverbs—Updated!
Real Kids: Short Cuts
Real Kids: The Real Deal—on Friendship, Loneliness, Racism, & Suicide
Real Kids: The Real Deal—on Sexual Choices, Family Matters, & Loss

Real Kids: The Real Deal—on Stressing Out, Addictive Behavior, Great Comebacks, & Violence
Real Kids: Word on the Street
Unfinished Sentences: 450 Tantalizing Statement-Starters to Get Teenagers Talking & Thinking
What If...? 450 Thought-Provoking Questions to Get Teenagers Talking, Laughing, and Thinking
Would You Rather...? 465 Provocative Questions to Get Teenagers Talking
Have You Ever...? 450 Intriguing Questions Guaranteed to Get Teenagers Talking

ART SOURCE CLIP ART

Youth Group Activities (print)
Clip Art Library Version 2.0 (CD-ROM)

DIGITAL RESOURCES

Clip Art Library Version 2.0 (CD-ROM)
Great Talk Outlines for Youth Ministry
Hot Illustrations CD-ROM
Ideas Library on CD-ROM
Screen Play
Youth Ministry Management Tools

VIDEOS & VIDEO CURRICULA

Dynamic Communicators Workshop
EdgeTV
Live the Life! Student Evangelism Training Kit
Purpose-Driven™ Youth Ministry Training Kit
Real Kids: Short Cuts
Real Kids: The Real Deal—on Friendship, Loneliness, Racism, & Suicide
Real Kids: The Real Deal—on Sexual Choices, Family Matters, & Loss
Real Kids: The Real Deal—on Stressing Out, Addictive Behavior, Great Comebacks, & Violence
Real Kids: Word on the Street
Student Underground: An Event Curriculum on the Persecuted Church
Understanding Your Teenager Video Curriculum
Youth Ministry Outside the Lines

STUDENT RESOURCES

Downloading the Bible: A Rough Guide to the New Testament
Downloading the Bible: A Rough Guide to the Old Testament
Grow For It Journal through the Scriptures
So What Am I Gonna Do with My Life?
Spiritual Challenge Journal: The Next Level
Teen Devotional Bible
What (Almost) Nobody Will Tell You about Sex
What Would Jesus Do? Spiritual Challenge Journal
Wild Truth Journal for Junior Highers
Wild Truth Journal—Pictures of God